PENGUIN BOOKS

THE MURDER OF CHILDHOOD

Tim Tate is an award-winning documentary film-maker and investigative journalist specializing in children's issues. He produced and directed Channel 4's acclaimed 'Dispatches' film investigating Robert Black's life and the police failure to catch him. He has also made films covering child pornography and ritual abuse; his investigations into organized child-pornography dealing led to the arrest of more than twelve active paedophiles. His documentary film on China's prison labour-camp system for dissidents won the Amnesty International Best Documentary Award for 1994. He is the author of four previous books: *What's Wrong With Your Rights?* (with Roger Cook); *Child Pornography – an Investigation*; *Children for the Devil – Ritual Abuse and Satanic Crime*; and *Murder Squad*. He is married with six children and lives in Yorkshire.

Ray Wyre is a nationally acknowledged expert in the sexual crime field. He began working with sex offenders as a member of the Probation Service in the 1970s. From 1981 to 1986 he established a group work programme for sex offenders in a top-security prison. On leaving the Probation Service he established the Clinic for Sexual Counselling, a hospital-based programme, until he founded the Gracewell Clinic and Institute in Birmingham in 1988. Ray Wyre was made a Churchill Fellow for his research in America into the treatment of both sex offenders and their victims. He is now an independent sexual crime consultant who works closely with the police services in profiling investigations and training police officers in interview techniques. He often appears in court as an independent expert witness for both prosecution and defence and has appeared in and acted as a consultant for many TV programmes and commentaries. He has published numerous articles on sex offenders and sex abuse and is the author of *Women, Men and Rape*; *Working with Sex Abuse*; *Sexual Crime Analysis Report*; and *Murder Squad*.

RAY WYRE & TIM TATE

The Murder of Childhood

PENGUIN BOOKS

PENGUIN BOOKS

Published by the Penguin Group
Penguin Books Ltd, 27 Wrights Lane, London W8 5TZ, England
Penguin Books USA Inc., 375 Hudson Street, New York, New York 10014, USA
Penguin Books Australia Ltd, Ringwood, Victoria, Australia
Penguin Books Canada Ltd, 10 Alcorn Avenue, Toronto, Ontario, Canada M4V 3B2
Penguin Books (NZ) Ltd, 182–190 Wairau Road, Auckland 10, New Zealand

Penguin Books Ltd, Registered Offices: Harmondsworth, Middlesex, England

First published 1995
1 3 5 7 9 10 8 6 4 2

Printed in England by Clays Ltd, St Ives plc
Set in 10.5/12.5 pt Monophoto Baskerville

CONTENTS

	Acknowledgements	vi
	Prologue	1
	Introduction	11
1	A Rush of Blood	17
2	Nobody's Child	50
3	A Kind of Madness	74
4	Ghosts in the Machine	100
5	The Price of Failure	135
6	Into That Darkness	168
7	Unquiet Graves	195
8	The Politics of Paedophilia	227
	Epilogue	257

ACKNOWLEDGEMENTS

My thanks are due to all those who supported us through this difficult project. In particular I owe an enormous – and unrepayable – debt to Chris Bryer and Grant McKee at Yorkshire Television, and to the 'Dispatches' editors at Channel 4 – David Lloyd and Francesca O'Brien.

The backing of a raft of lawyers was ultimately crucial in getting the documentary on screen: Jan Tomalin at Channel 4, Patrick Swaffer of Goodman Derrick and Patrick Maloney of counsel gave calm and rational advice throughout very difficult times.

Others, too, gave of their time and experience freely. To Magnus Linklater and Alan Hutchison of the *Scotsman*, and to our agent Caradoc King, I extend my grateful thanks.

Families played an important part in the long birth of our book and film. There are no words to convey my admiration, respect and affection for Liz and Fordyce Maxwell and for Jacki Harper. These feelings were unsolicited: I sought out the families, and the extent to which they allowed me into this painful corner of their lives is a testimony to their courage and commitment to a wider public understanding.

My family, as ever, have been the cornerstone of the four years it took to bring this project to fruition. Making films and writing books about the terrible things adults do to children leaves its own inevitable mark. Though at times they drove me to distraction, my own children and my long-suffering wife were a wonderful antidote and therapy. Thanks, one and all.

Tim Tate

PROLOGUE

Birmingham, December 1993

There was no such thing as a typical day. Each had its routine and schedules. But these were fixtures in an otherwise unpredictable round. And, in truth, that was how I liked it.

I leant, that winter morning, on the sill of the secretary's office window, staring at the human traffic passing by. The Gracewell Clinic, Britain's only residential centre for sex offenders, was ready to begin the day's work.

I watched as the first minibus pulled into the drive and fourteen sex offenders climbed out. They had spent the previous night, as they had spent every night since they had been accepted for treatment at Gracewell, in a residential hostel across the city.

They looked like a normal group of men, their ages ranging between twenty-one and sixty-three. I couldn't help noticing that some were in suits and carrying briefcases, while others were more casually dressed. One or two clearly had a limited choice of wardrobe, their clothes giving away the fact that they had recently been transferred from prison.

The heterogeneous nature of the group confirmed the fact that sex offenders come from all walks of life, all classes of society and all cultures. It is obvious to me, yet it seems impossible to get this vital piece of information across to people in the community at large.

I was often surprised how well these men got on together. Sometimes we had to watch the more 'caring' and intelligent men and limit the time they spent with those who were less able in the group. If we were not careful, it would have been easy for them to forget why they were with us.

Normally the men would be with us for a year – assuming they lasted the intense four-week assessment period. This stage was crucial, both for them so that they could begin the long process of confronting and controlling their offending and for us so that we could be sure that Gracewell was the right place to treat them. There are some offenders who are simply not suitable for a community-based clinic: these would be refused a place with us once their assessment was complete.

Once the formalities of each morning's arrivals were completed the clinic became very quiet. At 10 o'clock the men divided into three small sets – one set for assessment and two treatment groups run by experienced key workers.

These were trained therapists I had brought to Gracewell from the probation service, social work and other agencies involved with child care or child protection. They would be the most important figures in the men's lives, working with them intensively throughout their year at Gracewell.

It would be easy to imagine, as the groups got under way, that nothing of any significance took place within the clinic. A casual visitor would see only nondescript groups of men, sitting on institutional chairs in semicircles or loose ellipses and talking among themselves.

Talking, always talking. Words were teased out of the reluctant, the embarrassed or the defiant; torrents flowed out of others who sought a way to minimize the impact of their offences or to expiate their guilt for the pain they had inflicted on those smaller or weaker than they.

Talk – and its insidious antithesis, silence – had become the bedrock of our work at Gracewell. And the work was a crusade, self-imposed and often solitary, that had dominated every aspect of my life for more than a decade.

The basis of our effort was to bring out into the open the things that society refuses to recognize: the needs and influences that drive a man to abuse. Expose them to public view, and society can learn from them and become a safer place: expose them to the man himself, and change becomes a very real possibility. That was what Gracewell existed to achieve.

That morning, as on most mornings before it, a handful of

men split off from the rest and were directed into assessment. This was perhaps the least understood part of Gracewell's work. Press attention – and there was much of it – tended to focus on the rather more dramatic treatment: the seeming sorcery of turning habitual sex offenders away from their vicious cycle of recidivism. No other criminals had such a high rate of re-offending – some estimates put it as high as 99 per cent for the convicted fixated paedophile. At Gracewell not a single man, to our knowledge, slipped back into offending while he was with us.

The offenders in the assessment group that morning were a representative sample. Managed by the senior staff, they were Schedule 1 offenders (men deemed a high risk to the community) who had finished their prison sentences but were not allowed to go home before an estimate of the threat they posed to their children had been made. Sometimes men like this who have been returned to the community but who have had no family to go to (or no family that was prepared to accept them) have managed to find unsuspecting single mothers with children – and have moved in with them.

Social services departments are in a bind in cases like these: how can they protect the children without evidence of new abuse taking place? The dilemma is cruel: do they have to wait for the almost inevitable abuse to begin before acting? In times past they may have moved quickly to protect the children from the perceived threat by taking them into care or by seeking a court wardship order. Gracewell's existence allowed for men to be referred for a four-week assessment.

The other men in our assessment group had been referred by the criminal courts. They had been convicted of sexual offending – always abusing children – and the judge had asked Gracewell to take them on a month's bail while we assessed whether they were suitable for our treatment programme.

If so, they would avoid a custodial sentence and be sent to the clinic for treatment. Typically this would involve a minimum one year's residence as part of three years of probation.

This latter was no idle threat: if they committed any offence within that period they knew that they would be swiftly taken back to court and would receive a heavy jail term.

As I made my way to an observation area behind the main assessment room I reflected on how little the public understood the realities of this process. I knew, come lunchtime, I would have to settle down at my desk and patiently work through literally dozens of phone messages questioning the validity of, and need for, our work. Some would be from newspapers; increasingly radio and television sought our views on a daily basis. Others would be from the local community: many of these were likely to be brutally hostile.

The media were generally helpful and surprisingly constructive. But it was a tragedy that I could rarely get the message across to those who lived around us. In their lust for retribution people seemed unable to understand that the year some of these men spent with us was often likely to be longer than any judge would impose as a prison sentence. They saw therapy as a soft option for the men. And they couldn't grasp the strict conditions of their residence.

Probation orders imposed by the courts, as part of the order sending them to Gracewell, stated that if the offenders failed to cooperate in any way, they could be taken back to court and sentenced again for the original offence. One man was given a five-year prison sentence for precisely this.

That morning I had a specific offender to observe through the one-way mirror between the assessment room and my observation area. The man had been convicted of sexually assaulting his teenage daughter. I watched Charles Fortt, the clinic manager, work intensively with him within the context of a whole group of men.

At coffee break Charles and I sat together and reviewed the man's words and behaviour. He had been talking about his offending and had begun to disclose that the abuse he had inflicted on his daughter had not started when she was thirteen – his story to the court – but five years earlier. More important, his fantasies about her and the process of preparing her for abuse – 'grooming' the victim, we called it – had started when she was five.

It was a typical story, all too typical: a pattern we had come to expect and were able to predict. This was our routine, our business.

And yet, to an untrained outsider, it could be seen as a madness: how could a man harbour sexual desire for a five-year-old child, his own small daughter? And, if he did, was he not some sort of incurable pervert? How could simply talking to him serve any purpose?

I knew that it did. I climbed the stairs to my first-floor office to complete a report on an offender who had been at the clinic a week earlier. No two cases are ever identical, but the details prised from this man in his four-week assessment had a pattern that I saw almost daily.

I was convinced that they could hold out the prospect of changing the man's cycle of offending. Since it opened five years before, Gracewell had offered the only realistic hope of controlling habitual sex criminals.

After a hurried sandwich – low-calorie in deference to a stubbornly increasing waistline – and a predictable backlog of phone messages, I walked to the communal dining room where staff and clients sat eating their lunch. (It was very much an individual decision for the staff whether they ate with the clients. The men brought sandwiches every day from the residential hostel.) I normally went into the dining room for at least some of the lunch hour. By the time I got there they were usually sitting at the formica tables smoking and playing dominoes or cards. Informal contact with the clients was always useful and I frequently learned a great deal from discussions that took place over a cheese roll or a cigarette.

After lunch the men returned to the sessions, working sometimes on their own, sometimes in pairs or with their key workers. Every day at Gracewell offered many challenges to the staff.

In some ways the regime was harder for the treatment-group workers than for the assessment staff. The senior staff and I were often away from Gracewell, running training courses or attending conferences. This variety of tasks made our job much more manageable. But day in and day out, for up to a year, the therapists worked with a small group of offenders. Unlike me, they rarely had the chance to leave the clinic, rarely got to present their work in public or to place it within the bigger and highly politicized forums of radio and television debate. But, in truth, the learning and the development of our programme for dealing with sex offenders took place inside the clinic. The small rooms filled with child molesters were our coal face.

It is hard to express the pain that many of the staff experienced. The work can be very lonely, even when colleagues are doing the same job. The way each of us coped with similar sets of circumstances was quite different. There was simply no one correct way to manage it.

Watching the treatment groups I had very quickly learnt that sex offenders are masters at targeting vulnerability in the staff. It is almost as if they have a second sense of when their key worker or therapist is having problems. And because we worked within the criminal framework many of those problems were caused by time constraints.

The treatment programme was divided into five basic modules – distorted thinking, victim awareness, controlling fantasy, assertion training and female/male sexuality – that were run throughout the year. Not every offender stayed with us for the full twelve months, so we had to ensure that every man covered each of the modules.

But, even though they all worked through all five modules, we could not guarantee they would reach the objectives we set them. They would get halfway towards the mental state we wanted them to reach only to have the courts or the agency paying for their stay take them out of the clinic. The length of stay was determined not by the clients' needs but by criminal sentencing policies still based primarily on retribution – and by a constant shortage of resources to keep them with us. It was intensely frustrating for all of us.

One of the treatment sessions that December afternoon involved an offender working alone at a table. In front of him was a pad of A4 lined paper. At its head was a question: 'How did you groom your victim to stop her telling?'

I watched as the man began writing. On the sheet below, a second exercise was waiting: it would confront the offender with a victim's question and insist he write a response.

Later I collected both sheets and sat down to read. In answer to the first question the man had written:

> With Susan I had been giving her sweets and pocket money from the beginning. I began to give her more expensive presents, including bikes, so that I could touch her sexually.
>
> In the end she would lie on the bed and ask me how much I was going to give her. On one occasion, when she wanted £20, she undressed and said I could do anything I wanted.
>
> I suppose it's the effect of corruption.

The answer was short and typical of an offender halfway through the programme. There were hints, half-formed thoughts underlying the spare prose. The words seemed to imply – or at least to beg the inference – that the victim had to some extent been in control. Certainly the final sentence appeared to show that the man was gaining a degree of self-awareness. But there was still evidence of an offender seeking to blame his victim for the sexual assaults she endured.

The second exercise formed part of the process of forcing the offender to face up to what he had done: to confront the knowledge that lay somewhere within himself of how badly he had affected his victim's life. It prompted him to answer a question that the child might well have asked: 'I felt controlled – as if my life was not my own. How did you do that?' The man's reply was stark.

> You were controlled by me. Everything I did was taking away your control of your own life. Before, during and after every time I abused you I forced my actions and my needs on to you.
>
> I manipulated how you thought, how you behaved and how you acted – not just towards me, but towards everybody. I did this by deliberately shunning you and depriving you of attention and love, so that you would come to me needing attention. Then I would lavish you with love and affection, so that the

next time I shunned you you would need attention more.

Because I dumped all my guilt, shame and needs on to you I made you feel guilty and confused. I made you responsible for my moods and for making me feel better.

By acting normally towards your mother and other family members, and by talking about abuse in front of them, I made it impossible for you to turn to anyone to get help.

At other times I deliberately set out to make you a liar in front of your mother. I removed your ability to trust, and in doing so I made you believe that you had no control over your life or over what was happening to you. However, I did it in a way that left you with feelings that if you hadn't liked it you could have stopped it. This confusion led to the feeling of having no control.

It was a painfully honest account. Many clients began their stay at Gracewell by trying to please me or the treatment staff – mouthing words of regret and self-recrimination while refusing to confront the distorted thinking that allowed their aberrant sexuality full rein. This was different. This account, this letter to a child that would never be sent, had a sense of truth about it: a sense of an offender coming face to face with his actions and twisted mind games.

And I saw in it, that afternoon in December, what I always saw in such writings and in the treatment sessions we ran. I saw the possibility, the hope, of change. But, behind it, I saw the certainty of further abuse if we didn't work with these men.

It was 6 p.m. It had been dark for two hours. Outside, the city was lit up: Christmas was close at hand, and Birmingham was alive with its excitement. I had one more meeting to attend before I too could close the clinic and go looking for presents for my wife and children. It was not to be a happy meeting: no sense here of promise or of hope. I had received a letter that morning from the city council that threatened all that I and the Gracewell staff had tried to achieve for the past five years.

I thought back through those years. I was not ashamed to call them a success. Not one of the men who had stayed with us had been convicted of an offence during their time in treatment.

And yet they belonged to that most difficult category of criminal for society to deal with: the habitual recidivist. It had not been an easy five years. Logistically, financially and, above all, emotionally Gracewell had been a struggle. But we felt we had a mission – a mission to protect children – that overrode the personal consequences of devoting our lives to working with sex offenders.

I thought back particularly over the past two years. Years in which I had been given the unique privilege – and, with it, a burden of responsibility at times almost too heavy to bear alone – of working with an offender whose case encapsulated so much of the importance of Gracewell's message.

And now all this was threatened.

INTRODUCTION

High Court, Edinburgh, Friday, 10 August 1990

> 'Robert Black. The case against you is that you did on 14 July 1990, in the District of Ettrick and Lauderdale, abduct Laura Turner,* aged six years; and that you did assault her, seize hold of her, lift her into the front of a motor van, push her under a seat, cover her with a coat and blanket, order her to be quiet and convey her against her will to a lay-by on the A7 Edinburgh to Carlisle Road.
>
> 'There you did further assault her, place her in the rear of said motor van, take off her shoes and socks, and place your hand inside her shorts and pants; and you did place your finger into her private parts, tie her hands behind her back, stick pieces of plaster over her mouth, place a bag over her head, tie said bag around her neck and place her in a sleeping bag – all to her injury and to the danger of her life.
>
> 'How do you plead?'
>
> 'Guilty.'

This is the story of Britain's worst serial child sex killer and the process by which he came to talk candidly about his crimes for the first time in thirty-five years of offending. It is simultaneously the story of the process of entering the killer's mind for the first and only time in all those years.

It is not an easy story to read. It has not been easy to write or to publish. From the outset it aroused strong emotions both in ourselves and in those to whom we spoke. Sexual crimes, particularly crimes against children, arouse intense emotions within our society and yet are profoundly ill-understood phenomena.

* Laura Turner is a pseudonym used to protect the child's identity.

We did not enter this project lightly. We have written, broadcast and lectured extensively on paedophilia, child pornography and the policing of sexual abuse. None the less, from the first we each examined our motives in writing the harrowing pages that follow.

It was very quickly clear that Robert Black's case might spawn a number of 'quickie' books in the 'true crime' genre. These would inevitably dwell on the (genuinely) sensational details of his offences, offering up pain and suffering as a form of entertainment. To both of us such books seem to function as a type of pornography by which the reader is titillated with ever more gory stories as a means of achieving quick and easy profits. There is something deeply unsettling in the British public's voyeuristic taste for murder stories.

The genre of 'true crime' – particularly sex-crime reporting – has done little to heighten public understanding of its causes or effects and has simultaneously devalued the currency of serious attempts to enlighten an often over-heated public debate.

Why, then, the need for this book?

The story of Robert Black's assaults on very young children exemplifies – magnifies in grim clarity – many of the major issues of how society sees, understands and deals with men who abuse.

His offences stretch across thirty-five years. There is no authoritative estimate for the number of his victims: we can only guess, based on what he himself now says, that he molested hundreds of young children and abducted dozens. At least eight of them may have died.

Men who abuse children, especially if more than one child is involved or if a disturbing degree of violence is used, tend to be dismissed as 'beasts', 'monsters' or 'madmen'. These terms offer a convenient dustbin into which ordinary people can hurl their disgust and anger. Convenient, understandable even, but dangerously wrong.

The first purpose of this book is to highlight and challenge this knee-jerk response. Men who abuse may commit monstrous crimes, but they are not recognizably monsters. They do not have two heads, sloping brows and deep-set eyes. In the street, in the pub or at work they are not noticeably different from the rest of us.

Establishing an inaccurate stereotype is dangerous because it encourages children to believe that ordinary-looking men are 'safe' and not likely to abuse, assault or murder them. And families who accept that their children are in danger only from monsters are less careful about nice men – ordinary men who take a caring interest in their son or daughter and spend time with them.

The conventional warning from parents to children is 'Don't talk to strangers'. But children's understanding is different from that of adults': a stranger can become a friend within seconds if he is nice to a child. Day in, day out, there is a moral to learn. Those whom we call 'strangers' or 'monsters' don't get close to our children. 'Nice' or ordinary-looking men do. If this difficult, painful book teaches this point alone, it will have succeeded.

From the outset we insisted that our book must challenge the motives of its readers in buying it and its publishers for printing it. Equally we knew we must explain our own motives for writing it. Put simply, we have a mission to explain and demystify the nature of Robert Black's obsessive offending. This does not mean that we make excuses for what he has done. But there are lessons that all of us – the police, the public and our institutions – need to learn from his case.

Even when its aims had been so clearly stated, the project immediately ran foul of the very problem that it had set out to attack – the great taboo of wilful ignorance that has been erected around the subject of child sexual abuse. One publisher, whose fiction list includes semi-pornographic sado-masochistic books, told us quite bluntly: 'I do not want to be responsible for publishing this story. I do not think the world would be a better place for the availability of such a book.'

Maybe not. The world, and particularly the world as viewed by abused children, is not a good place. It is a uniquely bleak and horrible place. If our book doesn't make the world 'better', we hope it may make some parts of the world more informed, more aware and ultimately better equipped to deal with the problem of abused children and those who perpetrate the offences.

We do not set out to invite sympathy for offenders like Robert Black – although it would be an unfeeling reader who did not feel some shudder of revulsion at what happened to him as a child and as a teenager. Too often the debate about what to do with men who abuse centres on an (understandably) emotive argument about whether they 'deserve' expensive psychotherapy. Such moral judgements are, to an extent, irrelevant. Robert Black is not unpunishable but neither is he untreatable. If he is to be punished, then surely it makes sense to combine his life sentence with treatment that attempts to break his cycle of abusing?

No life sentence in Britain actually means life: twenty years is the most likely length of imprisonment for all but the most sensational cases. Failing to break the cycle of abuse means that offenders will leave prison and plunge once again into their abusive behaviour patterns. Time after time Gracewell has seen men in their sixties and seventies for whom a lifetime of imprisonment has not touched the basic problem of their paedophilia.

The only prospect of keeping children safe from abusers is to work extensively, painfully and expensively with those men in order to interrupt their cycle of offending. Such work – whether they 'deserve' it or not – is simply the best form of child protection we have.

It would be easy, with hindsight, to criticize the prison system for failing to address Robert Black's distorted thinking and behaviour during his early sentences. Equally it would be easy to criticize the police investigation of the murders of Susan Maxwell, Caroline Hogg and Sarah Harper for failing to take Black's record of similar offending into account. Certainly, had any one of the three police forces, which for almost a decade pursued the murderer of those three girls, understood the profile of this type of offender, then other small children might not have suffered.

None the less we did not set out to point an accusing finger at any individual agency. The problems of paedophilia and violent abusers are so widely ignored and misunderstood that the failures in the prison and police services simply reflect the wider public ignorance. Instead, we hope that, by reading and understanding Robert Black's history, future investigations may be better focused and more effective.

Finally, we know that in presenting Robert Black's own words to describe the methods he used in, and the motives behind, his murders and assaults we will inevitably be accused of causing unnecessary pain to the parents of his victims.

Indeed, the Home Office officially adopts the view that any interviews with men serving life sentences for murder will automatically cause great upset to the relatives of their victims, and it seeks to prevent publication wherever it has jurisdiction.

This stance is not, however, applied as universally as official Home Office statements suggest. Favoured journalists and film-makers are frequently allowed to record interviews with men serving life for murder.

And the premise itself – silence is golden – is dangerously flawed. Sex offenders frequently rely on the ignorance of their victims about how they operate. The paedophile needs public ignorance to carry out his abusing undetected. One aim of this book is to break the silence, the better to protect future victims.

Equally, the Home Office policy of protecting victims' families fails to understand one of their basic needs. Part of the reason may lie in the phrase itself: these mothers, fathers, brothers, sisters, grandparents, aunts and uncles are not merely relatives: they too are victims.

For the family of a murdered child there is a lingering, potent and corrosive compound of anger, frustration, loneliness and guilt. It is a tangible, solitary pain that can dissolve previously strong relationships, isolating the sufferers in a feverish and intractable memory.

The parents of two of Black's three proven murdered victims chose to speak with us. They did so voluntarily: we put no pressure on them or on the parents who did not wish to be a part of this project. We felt, and still feel, immensely privileged to have been taken into their lives, albeit for a short time.

But we also hope that we have given something back to them. Ironically it is sometimes those outside the family who can be a positive force for healing. Both of us had previously sat with, held and loved families who have lost a child, sat and talked night into morning with parents whose children have disappeared – and, in doing so, have drawn off a little of the sepsis that has spread through their spirit.

We have seen and, we hope, begun to understand the pain of abandonment, mistrust and depression. A need to blame, struggling with unshakeable guilt: an anger with others who misinterpret an apparently calm façade as 'handling it well'.

But, above all, we have experienced a weary and bone-deep sadness at man's apparently boundless inhumanity to children: a tangled puzzle because it begins and ends in ignorance of the motivation of the 'monsters' who steal a child's life. And these dark, miserable skeins weave back into the self-torturing web of guilt suffered inevitably by the families of those who suddenly disappear.

To the families we have talked to, to the parents of Robert Black's known victims, to those whose identities we cannot deduce from his own confessions – to all of them this book is dedicated with a simple message. There was nothing any one of you could have done, as individual parents, to protect your children from Robert Black. Susan Maxwell disappeared in a ninety-second gap during which she was out of an adult's sight. There is no twenty-four-hour security parents can give to their children.

Only we as a society can begin to protect our children from those whose desire is to abduct, abuse or kill them. But to do that requires understanding, understanding brought about by a willingness to work with those whom we call 'monsters' and to learn the lessons they have to teach us.

Which, ultimately, is the point of this book.

I

A Rush of Blood

High Court, Edinburgh, Friday, 10 August 1990

> The abduction of this little girl was carried out with chilling, cold calculation. This was no 'rush of blood', as you have claimed.
>
> This is a very serious case, an horrific, appalling case, and there are few words appropriate to describe the disgust with which one listens to the detail of this offence.
>
> You will go to prison for life and your release will not be considered until such time as it is safe to do so.
>
> *Lord Donald MacArthur Ross, trial judge*

Park Road, Moseley, is at the heart of Birmingham's red-light district. The area is sleazy and run-down: on almost every corner prostitutes bob and weave as they peer into passing cars in search of 'business'.

The terrace of renovated properties between numbers 25 and 33 once housed a popular casino. In 1988 workmen began ripping out the chandeliers and gaming tables and covering up the trademark red-flock wallpaper.

Eighteen months later the former casino was transformed into a dozen small offices, a canteen and a pair of linked conference rooms. But the meetings that would shortly take place in them would not be conventional business conferences. The expensive audio-visual equipment stacked up in the corridor outside would be installed behind a one-way mirror in what was to be called the observation room.

Numbers 25–29 Park Road were the new home of the Gracewell Clinic. As the prostitutes played hide-and-seek with police and clients outside, the talk inside was of a very different type of sex – an abusive, addictive variety: sex 'with' children.

Gracewell had existed for almost two years by then. It offered a formal, residential setting for pioneering work with men who abuse. It had begun to earn an international reputation for its intensive therapy and treatment and for undertaking risk-assessment reports of both convicted and unconvicted offenders.

In general, Gracewell's clients were sent by social-service departments, health authorities and the courts. Occasionally men, pressured by their families, would refer themselves for in-patient treatment. There were signs too that by summer 1990 the Home Office was beginning to consider recognizing the clinic's work officially.

That same summer Robert Black was locked up in a stark cell inside Edinburgh's Victorian Saughton Prison, awaiting trial for the abduction of, and assaults on, Laura Turner.

The Scottish legal system differs radically from its English counterpart in both structure and approach. The official in charge of Black's case was not from the national Crown Prosecution Service but the local Edinburgh Procurator Fiscal, a title and office that has its origins in Roman Law and for which there is no direct equivalent in the English legal system.

In June 1990 the Fiscal ordered a psychiatric assessment of Robert Black by Dr J. A. Baird, one of Scotland's leading forensic psychiatrists based at Carstairs State Hospital, Lanark. A month later the report arrived at the Fiscal's office in Queensferry Street.

> This man has strong paedophile tendencies. He has admitted to me a number of serious incidents with children, but has admitted to nothing serious between 1968 and 1990. In view of his inclinations the probability would be that he has had sexual contact with children on many other occasions in addition to those which he has disclosed to me . . .
>
> During the interview he made some mention of 'treatment', and told me that he had seen, on television, a documentary about, in his own words, 'therapy sessions with child sex offenders'.

There was a clear, and perhaps understandable, flavour of distaste running through Dr Baird's report. Yet within the fact that Robert Black had even mentioned treatment for his compulsion to abuse children lay the first fragile seeds of hope.

A month later a second, quite separate, psychiatric report was written about Robert Black. Andrew K. Zealley, Consultant Psychiatrist and Physician Superintendent at the Royal Edinburgh Hospital's Mental Health Unit, had been commissioned by Black's lawyers to write a defence assessment that would be shown to the trial judge. On 8 August Zealley visited Black in Saughton Prison and assiduously recorded what he heard.

> This report is based solely on my interview with Black, and I have no corroborative evidence upon which to base the opinions expressed.
>
> He is a forty-three-year-old man who was born in Falkirk. He understands that he is illegitimate. Having been in local authority care, he was fostered when aged six months and stayed with his foster mother until he was ten and a half years old. A large part of his life was spent up north in Kinlochleven.
>
> From aged 10 to 11 he was in a children's home near Falkirk, and then from 11 to 15 in a boys' home in Musselburgh. He never knew his father or mother and has no definite knowledge of any brothers or sisters.
>
> His later schooling was in Musselburgh, where he went to the grammar school. On leaving school he went to a working boys' hostel in Greenock for a year.
>
> Around that time, he told me, he first committed an indecent assault with a little girl, and that was the subject of a deferred [prison] sentence.
>
> He was living in Grangemouth by this time and then went back to Kinlochleven to live with someone he had known as an 'aunt'. A further offence occurred, he told me, with a small child, and he was sent to Borstal for a total of thirteen months. Subsequently he stayed in a hostel in Glasgow for ten months, and then went south to London. He has been based in London ever since . . .
>
> Since the late 1970s he has had some contact with child-sex

pornography and has made trips to Copenhagen and Amsterdam in this connection. He feels his interest in child sexual contact has been there for years . . .

His employment record has been substantially as a van driver, having had several jobs in the London area in this work. He did, however, work as a lifeguard in an open-air pool and then at an indoor pool for part of his adult life.

Your client was entirely cooperative with me at interview and was able to respond to my questions promptly and entirely sufficiently.

He revealed no evidence of abnormal thought processes, is not suffering from a mood disorder such as depressive illness, and his demeanour when describing sexual deviant activity was muted.

He did not, however, decline to provide me with information when I asked for it. There is no evidence that he suffers from any organic brain disorder.

I consider that this man is sane and fit to plead. He would appear to have a life-long interest, of a pathological type, in sexual activity with young children. It is possible to speculate that this sexual deviation may have been predisposed to by the lack of normal family care when he was a young child, aggravated by his experience at the hands – so he says – of an apparently homosexual member of staff at Musselburgh Children's Home when he was a teenager.

I can offer no other extenuating medical explanation for the sort of offence with which he is now charged. Your client has himself recently learnt of the existence of a treatment clinic for child sex offenders somewhere in England . . .

Because the man is free of any formal psychiatric illness, psychiatric treatment of the conventional type does not have any relevance.

On the basis of this report the Rt Hon. Lord Donald MacArthur Ross, Lord of Session of the Scottish courts, sentenced Robert Black, van driver, to life imprisonment.

It was, on the face of it, an unusual sentence: sex offenders rarely receive life sentences, and those who do have generally been convicted of more serious charges than a limited sexual assault, even when that has involved abduction, and are generally given some indication of the number of years they must serve.

By admitting the sexual assault – for which otherwise there would only have been Laura's word – and the abduction Black had neatly ducked the potential charge of attempted murder: there was simply no point in attempting a contested prosecution on the more serious charge if he accepted the lesser ones.

Robert Black might even have expected a lenient sentence because he had pleaded guilty – though only, as he made plain to Dr Baird, 'because they caught me red-handed: I've no choice'.

But Laura Turner had been within ten minutes of suffocating when her bound and gagged body was discovered under the seat of Black's van. And the tenor of both psychiatric reports convinced Lord Ross that Black was something more dangerous even than a 'normal' sex offender.

A paedophile is usually defined as a man (or, occasionally, a woman) who is sexually attracted to children. Not all paedophiles put their fantasies and desires into practice, though most will probably abuse in some way at some point in their lives.

But paedophilia is merely an umbrella word, a catch-all description that itself breaks down into a number of subcategories. On the basis of behavioural studies, abusers tend to fall into one of two main types – 'non-predatory' and 'predatory'. The former will target and groom a potential victim and then gradually ensnare or seduce the child into an abusive 'relationship'. The latter – and it is the rarer of the two categories, despite the acres of press coverage that frequently accompany its incidence – typically involves an unexpected physical assault (the classic 'pouncing' child molester) prior to the sexual abuse.

Paedophiles in both categories generally profess a 'love' of children and frequently exhibit a lifelong pattern of seeking out work and leisure opportunities to be near them. Almost invariably they seek out and collect a large quantity of child erotica and, sometimes, child pornography.

But for some men within both typologies simple sexual abuse is not sufficient: there are abusers for whom the torture, and even murder, of a child is sexually arousing.

In addition to the predictable behavioural evidence of their aberrant desires, these men generally collect and maintain child pornography that reflects their sexual drive: photographs, films and videos that depict the cutting, strangulation and, occasionally, death of the young victims.

Lord Ross's life sentence reflected the official suspicion that Robert Black might belong in this category of sadistic paedophile – a view born of the image of Laura Turner's red and gasping face as she struggled for life, bound and gagged inside Black's van.

None the less, Black and his lawyers decided to appeal against the judge's sentence. No prisoner likes an indeterminate sentence hanging over his or her head: sex offenders, who routinely live out their sentences in isolated segregation units, have a particular need to know how long are the prison sentences that they must serve.

To prepare for the appeal Black's lawyers telephoned Gracewell to ask for an independent assessment of Robert Black and the risk he posed to children, a second opinion with which to contest Dr Baird's initial report and the life sentence to which it led. I had no idea just how the phone call would alter my life or how profound its effect would be on Black and the families of his victims.

From the moment a call like that comes through I experience an intense fusion of emotions – excitement, anticipation, privilege, fear. Can I get close enough to the man to build the relationship I will need? How long will it take to establish a rapport? There is no reason for him to be honest: his best defence is silence. How can I give him some hope that, by talking, we can achieve something positive?

How cooperative will the prison staff be? It's quite common for prison officers to be hostile to anyone prepared to work with sex offenders: will they see me – quite wrongly – as someone who is being paid to get Black out of prison?

Above all I know I will have to go through yet another harrowing case on my own, isolated and exposed. Until after the appeal I will be legally bound not to say anything, even to my closest colleagues.

I can't even tell my partner: and if I *were* free to speak to her, how could I share with her the details of what Robert Black has done when our own daughter is only a few years older than Laura?

Hearing the details will be painful. People often ask how I can sit with men who abuse children and listen to their stories without showing anger or revulsion. The answer is always the same. Of course I have those emotions, but I have to use them: I have to deal with them in such a way that I can be angry and yet maintain a rapport with the man. Eighty per cent of the way we communicate with each other is non-verbal – we express ourselves through body language, posture, expression, even the way we breathe.

I have to be aware constantly of how my own feelings are being interpreted by the man I am facing, so distancing myself from him, or showing my very real anger, aren't realistic options. I have to enable him to tell me what he has done – and that means letting him know that, whatever he says, I will not abandon him. To acknowledge my feelings, and at the same time to ensure that my client feels cared about, is the skill of the therapist.

His greatest fear is that, if I really know the sort of man he is, I will reject him. This is the central problem I know I will have to overcome. I have to convince him that there is nothing he cannot tell me, no part of his mind that we cannot explore safely.

I know too that most offenders try to depict themselves as victims and sometimes give me graphic accounts of how they themselves have suffered. I have to resist the lure of allowing the offender to take on the role of victim and yet, simultaneously, not reject his suffering (quite often it is genuine).

To help me I keep a separate mental box in my head – I call it the 'victim box'. It is here that I test constantly every word the offender says against what I know he did to the child. I try to feel what it must have been like for a small child, terrified and hurt by the big adult in front of me. It's not easy. Yet I need to be able to feel that trauma, experience that pain, if I am to work successfully with an offender. It is exhausting, mentally and physically, and a constant demand on the time I would like to reserve for my own family.

When I was asked to see Robert Black that day in September 1990 all of these conflicting emotions ran immediately through my mind.

For a moment I wondered whether I truly wanted to take on the job, to trek into the mind of an apparently sadistic abuser inside a prison where the staff might well be hostile to my very presence.

In the end I knew I had to. Not for any financial reward, nor yet from any self-righteous sense of 'do-gooding', but for the sake of Laura, her parents and the potential queue of Robert Black's future victims. Even if Black was never to be released, I could learn valuable lessons from him and use the information I gained to protect other children.

The short flight to Edinburgh, and the time away from home, would be just the start of it: the journey into his mind would be much longer, darker and more terrible. But it was one I had to make.

My own journey through life had been, by any standards, eventful. I was born in Bournemouth in 1951 and attended the local primary and secondary modern schools. Then, as a twelve-year-old boy I moved to Belfast, where my father, a serving chief petty officer in the Royal Navy for thirty-three years, had been posted.

A posting to Northern Ireland in the early 1960s was a much less daunting prospect than it later became. The Troubles, which divided communities along a strict, if arbitrary, religious front line, did not erupt until 1969. Two years before then I left Belfast, following my father's footsteps into the Navy.

At the age of fifteen Junior Control Electrical Mechanic (2nd Class) Wyre had seen nothing of the world and little of its wickedness. Within a year the Royal Navy would have all but completed an education in a life that had hardly begun.

From 1968 to 1970 I served on HMS *London*, flagship of the

Far East fleet, patrolling the warm waters around Australia, Japan, Hong Kong, Singapore and the Philippines. Shortly before my seventeenth birthday my crewmates decided on a traditional induction to naval manhood. The ship was anchored at the naval base in Singapore. A shore party was organized: the first destination a blue movie show in a nearby village, the second, a brothel in Jahore Barau.

It was to be my initiation. I was to be a 'cherry boy' (virgin) no longer. We went in, and the women were paraded before us. The two experienced sailors chose their women. I sat there, covering my fear with the veneer of the macho sailor. Someone negotiated a price for the three of us: it was $36 Singapore each – about £15 in all. I remember that I paid.

My friends disappeared with some of the prostitutes. A woman at the end of the line came and chose me. She took my hand and led me to her room.

The room was dull, the bed unmade and the bin overflowing with paper tissues. The smell of sex was everywhere, and I was terrified. I stayed for a few minutes, but I couldn't do anything: I just couldn't do it to her.

I had seen so much by then that disturbed and stunned me. I'd been in the bars where women attempted – on pain of punishment if they failed – to get sailors to buy them a drink. The dark-brown watery liquid was the price for fondling under the table. I'd faced the reality of death for the first time when, during an exercise, one ship literally cut another in half and we spent the rest of the day searching for bodies in the water. But above all I'd experienced the way men's power and desire for sex can distort what is right and natural.

Singapore in the 1960s was a very different place from the one it is today. Wherever the West had its naval bases a corrupt trade in sex would emerge. In Singapore a young boy had come up to me – he saw I was a Western sailor – and offered to sell me his sister. The boy was about eleven; the girl a year younger. I remember thinking even then that this was crazy: how could anyone do this to another human being?

Such sensibility was unlikely to find favour in the raucously macho atmosphere of the ratings' mess. I kept my misgivings to myself and stayed silent, above all, about my inability to have sex in the Singapore brothel.

The mess was informed that I had gone through the rites of 'manhood'. No one was ever to discover that nothing had happened between the prostitute and me. It was very clear to me that I couldn't be seen to fail: I was a sailor, I was one of the lads.

Instead, on my next shore leave I got royally drunk and was persuaded, for the first and last time, to undergo the traditional naval ritual of being tattooed.

On my right forearm the Hong Kong tattooist engraved a small and sinuous motif. It was an attempt to translate my Christian name into Chinese characters, using the pictographs for 'thunder' and 'door'. In Cantonese the words 'thunder' and 'door' are pronounced 'laymond'.

For the next three years I served my apprenticeship on HMS *London*, touring all the major Far Eastern ports and being shown the extremes of the naval rating's shore leave by 'Sea Daddies', older and more worldly wise sailors. In those three years I became ever more disturbed by what I witnessed. And then in 1970 I returned to Belfast to find a city beset by the Troubles – divided and at war with itself.

When I got back to the city I wanted to contact my old friends – I'd been away for three years and had any number of stories to tell. But they lived in Andersonstown: I found myself excluded, suddenly cut off from all my peers.

Andersonstown was – still is – in the heartland of Belfast's Republican district. In and among its housing estates, unemployment and poverty the IRA first recruited, then hid, the volunteers who were waging war on the police and the British Army.

For me, a serving British naval seaman, to have ventured across its arbitrary borders would have been suicide. No longer could I call Belfast home.

Instead, isolated and lonely, I signed up for submarine duty, first on a conventional boat and later for a tour of duty on HMS *Valiant*, one of the Navy's nuclear submarines constantly on patrol under the world's most remote and inhospitable seas.

Control Electrician Mechanic (1st Class) Wyre was set to work on the control units for the submarine's torpedo-guidance systems. At the age of twenty I was one of a handful of men in control of the world's most sophisticated weapon of mass destruction.

Life on a nuclear submarine is unlike any other form of military posting. There are few, if any, opportunities for what the Navy calls 'R & R' – binges of beer and women in traditional sailors' ports. The entire world is compressed into the confines of a surprisingly small boat. At the very least, it leaves plenty of time for thought.

Those thoughts steered me towards religion. So, when at the end of the tour I was given a medical discharge (bad feet) and a war pension (£26 per week), I promptly enrolled as a student at a Birmingham Bible College.

In between studies I began working as a probation volunteer in the Family Centre at the city's Winson Green Prison. My job was to make and serve tea to the sad flotilla of mothers, wives and children on their weekly visits. Among my first clients were the relatives of the six Irishmen arrested – wrongly – for the Birmingham pub bombings.

The bombings, and the deaths and maimings left in their wake, had caused a fever of anger and recrimination within hours of the first news reports.

The climate of opinion in the city and throughout the country was violently hostile. The police responded by seeking 'confessions' from the 'Birmingham Six' – confessions that would, twenty years later, be found bogus and false.

Looking back, it seems a curious twist of fate: my professional life all but began with the victims of a case built on prejudice, anger and spurious confessions. Within ten years I would be struggling daily with the same problems and ethical dilemmas. How, after all, does the professional approach cases that seem to require a suspect to implicate himself?

The prosecution of child-abuse allegations all too frequently founders on the rock of a suspect's inalienable right to be proven guilty beyond all reasonable doubt. And yet, when the only evidence is the word of the child accusing him, how can his civil liberties be reconciled with the very real needs and rights of the alleged victim?

The main purpose of our legal system must be to protect an individual from the abuses of the state. Better that a hundred guilty men be found innocent than one innocent man be found guilty. But the tragedy with sexual crime is that it is never simply the state against a citizen: it is one individual against another.

In the case of sexual crime, if we sustain the nostrum that a person is innocent until found guilty, we have to accept that the person who claims to have been abused is guilty of lying and deception until a conviction proves him or her truthful. Put so bluntly, this is not an appealing concept – yet neither is the option of assuming the accused's guilt on the basis of one person's allegations. There is no comfortable route through this dilemma.

All that can be said is that when a man is acquitted it does not always follow that his accuser was lying. With sexual crime, not having sufficient evidence to convict does not automatically signify innocence, a civil liberties nightmare that is impossible to resolve. In sex-abuse cases I would like the verdict of 'not proven' added to 'not guilty' and 'guilty'.

And the problem is exacerbated by the existence of two parallel justice systems in child-abuse cases. When an alleged murderer or burglar is acquitted his ordeal is over. With child abuse it can be only the beginning: civil courts are invoked to consider the man's position in his family and how to ensure the future protection of children. These courts operate on a lower standard of proof – the balance of probability as opposed to the criminal courts' requirement for proof beyond all reasonable doubt. An acquitted man can still be 'punished' by the rulings of these civil courts.

This was a dilemma I would soon have to face. There was never – is never – a neat and easy answer. While part of my job would be to encourage honesty in alleged offenders, any 'confession' might not be strictly accurate, even if it was admissible in court.

The rage and impotence that society instinctively feels about child abuse are no justification for bad justice. The lesson of the Birmingham Six – though at that time no one was prepared to listen to the men – was precisely the same.

Given the public anger and demand for revenge in the wake of the pub bombings, it was, perhaps, not the happiest timing for a public debate on the reintroduction of capital punishment, much less for me to oppose it.

The debate had been planned for some time by the Birmingham Bible Institute, part of the theological college where I was studying. My own resistance to the death penalty was no secret, and I was picked to oppose the motion calling for its return. It was not a popular view that night.

But even then, and subsequently as I handed out cups of tea to the families of the men charged with the bombings, I felt no rush of anger towards those who kill. My overriding emotion was sadness. Anger seemed a sort of luxury – an intense reaction we cannot generally afford. Quite simply, it is impossible to produce change, or at least positive change, in people's behaviour if we let anger take over.

I stayed at the Bible College for three years, working throughout as a probation volunteer. If the experience affected me, it was not by way of channelling me into the clergy.

Having worked as a volunteer – against the college's wishes – I no longer saw my vocation in the professional clergy. The Church, for me, had become an institution that concentrated on minor issues rather than rooting itself in the real life I saw around me.

I had met, and been deeply impressed by, a visiting speaker from the probation service. I had only attended his lecture by chance, but he planted within me the idea of working for the service. It would mean another two years as a student: to join the service I would need a Certificate in Social Work. It was no easy option. I was married, and we had two young children: funding would be crucial. At Bible College I had survived by selling rewiring, and, if all else failed, this would help make ends meet.

I saw in probation the hope of effecting change in offenders.

It was, and remains, the only arm of the judicial system dedicated to working with offenders rather than simply containing them. But if *I* knew I should become a full-time probation officer, the service itself was less convinced.

I applied for a grant to fund my two years of training: the Home Office, which is responsible for probation, awarded a few bursaries every year.

But it rejected my application swiftly and without giving a reason. It seemed my chosen career was to be over before it started.

I decided to give it one last try. I phoned the Home Office, not knowing whom I needed to speak to or even which department I should ask for. Eventually I was put through to the right section. I gave my name, and the voice at the other end asked me to repeat it. He seemed astonished that I had called and explained that literally five minutes earlier a decision had been taken to reconsider and approve my application. The extraordinary coincidence of timing appeared to be a good omen for my career in the probation service.

Between 1977 and 1981 I worked as one of many generic, or non-specialist, probation officers in the West Midlands – in divorce-court welfare, juvenile supervision and the supervision of men on parole. I was learning the rules of the criminal justice system and, most important, listening to offenders discuss their crimes.

After three years I was transferred to Albany, the highly secure and fortress-like prison on the Isle of Wight. My clients came from two of the 'wings' into which the prison was divided.

C Wing housed long-term prisoners deemed to be in need of special security attention. There was a smattering of convicted terrorists – including Patrick Hill, one of the Birmingham Six, by then jailed for the city bombing, the leader of the Balcombe Street siege, one of the Islamic extremists arrested after the SAS stormed the Iranian Embassy – together with a handful of celebrated murderers.

In prison I found the probation officer's role lagging far behind that of probation officers in the world outside. Even the jargon used was archaic: we were known by the old job title of 'welfare officers' and were expected to be little more than glorified secretaries to the prisoners. We were the link between the prisoners and the outside, liaising with their families and writing the reports that determined who got home leave or parole. While many of us wanted to be genuinely useful – to have a rehabilitative function – the prison was more intent on using us to handle the humdrum tasks associated with keeping a large body of men incarcerated. Far from effecting change, we were there to administer daily routines and work rosters that hadn't been altered in a generation. It was immensely frustrating for me – and for the men on C Wing.

But my experience with the other wing for which I was responsible was to prove formative. E Wing was officially classed as a Rule 43, or vulnerable-prisoner, unit. In it, segregated for their own safety, thirty-six sex offenders served their sentences largely untroubled by any official attempt to understand – much less change – their behaviour.

At that time little or nothing was being done with sex offenders. Their daily routine was mundane: most were employed in painting toy soldiers. Their life had none of the rewards that even the men on C Wing enjoyed. There was hardly any recreation, and their exercise yard was an enclosed concrete compound otherwise used by prisoners on punishment fatigues. It seemed that they had been just dumped inside the wing and were kept there until their release without any attention being paid to their paedophile or other sexually aberrant tendencies. Somehow the prison and the Home Office seemed to think that simply imprisoning these men was enough – that, on their own, their sentences would cure the problem.

Clearly, they could not and had not. Many of these men had offended many times, had abused a large number of children or women and revived their old patterns of offending almost as soon as they were released. Inside the wing they had the opportunity to mix freely with other paedophiles, and little or no attempt was made to attack the cause of their behaviour. The same was true throughout the prison system. Some work had been done with sex offenders inside Maidstone Jail, but when the officer who initiated the sessions left, most of the efforts stopped.

The Home Office wasn't interested in setting up new programmes or even researching the possibility of a different approach. As late as 1987 the Home Office told me it had no intention of backing research into the treatment of sex offenders because it put effort only into areas where a change of policy was expected. In those days there was absolutely no intention of changing policy.

Bemused by this apparently cavalier attitude, I began working intensively with the group of sex offenders. At first the process involved a good deal of simple listening to what the men had to say about their own lives and their offending. In Albany it was felt that, as a group, the men posed a security risk, so initially I had to meet them in my office (two cells knocked into one) on the wing.

The first pattern I discerned was that, faced with someone in authority over them, all the men either denied the facts of their offences or put the blame on someone else. Most understated what were quite often serious sexual assaults; some minimized the effects on the children; others suggested that by abusing the youngsters they had been helping them to understand sexuality or the facts of life.

It was clear that within this one wing of sex offenders was an entire community of men – men whom our society viewed as a danger to its sons and daughters – who had a completely distorted view of children and sex. Yet that same society was apparently content to let these offenders hold on to their twisted beliefs in the knowledge that most would go out and abuse more children as soon as they were released.

We were releasing habitual paedophiles back into the community, often without even basic subsequent supervision. Sometimes the only way I knew where they were heading was by the destination stamped on the regulation railway warrant handed to them at the gate. The result was dangerous men, often resentful about being punished, with no supervision, a bigger set of paedophile contacts and no official record of their whereabouts. It was complete madness.

I had no formal training in working with sex offenders. No training was available anywhere in Britain. All I had to go on were my own instincts and a belief that there had to be a better way of protecting society than simply locking men up for a few years and hoping that prison would cure them.

At the time the main responsibility for any group of sex offenders lay with probation officers. For years the psychiatric profession had not been concerned with paedophiles or rapists except when an individual's psychopathy was so disturbed or extreme as to make him 'interesting'.

Throughout the 1970s psychiatry moved towards a medical model, increasingly orienting its work in studies of the chemical function of the brain. Unsurprisingly, drugs became the method of choice for controlling patients. Behavioural problems were treated as a biological challenge to be confronted with a definably scientific chemical response. But for this to work within the existing legal structure offenders had to be dealt with under the mental health rather than criminal justice system. The reality was that relatively few men were accepted as mental health patients, and the rest were left within a rudderless prison system.

Psychology, as a profession, spent much of the decade in conflict with psychiatry. And while the academic research produced in the 1970s, particularly studies of methods of assessing patients, moved the debate forward, there was little effort to improve treatment. The clinical psychologist within a prison became a very rare breed: a few years later, by 1988, there were just three in the entire service.

The work I did with the men in Albany began to challenge the way in which they justified or validated their offending and tried to make them understand the effect of their crimes on their victims. From 1981 onward I began to specialize in working with the sex offenders on E Wing. Gradually more offenders were placed in the unit, yielding more information about how and why men abuse children.

In 1983 a series of prison riots led to the dispersal of all my non-sex-offending clients to other high-security jails. Purely by chance, I was left as a *de facto* specialist working with an enlarged community of seventy-six convicted sex offenders. Out of the seventy-six men, fifty-six wanted to join a new treatment programme I proposed. The vast majority had been in and out of the prison system for years, some since they were adolescents. It was clear that no one had had done anything with them during their previous sentences. The issue was not seen as a psychiatric problem, and only one of them was regularly seeing the prison psychiatrist.

The new programme involved a continuation of the previous groups, but this time it was properly timetabled. I was officially running seven groups a week. But from the outset much of the work was viewed with alarm and distrust by other staff within the prison.

The Prison Officers Association at Albany wasn't happy. Its members couldn't understand why anyone wanted to work with these men. They thought of them as dirty, perverted monsters: many prison officers thought they should be killed or, at the very least, left to rot in prison.

In this the officers and the other prison inmates were united. There is nothing lower or more despised in British prisons than the 'nonces' (prison slang for sex offenders). If left to serve their sentences on the general wings, they run the very real risk of serious beatings, even death. But putting them together for their own safety on the Rule 43 wing had its own drawbacks. By concentrating so many paedophiles together in one place, with relatively light supervision, a safe haven was established in which they were able to form alliances and new child-sex rings in anticipation of their release.

There were also personal consequences for me. So great was the hatred of sex offenders, and so little did my colleagues understand about the nature of paedophilia, that merely by working with these men I somehow became tarred by their crimes. Many people either assumed or suggested out of spite that I must be a paedophile to want to work with them.

Nonsense, of course – but dangerous and insidious nonsense none the less. I discovered that some of the prison officers would try to dissuade offenders from joining my groups. They told the men, 'Don't go with Wyre – he'll only have you wanking.'

Much of this antagonism was caused by the shift in the balance of power between the prisoners and the officers that my sessions caused. As they began, for the first time, to understand what was causing them to offend, they also began to feel they had some power over their own lives. That led them to question the prison officers' daily aggression. They felt sufficiently empowered to ask their jailers: 'Do you really think your attitude is helping me?'

But there was also perfectly understandable reasoning behind some of the officers' hostility. One prison officer in particular was vehemently opposed to my work with offenders. One day I confronted him and asked why he was so hostile. The answer was brutally simple: his daughter had a terminal illness. It would respond to treatment, but treatment was in short supply because of the cost. For him, to devote scarce resources to treating men who abused children, while at the same time failing sick youngsters, was a kind of madness. It was for me too, but I saw a greater stupidity in not treating sex offenders and allowing them to abuse yet more children.

It was not the only idiocy that quickly became apparent. The prison system seemed to have developed a self-protective shell over its handling of sex offenders, a shell that worked fine for the jail and its staff but less well for the community outside. There appeared to be a complete inability to understand the basic issues. This reached its apogee in the practice of early releases.

No community surrounding a prison wants sex offenders released before they have served every single day of their sentences – which is, perhaps, an understandable emotional reaction. But without early release the prison system does not provide for any supervision, merely voluntary after-care which places the burden of seeking help on the released prisoner. To complicate the matter further, in Albany the boards that operated the parole system, which processes early release for offenders, didn't want to be seen to fail. And, given that a high proportion of untreated sex offenders routinely reoffended very quickly after release, there was a general fear that all the blame for any new offences would be heaped by the community on the parole boards.

This is a problem that constantly faces community-based programmes. No one wants dangerous men in their midst, but at least with early release the offenders are supervised. The result of the politics and the policy deficiencies was that dangerous men were released routinely and with no supervision whatsoever. The chaos that ensued from an official reluctance to take responsibility for these men was graphically illustrated by one man who was due for a scheme called 'terminal home leave'.

Under this system a short home leave is granted when the offender is four months from the end of his sentence. The man in question was at the time in the punishment block, but was none the less put up for terminal home leave. I did something that was considered very unusual for a probation officer: I argued that the leave should not be granted because he seemed to me to be highly disturbed. He had told me that he intended to commit suicide by hanging himself from a lamppost outside the prison. On that basis – and because I was convinced he would re-offend unless carefully supervised – I opposed the home leave.

Within days, I was due to take my own annual leave. While away on holiday, I discovered that the home-leave board had overruled my recommendation. I was so worried that I arranged for a probation volunteer to meet him outside Albany and put him on the train. Then I called the probation service in Manchester and asked one of the staff to meet the man off the train and take him to the hostel where he was to stay. Finally, I rang the hostel and told them that when the prisoner went missing (as I was sure he would) they should phone me immediately.

Within twenty-four hours the hostel was on the phone: the man had absconded the same evening and had never returned. Immediately I put a call through to the Home Office to fix an official 'recall' of the home leave, which would allow him to be picked up by the police. But it was too late. By the time he was caught he had murdered three teenage boys.

Experiences like this burned into my mind. They became the fuel that drove my arguments with the Home Office: something had to be done.

In 1984 I was given a scholarship to study the way in which sex offenders and their victims were treated in the United States. It was to be a formative experience. I had always believed that there must be someone who knew how to tackle the problem. In America I met the same set of issues and some of the same bureaucratic difficulties. But I also discovered that there people had begun to address the subject.

My most influential experience was working with the men and women who profile serial killers. At the time I was based in New York with the city's Rape Crime Squad. On an FBI course I began to learn about the patterns within offending by studying the scene of crime and working out an offender's motivation from what he had done to the body. Simultaneously I was confronted by the reality of what these academic analyses meant. Working with the Squad I saw what the rapist-killer did to his victims; I saw the bodies – the mutilated women and damaged children.

The course gave me invaluable experience. But it also gave me two other enormous boosts. I came back to England convinced that we had to do something more than to contain our sex offenders temporarily. And I came back with the confidence to try. It was a confidence I would shortly need to draw on deeply. In less than two years the ignorance and prejudice confronting me and blocking my efforts became unmanageable.

The Prison Officers Association, never happy with the idea of working with sex offenders, threatened to strike unless I left the prison. I was swiftly transferred from Albany to a community probation office. The sex offenders' groups were terminated.

The prison officers saw me, in the final analysis, as no more than a voodoo worker (the governor at that time actually used precisely those words), a soft touch who challenged the macho approach. And, of course, I made mistakes: the work I was doing was new and was taking place within a societal and professional context that held that working with sex offenders could not achieve anything worth while.

I was breaking new ground, however inexpertly. Failure, for me, was an important part of learning. But what I learnt was invaluable. I learnt one lesson above all else: I recognized that the sex offender was the expert, not the professional working with him.

And from that followed a vital principle. Therapy is not something a therapist does to a sex offender: a therapist is, instead, a person who facilitates change and sometimes, in some ways, motivates it. A therapist can help an offender to understand, maybe even to face the truth of, who or what he is. If the therapist can do this, it can lead to change. I realized early on that what can be achieved is not a 'cure' but a control. And although not all offenders want to change, they can gain control of themselves and of their actions – and they can enjoy the feeling of being in control and not abusing.

I learnt also that there was a way of obtaining information from the offender in a way that could give him the hope of changing. The effect of abuse on women and children had already convinced me that information from their abusers could help them. Prison taught me that the release of this information could also help the offender. Rather than seeing no way forward, they could begin to see the possibility of living a life without abusing. They could begin to understand that, in some way, the abuse of someone else was also an abuse of themselves.

Looking back, I know that I was never so naïve as to believe that all offenders would be willing to embrace, or be capable of, change. But I was, perhaps, naïve in thinking that what I was attempting would easily be accepted. It wasn't, and I wasn't. At the end prison officers told me bluntly that if I ever spoke to a sex offender again, they would not speak to me.

I have often wondered since if it could have been different. Could I have made other decisions? In the end I simply tell myself that since I raised my head above the parapet, I should have expected to be shot at.

A parting of the ways seemed inevitable. In 1987, at the age of thirty-six and now with three children, a wife and a mortgage, I left the security of the probation service to work where and whenever I could with sex offenders, convinced that in such sessions lay the best hope for protecting children. To fund the work, I borrowed heavily from the bank.

I will never forget those early days. I had resigned from the probation service with no grand business plan, no idea where I would find the money to fund my work. We moved to Northampton, where my sister-in-law lived. The next few years were going to be hard on my wife Shirley, but at least she would have the support of her family.

I knew that I could continue counselling offenders and develop a secondary income from running training sessions. But the most important thing was my need to keep working with the offenders: I had so much to learn from them, so much they could teach me, that I could pass on to society at large.

I went to see our bank manager and asked for an overdraft. I had no collateral, no security. He agreed. Somehow I must have convinced him my vision was worth backing.

I was approached almost immediately by a psychiatrist at St James's Hospital in Portsmouth. He suggested that I should run a twice-weekly clinic for sex offenders who were living in the community. I would be paid just £50 a week, but the money seemed irrelevant. The clinic was my vital first step as an independent therapist.

The clinic was established in the outpatients department and began with only a handful of offenders. Within three months twenty habitual paedophiles were attending every weekly session.

In the past, whenever sporadic efforts had been made to work with sex offenders, it had always been on an individual basis. I began to see that group sessions, with a number of men at different stages in their treatment, might offer some hope of change.

The groups began to develop their own internal dynamic. There was nothing cosy or gentle about many of the sessions: no one knows better than an abuser the excuses and lies a fellow abuser may try to put forward, and gradually the men in the groups began to police each other's distorted thinking.

Initially the men challenged the self-justifications each of them offered. When a new man joined the group and, as was typical, either denied his offence or blamed his victim, it would frequently be the other men who jumped in to demolish his excuses.

In Portsmouth I saw for the first time in Britain a realistic prospect of preventing habitual paedophiles committing offence after offence. For a long time I had been curious about what stopped some men from committing, say, a full-blown rape and of being convicted instead of attempted rape. At some point during the offence they must have stopped, pulled back from the brink. I wanted to know why and how that process worked.

In trying to understand that process I wasn't in any way attempting to diminish the effects of even attempted rape on the victim: it wasn't a question of praising an offender for 'only' committing the attempt. But, clearly, there was some mental process going on – a sort of internal dialogue – that put up a barrier or recognized an inhibition. And this stopped the men going through with the full rape. If I could get into offenders' minds and somehow find a way to trigger these internal inhibitors, then the cycle of offending could be interrupted and perhaps broken for ever.

The Portsmouth group operated quietly and without any media attention. All the men who attended its weekly sessions had lengthy histories as active paedophiles. (One, a seventy-year-old former foster-parent, had been carefully selecting young boys to abuse all his adult life. Until a few months earlier he had never been caught.) All of the men lived, as they had before the clinic started, largely unsupervised in the community. There was no legal method by which the police or the probation service could monitor any of them.

Had anyone known about the group, there would almost

certainly have been a public outcry – not because what we were doing was wrong or putting people at risk but simply because no one wants sex offenders in their midst. The irony was that the work I did with these men actually reduced the risk, which was otherwise very high, of their abusing more children. It was a paradox that I was to see again and again as my work with paedophiles developed. It was as though only by remaining wilfully ignorant could a community feel safe.

But if it attracted no publicity, the work had been noticed by police forces and social workers. By 1987 I was dividing my time between the Portsmouth group and an ever-growing case load. Simultaneously I found that I was in demand for conference speeches. And conferences led to training sessions. Individual social workers sought advice; police forces began calling me in on difficult investigations.

It seemed as though the message was at last beginning to get through. Social workers and probation officers responded positively quite early; the police were initially more sceptical but very soon began to see how offender information could help them in their investigations and interviews. They had spent so long listening to the lies offenders fed them, and so little time listening to what the victims of these men were saying, that when my work was acknowledged it was a real breakthrough. Even some of the most reactionary newspapers carried editorials demanding that we work with offenders rather than simply incarcerating them.

But recognition did not bring financial security. All the while I was working out of a tiny and cluttered bedroom, shared with my eldest son, in our little town house in Northampton. The battered Lada in which I spent an increasing part of my life was accumulating an alarming number of miles on the odometer.

Gradually – month by month, conference by conference – the word spread. By 1988 my work was becoming so widely recognized that I was able to formalize the treatment programmes within a residential centre for sex offenders. The Gracewell Clinic, with financial backing from a local entrepreneur, was born.

From its inception Gracewell carried a full complement of twelve staff. Four of us had extensive experience in the field of sexual abuse. Jenny Still had been with the NSPCC and Great Ormond Street Children's Hospital; Hilary Eldridge came direct from Nottingham probation service, where she had been working with sex offenders; and Ian Henderson was a psychiatric nurse who had helped me to run the groups at St James's Hospital. Together we set about creating a coherent treatment programme. The other staff came from a wider background: from probation, inevitably, but we also attracted social workers, psychologists and a consultant psychiatrist. Charles Fortt, who had been senior probation officer at Parkhurst Prison before coming to Albany as my senior, joined us as clinic manager.

Very quickly Gracewell received a steady stream of 'clients' – offenders sent there by the courts, prison or social services departments. Subsequently, a training unit was set up to teach others the skills used at Gracewell and to analyse the swathes of information its clients were yielding. At times the power and importance of this data were almost overwhelming. In one of Gracewell's earliest days I turned to Charles and asked, 'Why are they telling me all this? What's in it for them to be so open?'

The clinic provided a rapid learning curve, as much for me as for the staff. Our guiding principle was that the offender was the expert. But I also saw quickly that simply facilitating the outpouring of information wasn't enough: the men had to get beyond a cognitive response. I wanted them to feel, and I sought out ways of taking their thinking into feeling and then of diverting their feeling into new ways of thinking.

I was cautious too. These men were among the most manipulative of offenders, and there was an old saw which ran repeatedly through my mind: 'Educating a devil may just make a clever devil.'

Exploring the offender's fantasies became a key part of our work. It had always struck me that to understand what motivated an offender I needed to get inside his head. At Albany I had once been approached by a sex offender who asked me whether he was certain to abuse when he was released. There was no way I could make any prediction, but I had learnt never to give a negative response. Instead I asked him what he thought about when he masturbated. He considered this and then said 'Oh, I see what you mean.' At the time I had no idea what I had actually meant – or at least not its significance. But as we discussed the matter further he described how he lay in his cell masturbating to mental images of young girls, fantasies that were becoming increasingly worse.

I began to see how we could evaluate offenders by entering their fantasies and how important it was to be able to control them. I also began to see how certain types of offender used fantasy and how, for others, it seemed less important.

At Gracewell we ended up with a profile of four types of offender with a breakdown of how fantasy operated in their lives.

The first were men who were sexually oriented towards children, of either sex, who presented as fixated offenders. They seemed to show a steady level of illegal fantasizing.

The second group could be described as binge fantasizers, men whose fantasies came, like their offending, in bursts. Many rapists, both those motivated by sexual desire and those driven by anger, fell into this pattern. Most spoke about fantasy as a problem.

Sadistic offenders formed a third category. For these men the sexual element seemed less important than the violence that accompanied it. It was as though what they truly wanted to do was to hurt, and in the hurting they were aroused by their victim's reactions. Clearly, it would be important to understand how violence had come to be involved in their fantasies – important but immensely difficult: this group above all were reluctant to discuss the images in their minds.

Finally there was a group of offenders who insisted they had no fantasies involving sexual abuse. In prison, had anybody bothered even to explore this area in the first place, such a statement would have been taken at face value. But we were working with men who did not want to volunteer information: the question we had to ask was whether they were telling the truth or were simply still in denial.

At Gracewell our inclination was never to accept unquestioningly what an offender told us. And as time went by these men did begin to talk about fantasy. Their refusal to discuss it was caused less by the nature of their fixation than by a realization that, if they admitted fantasies in the context of their offending, the criminal justice system would perceive these fantasies as evidence of the deliberateness of their crime and impose a harsher punishment.

Our society punishes those who plan their offending more severely than those who do not. Consequently, the abusers tried to convince us that somehow the offences 'just happened'. I came to the conclusion that the only way to deal with this was to approach all sex offenders with the assumption that their behaviour was deliberate and premeditated. If we took this route, we might discover it turned out to be correct, but if we approached them as offenders who had committed one-off offences that happened out of the blue, every single one of them would gratefully confirm this.

So by the end of 1990, when the phone call came through from Robert Black's lawyers, I could almost predict what would be waiting for me in Saughton Prison, Edinburgh. I knew primarily that Black would, if he admitted the Laura offence at all, insist that it was a one-off, something he had never done before that was completely out of character. All offenders are, initially, in this stage of denial. I knew too that he would be minimizing the offence: trying to find words that made it sound not too serious. He would try to normalize it, to make it seem as though it had happened in a very ordinary, even understandable, way.

He would take examples from the society around him – from newspaper articles to the behaviour of other people – to make his actions seem normal. He would be looking for excuses for the offence and justifications for these excuses. One excuse, inevitably, would be to blame the victim in himself.

Most people, if seeking to excuse their own illegal sexual behaviour, can identify a past experience of unwelcome sexual advances or even abuse. Sex offenders routinely use their own past experiences – and many have been abused as children – to legitimize what they have done to their victims. One way to circumvent a list of excuses and prevarications, the outer defences of a cornered paedophile, would be to explore Black's fantasies, the sexual images inside his mind to which he masturbated.

At one level the fantasies would show what aroused him sexually and thereby reveal the type of paedophilia – sadistic, seductive, opportunist – to which he conformed. At a deeper level they might offer a 'safe' way for him to tell me not only what he dreamed of doing but what he had actually done.

The only information about Black I had to go on was the bare bones of the police case, as presented in court, and the life sentence imposed by Lord Ross. On the surface it was a one-off offence. But what was below the surface?

That was precisely the question that I was asked to answer – and Robert Black had a strong vested interest in my response: if he convinced me that he was not as dangerous as Ross believed, the appeal against sentence could progress. If not, an unknown number of years in prison was all he could look forward to.

I suspected I knew why he wanted to see me: he probably regarded me as a possible means of escape from his indeterminate sentence. He would have an image of himself that he wanted to persuade me was accurate. I call the process that his mind was doubtless going through 'psychological situational'. Anyone faced with a difficult situation is going to spend a great deal of time thinking about what he or she will and will not say in response to questioning.

In simple terms he would be working out the best way to con me. If he discovered I had some knowledge of his pattern of offending, or if he recognized my experience of sex offenders, I could expect an intellectual cat-and-mouse game. And because I had to assume that Laura was not an isolated offence, I expected to meet someone of considerable mental abilities.

These thoughts were running through my mind as I took the plane from Birmingham to Edinburgh. I was preparing my own strategy: how to reach across his defences enough to get a hold on the man within, how to find the right part of myself to offer him as a trigger to make him tell at least some of the truth.

I knew that our meeting would take place in an unforgiving prison cell, 16 feet long by 12 feet wide. Saughton Prison, built in the 1920s, was a grim and archaic reminder that our penal system values retribution more than the notion of rehabilitation to which it occasionally pays lip-service. To look at Saughton, and at countless prisons like it, is to look at a cage built to confine rather than counsel. Little wonder that its inmates often seemed to want to earn the misleading public image of them as monsters, not men.

Yet if I knew one thing above all that day in September 1990, it was that, whatever Robert Black had done, he was not a monster. He was just a man, as I am. And it was my job to get through to him somehow.

At 9.30 a.m., on 8 September 1990, I was led through the dank Victorian corridors of HMP Saughton. I passed through the admissions hall, a daunting and bleak induction to an antique penal system, with its strip showers, holding cubicles or 'dog boxes' and the tiny room furnished only with a cold stone bench and powerful lamp by whose beam each new inmate was subjected to a dehumanizing search for lice.

I walked alongside the uniformed warder, his keys jangling against regulation blue serge trousers, to a drab and functional interview room. In it two chairs had been placed on opposite sides of a small, standard-issue prison table. I immediately shifted the table to one side. A small and heavily used ashtray was the only other furniture.

A few minutes later Robert Black was led in quietly by two uniformed prison warders. The man who greeted me, shaking my hand firmly and thanking me for coming, was small – no more than 5 feet 7 inches – but powerfully built. A full beard and moustache contrasted with the advancing bald patch at the back of his head; behind a pair of silver-framed glasses Robert Black's eyes were wary and watchful. His voice was calm and well modulated; the accent was distinctive – Lowlands Scottish, with a bias towards Edinburgh and the east coast rather than the harsher tones of Glasgow in the west. It reminded me of a familiar voice, that of a politician, perhaps, a television personality or an actor. I racked my memory to put a name to the accent. Suddenly it came: the soft, even seductive, brogue sounded almost identical to the tones of Sean Connery, the film star.

Black's behaviour at this first meeting set a pattern for what was to follow. He was always slightly withdrawn but never uninterested. He looked directly at me, his eyes never wandering around the room. He never once glanced at his watch, wondering how long I would continue. He never seemed tense and hardly ever expressed any emotion.

Only when I faced him with a difficult question did he break eye contact and drop his head. He struggled to hold on to his feelings, to regain control of himself. As he did so, I kept quiet. Sometimes he raised his head to look at me again, clearly hoping I would break the awkward silence. I didn't. Instead I made facial gestures that let him know I wanted an answer. The silences became deafening. I moved closer to him, offering him a caring movement. I wanted to let him know that I knew how difficult it must be to face up to what he had done.

But what exactly had Robert Black done? My brief for this first encounter was quite clear: I was to assess Black's state of mind, his paedophilia and, above all, the threat he posed to children. The only known ground for this exploration was to be the case for which Black had been sentenced: however much I might harbour suspicions – suspicions based on experience – that the Laura offence was part of a pattern, I had initially to focus on it alone.

At the trial defence counsel had argued that the abduction had been an 'opportunity of the moment' and that Black had tied up the girl only to keep her secure while he made a delivery in a nearby town. This was in keeping with the statement he had made to the police as soon as he was arrested.

> It was a rush of blood. I have always liked young girls. I'd just seen her and got her into the van. I tied her up. I wanted to keep her until I delivered a parcel.
>
> I only touched her a little. I wanted to keep her to go somewhere like Blackpool, where I could spend some time with her.

On my way to Saughton I had methodically worked out what I needed to achieve in the two four-hour meetings I would be allowed. The purpose of my visit was to complete the assessment commissioned by his solicitors. Although they were paying, I was strictly independent: there was no question of my being part of their effort to secure a successful appeal against Black's life sentence.

Because of this almost unique position, I had been able to ask the police for basic details of the Laura case without compromising them, Black or me. The information had been revealing but had raised more questions than it had solved. For example, why had he put Laura through a limited sexual assault just outside the village? Experience told me there might be something significant in that behaviour. Why had he then bound and gagged her after his initial assault? Why was there an apparent inconsistency between his actions – which could clearly be interpreted as sadistic – and the child pornography found in his flat by police after his arrest, none of which depicted the torture of youngsters, as I might have expected?

My report had to deal with what I could find out from Black about his offending and his evident paedophilia and to assess the risk he posed to the community. It followed, then, that I also had to put forward my view of whether the indeterminate life sentence was appropriate for the Laura offence in the context of Black's general sexual behaviour.

What transpired in these earliest meetings with Robert Black remains confidential. I was, after all, seeing Black at the request of his defence team, and the details of what was said in the small and shabby interview cell are covered to this day by the legal doctrine of confidentiality. But by the end of our two meetings in HMP Saughton that September I had begun to get a picture of Robert Black that disturbed me greatly.

Far from feeling able to support the appeal against sentence, I suspected that, given time and encouragement, Black might divulge details of any number of abductions and assaults. There was something too about the way Black discussed the Laura case. He was neither unusually forthcoming, in the hope of winning me over, nor particularly reticent. Instead he gave the impression of a man tormented by the secrets in his mind, a man desperate to find someone who could make sense of his confusion.

This was something I hadn't expected, hadn't prepared for. My experience of paedophiles and killers had led me to assume that Black had only one motive for seeing me: to influence my report for the appeal hearing. With that in mind I had thought that we would meet, I would assess him, I would write the report and that this would be an end to it. But an unmistakable bond was beginning to grow between us: a fragile thread, no doubt, but a thread none the less. And it hung on Black's genuine desire to discover what drove him to abuse children.

By the close of the second interview both of us were mentally exhausted. We had been through a total of eleven hours of deep and painful probing at the mystery of Black's mind. As I got up and moved to signal the prison officers back into the interview room, Black asked an unexpected question: would I come back again, after I had submitted my report, and continue the work we had begun together? I agreed without hesitation.

It was to prove a crucial decision. For both of us.

2

Nobody's Child

As I left Saughton Prison via the heavily fortified modern brick blockhouse, through large, heavy wooden doors that sealed behind me with a deceivingly calm hiss, I was anxious to return and continue the work. But such a meeting could take place only after the report for Black's appeal against sentence had been written and submitted.* I was very aware that the report I knew I had to write might close the door for ever. Black had said enough to convince me that I should not – could not – support his appeal.

In carrying out any risk assessment I have to look at five major areas. The first is motivation: what is it that makes a man choose to abuse a child sexually?

In Black's case all of his past history, including his own abuse as a child in care, had clearly influenced his later offending. This is not to excuse what he did: it simply shed some light on the complex multiple causes of his behaviour. Those early experiences fed into the next area I had to assess – the fantasies that surrounded his actions and titillated his masturbation.

I had known before I met him that he would be masturbating at least once a day to mental images of young girls. Before going to prison this practice had been reinforced by his collection of child pornography and other paedophilic writings. The point about his masturbatory fantasies is that, rather than being harmless safety valves, they represented both what he wanted to do to children and, in some cases, what he had actually done.

The third area for me to look at was his distorted thinking

* Although the precise details of what Black revealed in our first meetings remain confidential, in subsequent sessions he would confirm all that I detailed in my report to Black's lawyers.

and beliefs. It was these that, at an intellectual level, must surely have nurtured his physical actions in abducting and abusing a child. This was where I had encountered the apparent contradiction between Black as a genuine paedophile and his behaviour, which almost led to the death of Laura.

It was a paradox that on the surface made little sense unless it was linked with his fantasies. I suspected (and it later became clear from our subsequent discussions) that one of his obsessions was to explore the vaginal size of his victims – and that he realized this would hurt the child. So he rationalized the conundrum within his distorted thinking, effectively saying to himself: 'I do not want to hurt the child, therefore she has to die so that I do not hurt her.' However bizarre that proposition may seem, he himself suggested it during numerous interviews. He also implied that so long as the child was unconscious, it would be all right for him to hurt her.

I knew that one day I would have to challenge him on this most difficult of concepts: for the moment I simply included it, unchallenged, in my report. But I had to go further. I had to explain how Black's aberrant thought processes would rationalize his victim's pain afterwards: that pain would have been enough to make normal people abandon their actions.

All sex offenders reinterpret their victims' behaviour in a distorted way. If, for example, a child does not scream during an assault, the abuser tells himself that she has 'consented'; if she doesn't tell anyone afterwards, in his mind she has 'willingly' entered into some form of relationship with him. Robert Black was reinterpreting his victims' behaviour. In Laura's case it was clear that the little girl must have endured terrible pain and terror. But Black was telling himself that her enforced silence meant that she was *not* terrified: he used this assumption to ease the pain that his own actions were causing him, and it enabled him to carry on.

This distorted thinking was part of the next area I had to assess: the way in which Black overcame his internal inhibitors – the mental barriers, like conscience, that would otherwise have prevented him from abusing. All of us, sex offenders and normal people alike, are governed to a greater or lesser extent by internal inhibitors: for example, a man or woman who has the opportunity to have an affair but resists the temptation. Part of the reason is that their conscience stops them. If I could have pointed to a viable, dominant internal inhibitor controlling Robert Black, it might have worked in his favour for the appeal. But I had to write about what I had seen and what he had told me. It was crystal-clear that his distorted thinking, his fear of being returned to prison, his sexual arousal by, and his fantasies about, small children and, above all, his constant rehearsing of abductions were all sufficient to overcome any conscious or internal check on his offending.

Of course, external factors govern behaviour – for example, the opportunity to do what one wants without risking unacceptable consequences. (In the example of an adult contemplating an affair, this comes down to the chances of getting caught by their spouse.) In Robert Black's case these were the circumstances that prevented him from abducting and abusing children. I had to deal with his reaction to these external inhibitors.

I had to explain that he targeted children in places he thought suitable – always girls and generally between the ages of six and twelve – and then made an approach when he believed it was safe for him to do so. But his awareness of the dangers was such that if the circumstances were not perfect, he would pull out of the abduction, just as, I discovered, he had done earlier on the day he snatched Laura. This showed how calculating he was, how mindful of the external inhibitors and how far he would go to ensure that the circumstances were ideal.

I carefully documented all these aspects of Black's offending in a closely typed eleven-page report to the appeal solicitors. It ended with an uncompromising assessment of Black's aberrant sexuality. The document was posted on 8 October 1990. One month later Robert Black's appeal was listed at Edinburgh High Court. That morning his barrister showed him the report in the cells beneath the court. Black read it without emotion and abruptly told the lawyers to cancel the appeal.

*

Robert Black – he has no middle name – was born in Falkirk Royal Infirmary on 21 April 1947. His mother, Jessie Hunter Black, had been a munitions worker during the war before drifting through a succession of factory jobs in Grangemouth, a small port on the Firth of Forth.

Jessie was twenty-four years old and unmarried, living in rented accommodation in a small and unyielding Scottish town. Within a year she left Grangemouth, moving the three miles down the coast to Falkirk. She quickly agreed to leave her son in the care of the local adoption and fostering agency.

Soon she met and fell in love with Francis Hall, a boilerman at the local colliery: they married shortly after Robert's first birthday, but Jessie never told her husband about her first child. None of the couple's subsequent children were ever told they had a half-brother. Jessie's sister, Minnie, knew only that Robert had been born and probably adopted.

It was a common enough pattern of the times. Babies born out of wedlock were all too visible evidence of the sin of premarital sex, a source of great and enduring shame. Mothers in that pre-sexual revolution era routinely abandoned their illegitimate offspring in the face of an unforgiving community determined to heap notoriety and scandal on top of the difficulties of single parenthood. And so Robert Black was put up for adoption. Jessie's only bequest to her son was to name him after her own father.

It took only a few months before new parents were found for Robert. Jack and Margaret Tulip were in their fifties, perhaps a little on the elderly side to be bringing up a first child; certainly no adoption agency today would consider them suitable candidates. But they were solid, Godfearing Christians, and their home seemed eminently suitable. The Tulips lived at Kinlochleven, a small town set in breathtaking Highland scenery at the head of Loch Leven. Young Robert Black was assured, at least, of plenty of bracing fresh air, good clean water and the tranquillity of a landscape dominated by forests and mountains.

Whatever happened to him in the eleven years that he lived

at the Tulips' home – and I had already sensed an undercurrent of tension – there were few outward signs of anything untoward.

Villagers later recalled that Robert was somehow 'awkward' as a boy and that his legs were frequently disfigured by ugly bruises, but at the time most simply assumed that Margaret had 'skelped' her son for any one of a number of juvenile misdemeanours. Instant and very physical retribution was the order of the day in a small post-war Highland village.

Jack Tulip was English and had moved to Kinlochleven from County Durham at the end of the war. He had taken a job at the local aluminium smelter. Margaret was Scottish but, like her husband, was regarded as an 'incomer' by the tight-knit community: she had moved there from Motherwell, close to the urban squalor of Glasgow.

Robert Black grew up, by all accounts, into a lonely and isolated small boy. From early on he needed thick, strong glasses – always guaranteed to attract the wrong sort of attention from his peers – and the fact that he never took his adoptive parents' name ensured that he was recognized as an orphan.

When Jack Tulip died Robert and Margaret continued living in the old house in what had become known to the police as the 'rough end' of the village. Robert steadily earned a reputation as a tearaway, hanging around the bus shelter with the local toughs and moving ever further outside Margaret's control. He learnt how to take care of himself and variously beat, or was beaten by, his opponents in the periodic rough-houses that erupted on the streets. But it was all minor misbehaviour. Certainly the young Robert Black was known to the police, but then so were most of the local boys. Those were the days of village bobbies who knew their patch and, for good or ill, treated delinquent youths to a swift clip round the ear. Robert received his fair share.

Margaret Tulip died when Robert was eleven. An orphan for the second time in his short life, he was packed off back to Falkirk and the local children's home. It was not a happy move, and in 1959 Robert, by now an adolescent, was summarily expelled and sent down the road to the Red House in Musselburgh. The Red House was an imposing brick-built mansion overlooking the River Esk just six miles outside Edinburgh. Two miles away was the town of Portobello where, twenty-four years later, a small girl called Caroline Hogg would be abducted.

In the early years of the nineteenth century the Red House was pressed into service as a lunatic asylum. Then, in 1874, its status was changed to a home for 'destitute boys', a chilling and unforgiving phrase very much of its time. By 1959 its role was interpreted a little more kindly than its Victorian inventors had intended. But there was still something of the flavour of a grim and punitive institution about the Red House when Boy 28 – each new arrival was issued with solid black boots, rough tweed shorts and grey woollen jumper bearing his identification number – took up residence in an attic room.

Perhaps the retributive flavour of the place was understandable in Robert Black's case. The circumstances of his departure from the Falkirk home were never made clear, but the staff were told that he had in some way interfered sexually with a young girl living under the same roof.

The regime at the Red House was regimented, disciplined and swift to punish those who infringed its rules. Bullies were routinely beaten by the home superintendent who, on taking up the post, had described conditions there as 'Dickensian'.

Like all the boys at the Red House, Robert Black attended the local secondary school, Musselburgh Grammar. But academically he was never to shine. He was neither better nor noticeably worse than his companions. In fact, aside from projecting an air of a boy all too used to ducking blows from his elders, only his prowess at sport made him stand out. Football, billiards, table tennis, athletics, weightlifting and swimming became passions for him. Every Sunday, after attending the compulsory church service, he slipped away to swim in the seawater baths at Portobello. Monday afternoons would find him training for a life-saving badge in the pool of a nearby private school.

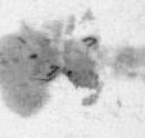

What little spare pocket money he had was spent on music. Robert Black was a child of his changing times: rock and roll, with its back beat, electric guitars and rebellious attitude, had arrived. A black leather jacket in the style of James Dean hung proudly in his cupboard. Records by Johnny Kidd and the Pirates began to accumulate on his shelves. But a decade later he would confide to friends that one of his favourite records was the plangent Hank Snow Country and Western number 'Nobody's Child'. The mawkish lyrics of the singer's loneliness and abandonment – no 'Mommie's kisses' or the smile of a father – and his conclusion that nobody wants him. He has become 'nobody's child'.

If, as he confessed to defence psychiatrist Andrew Zealley, one of the male staff at the Red House abused him, his contemporaries in the home can recall few outward signs of trauma. But this was an era when sexual abuse was an unspeakable taboo, and its victims were sealed in a destructive straitjacket of silence. If Robert Black had been molested, it was almost inconceivable that he could have told another staff member, much less his fellow inmates. And certainly they recalled of Black that rumours about his supposed homosexuality had begun to flourish in the home's hothouse atmosphere of adolescent ignorance and frustration.

Care in the Red House ended when its boys left school. Those who wished to stay on in the Musselburgh area were generally helped to find accommodation and employment. The home superintendent arranged a welding apprenticeship for Robert Black, but a summer holiday intervened, and by the time he returned the job had evaporated. Instead he travelled across to the west coast of Scotland, to Greenock on the Firth of Clyde, just a few miles outside Glasgow. Here he found work as a butcher's errand boy, sleeping in the local working boys' hostel. Robert Black was fifteen years old and alone in an adult world.

Within a year he lost his job. On 25 June 1963 he was convicted at Greenock Juvenile Court of 'lewd and libidinous behaviour'. The official record shows that the offence involved an indecent assault on a seven-year-old girl. The court, plainly unsure of what to do with him, imposed a deferred sentence, effectively suspending punishment for a year. Robert Black walked away from his first conviction and into a dreary succession of labouring jobs in his natural mother's home-town of Grangemouth. These would keep him alive for five long years.

In 1967, at the age of twenty-one, he returned to Kinlochleven when his firm won a contract to work in the area. He lodged with a family whose parents had been friends of Jack and Margaret Tulip. At first all went well: so well that Black spent many a night babysitting the family's six-year-old daughter. But late one night local police arrived at a bar where he was drinking to arrest him. At the nearby station he was charged with three counts of indecent assault. The victim was a six-year-old girl.

On 22 March 1964 Robert Black was sent to Borstal for one year. It was to be his last prison sentence for twenty-three years: the last chance to analyse and influence his emerging pattern of sexual offending.

Inevitably it was a chance that came and went unheeded. At the end of his year in Borstal he moved into a probation hostel in Glasgow. But there all official records of Robert Black cease. When he left the hostel, aged twenty-one and with two convictions for sexual offences against young children, he simply disappeared: no supervision, no follow-up, no trace.

In fact, after a brief period in a nearby bedsit and an apparent brush with Glasgow's uniformed police for 'loitering with intent' to steal from shops, he slipped across the border and headed south to London. For the next twenty-two years Black lived at one of three addresses in Stamford Hill, north London. His first home was a bedsit in Bergholt Crescent; very quickly he moved just a few streets away to Albion Road.

Finally, in 1971, he settled in an attic room at 7 West Bank, a modest terraced house running up one side of Amhurst Park and less than half a mile from his first home. Once a quiet, genteel neighbourhood, the area has gradually sunk into the malaise of drugs and prostitution creeping insidiously across the outer reaches of both north and south London.

Number 7 belonged to Edward and Katherine Rayson and their family of seven children, five boys and two girls. Black's room had a converted dormer window looking out on the street, and it became a sanctuary for him.

His childhood interest in sport had graduated to a determination to keep fit and strengthen his upper body muscles. He turned his room into a make-shift gym and worked out in its confines most days.

At first he took attendant jobs at local swimming pools, boosting the poor wages by working as a part-time barman. Bars simultaneously came to be the centre of his limited social life. Either as a regular drinker at any one of a dozen pubs, or as a member of their darts teams, Robert Black came to be accepted as a fixture in the neighbourhood. But almost invariably his night's drinking ended with a solitary walk back to the attic room at Number 7. If Robert Black had friends, he kept them well hidden.

Other pub regulars took pity on the lonely young man, inviting him to their homes for that staple of English hospitality, the traditional Sunday lunch. But these invitations quickly dried up. There was something in the way he played with their children – bouncing them on his knee or 'pretend fighting' with them – that was unnerving.

Not that there was anything overtly wrong: the children didn't complain, and in truth there was nothing more boisterous to the games than might be expected from a family friend with a genuine interest in the youngsters. And Black did get on well with children – so well that at least one of his employers was happy to leave him babysitting his six children in the flat above the pub he and his wife managed. All the same, there was something about Robert Black that made most parents uneasy.

He began too to accumulate a wider criminal record. On 22 September 1972 he was convicted at North London Magistrates' Court of stealing cars, theft and driving without insurance. For a total of seven offences he was fined £45 and put on probation for two years.

In 1976 he began working as a delivery driver for a company called Poster Dispatch and Storage (PDS). The wages were better than those he had earned as a swimming-pool attendant, but the job involved long hours, driving all over Britain and frequently sleeping rough in the back of his van. Sometimes the destinations were halfway across Europe.

Black didn't object to any of those drawbacks. In fact, colleagues found he became almost obsessive about the driving, anxious to tell them endlessly about new routes he had found – routes that took him away from motorways and main roads and through quiet villages. The other drivers were bemused: most liked to drive the shortest route at the highest possible speed, drop off their cargo of advertising posters and get back to their homes and families as quickly as possible.

Robert Black was different. Though he habitually drove excessively fast – and collected a number of dents and scrapes on the chassis of his dark-blue van to prove it – he would take extraordinarily complicated routes between delivery addresses, often earning warnings for bad timekeeping.

The van – or rather vans, for Black progressed through a number of similar transits – was kitted out with a sleeping bag and a mattress in the back. If a van had windows in the back, curtains were fitted. Although Robert Black lived at 7 West Bank when in London, increasingly his van became his home, his life peripatetic and rootless.

In 1987 he became his own boss: PDS issued the delivery instructions and held the goods until he picked them up, but Black became a self-employed, freelance driver, paid by the job and largely free to choose his own routes and timetables.

The arrangement, although imposed by a new management, suited Black well. It formalized what had been his practice for the past ten years, doing jobs in his own time and via his own tortuous routes. Frequently these were managed so that they took him through the Midlands, where he had friends, or, on a Friday afternoon, on to Blackpool where he would stay for the weekend. This was the pattern of his life for the next thirteen years. For all anyone knew – and for all most cared – Robert Black was simply a van driver who disappeared for lengthy periods from his bedsitter and the bars he frequented.

He was, however, no stranger to the police. Between 1979 and 1986 he collected four new convictions – three for speeding and one for assault causing actual bodily harm (to an adult man). If the succession of magistrates' benches were informed of Black's previous record, the sentences they imposed did not reflect it. The assault cost him £140 in fines, the motoring offences a further £110.

In a sense he slipped through the gratings of the urban streets in which he existed: another grimy worker in a part of the city rapidly crumbling away, a loner, a man with no girlfriend, wife or family and no apparent prospect of finding any one of them. His only real friends in London were Edward and Katherine Rayson, the couple in whose attic he lived for nearly twenty-three years. But they never saw the contents of his room, nor did they know what it was he did when he travelled throughout Britain and across Europe. Even from them he kept his secrets.

Those secrets began to unravel early on the morning of Saturday, 14 July 1990, in a small village in the Scottish Borders when he abducted Laura Turner.

When I heard that the appeal against his sentence for the Turner abduction had been withdrawn, literally at the doors of the court, I assumed that Black would cancel the meeting he had proposed back in September. The date we had set was 11 November, but as the days ticked by there was no message from Saughton Prison. In the absence of any other instructions, I booked tickets and advised the prison of my impending arrival. I asked the governor to ask Black whether he wanted to see me. This became the procedure for every visit. Not once did Black inform the prison staff that he did not want me to come.

I wondered how he would greet me this time. After all, I was the reason why he had abandoned the appeal and now had to face up to an unknown number of years in prison. And I was no longer anything to do with his solicitors. I was there on my own initiative to explore with him the nature of his sexuality.

I was shown to the interview room. He walked in, calmly shook my hand and sat down. We began to talk as if nothing had happened. He readily agreed to my tape recording the interview.

I began by asking him about the appeal, and he told me that, having read the report, there was simply no point in proceeding with the case. There was something – a marked lack of anger – in Black's voice as he explained the decision that had cost him any chance of a determinate sentence. It seemed that the man slouched before me in shabby blue prison denims and a ribbed acrylic blue jersey had been resigned to this outcome almost from the start.

RAY: Why did you agree to see me today?
BLACK: Why not?
RAY: Because your opening comment [was] ... 'You're the person who is the reason I may never get out ...'
BLACK: Well, at the moment you're the only one that might be able to solve any problems I've got ...
RAY: Can you identify what those problems are?
BLACK: Just (*pause*) ... my problem is the fact that ... I've got this thing about children, little girls. Like, what's the reason for it?
RAY: And there's your obsession with orifices.
BLACK: Well, there's that as well, I suppose ...

These opening remarks set the pattern for my conversations with Black over the next eighteen months. Each started hesitantly – I probed, he parried or allowed out only a morsel of information at a time. Our statements, frequently disjointed and fractured by long silences, were opening gambits in a complicated game of intellectual chess.

We had already been over much of the ground in our first two meetings. From then on I was to press him more closely from the security of a knowledge base, albeit a small one. This, and the understanding that I was not constrained by any procedural boundaries about the way in which I conducted the interviews, allowed me to ask what, if asked by a detective, would be viewed as leading questions.

My first task was to get Black to retell his version of the abduction and assault. I pushed a sheet of plain A4-sized paper across the desk and asked him to write down all that happened, and all that was going through his mind, in the hours before he forced Laura into his van. It was a technique called 'thinking, feeling, seeing', and I asked Black first to write that at the top of the page.

I wanted to climb completely inside his head and see everything that he saw, think everything that he thought, feel everything that he felt. I wanted Black to take himself back to the day of the offence, relive it and record on the paper everything that went through his mind. I sensed that it might be important to start him off a little while before the moment at which he abducted Laura. So I suggested he began his recollections from six o'clock that morning. In playing my hunch, together we began the process of opening up Robert's mind. What he wrote, in careful block capitals on a piece of cheap lined A4, was a revealing stream of consciousness. It began as he woke early inside his van.

> 6 a.m.: Well, I've had two hours. Anyway, can always have a kip later on when I'm finished. Drive into Kirkcaldy; find a garage; get directions to delivery. Find a café for breakfast.
>
> Drive back to that new Asda I spotted coming out of Dunfermline and get some tobacco: should be open by then. Then on to Edinburgh. Two drops to do there; one I have to find, one I know.
>
> Café in Kirkcaldy. Not sit down. Roll and cup of tea: can get something later. Decide to do unknown Edinburgh drop first.
>
> Find it at last. Should have done it second. Do known drop; one to do in Galashiels. Have accident with bus on roundabout in Edinburgh. Upset. Just had it repaired in January. Cursing myself, bus driver, my luck, everything.

Start down A7 to Galashiels. Sun comes out: looks like it's going to be a good day. Might go to Blackpool if it looks good further south.

Stop in lay-by to take off sweatshirt. Look at damage: hub cap all dented. Take it off, examine well. Cap won't go back on: throw it away. Cursing bus driver: he could have stopped.

Roll a couple of fags. Have to find café, have a meal, roll a few more, get a paper.

Come to village. See girl with dog: stop and watch her in mirror till out of sight. Turn round: see if any chance of pick-up. Can't find her.

Out of village. Find place to turn round. Back into village. See side street. Look up there. See girl and dog again, park.

Get out of van and ask her if there's a café in village. She directs me to café.

Thank her. Get back in van. No chance there.

As I read the words I realized that the girl with the dog was not Laura. What Black was describing was another attempted or aborted abduction earlier the same day. And with a growing sense of excitement and unease I saw the beginnings of a pattern of offending, a pattern that promised both the prospect of treatment and the likelihood of many more victims.

It seemed as though Black had set out to abduct a girl that day but, for some reason, had pulled out at the last moment. Clearly, if he was capable of stopping himself during the course of an offence, then there might be a way of working on whatever triggered that. But there was also a sense, in what he wrote, of a man going through a familiar routine, a routine in which, unless all the circumstances seemed perfect, the abduction would be aborted before any abuse could take place. If so, the implication was that Laura was very far from being an isolated offence: there would have been many more rehearsed but aborted attempts – and almost certainly a number of other successful abductions.

Further down the sheet Black began to describe the build-up to the snatching of Laura herself. Again I was struck by the meticulous preparation that preceded the abduction.

Find café and newsagent's. Have breakfast, read paper, roll fags. Come out of café. See girl [Laura] across road.

Go to van, turn round: girl out of sight. Go up road and turn round. On way back see girl coming down path from house.

Pull over and park with wheels on pavement. Get out and start polishing windows, mirrors.

Go round to passenger side door. Girl coming towards me. Open passenger door (blocks pavement) as girl comes near . . .

The village that Black targeted that morning (for legal reasons it cannot be identified) sits in the rugged tranquillity of the Scottish Borders, beneath the Moorfoot and Lammermuir Hills that lie south of Edinburgh. Forty miles west is Coldstream, the town that marks the border between Scotland and England where, in the summer of 1982, an eleven-year-old girl called Susan Maxwell was abducted.

It is a quiet place, neighbourly and observant of strangers. That Saturday morning Laura Turner was on her way to a friend's house as Robert Black drove back into the village from the café where he had earlier eaten breakfast. It was close on midday: having failed to abduct the girl he had seen a few hours earlier, Black had none the less decided that this was a suitable place to find a victim.

As Black drove into the village, Laura Turner was walking in the opposite direction towards him. He saw her immediately but drove past her and up the road to find a lay-by in which to turn round. By the time he had executed a three-point turn, Laura had disappeared into her friend's house. Black repeated the 180-degree manoeuvre and began the process of quartering the village streets in search of his quarry.

Laura had emerged from her friend's house and was half-way down the garden path as he caught up with her again. He drove on and pulled the van on to the pavement on her side of the road but some yards ahead. To get past, Laura would have either to walk along the road or to squeeze between the van and a wall.

As she approached, Black swung open the passenger door, blocking her path; when the six-year-old stepped uncertainly towards him, Black grabbed her and pushed her small frame into the front of the van. Laura screamed. Black silenced her with an angry warning. He forced her under the passenger seat, struggling to free her foot, which had been trapped in the door. Running round to the driver's side, he gunned the motor into life and drove out of the village, shouting again at the terrified girl to shut her mouth.

As he drove past the quiet houses and neat gardens, he noticed a car parked ahead; a woman was sitting in the passenger seat. He quickly changed direction and sped away from the village by a circuitous northbound route. Two miles further on he pulled into a lay-by. He needed to turn around and head south towards the English border. But first he took the opportunity to examine his captive.

Methodically he tied her hands behind her back, strapped sticking plaster across her mouth and tied a cushion cover over her head. Then he lifted her clothing and forced his fingers into her vagina.

Momentarily satisfied, he pushed her, head first, into his sleeping bag, swiftly zipped and tied the ends and slung the tiny parcel into the back of the van.

As he drove back through Laura's village and on towards the A7 to Galashiels, Black was unaware that police were already searching for his van. A villager had been out in his garden, cutting the lawn, when Laura was abducted. He noted down the registration number of the van and ran inside to dial 999. As he stepped back outside to resume his gardening he saw the van heading back towards him; almost simultaneously a Lothian and Borders Police patrol car swung into the road.

There was not, in the event, much of a chase. Black pulled over as the police car's siren shrieked and its blue light flashed. A uniformed officer stepped out of the car and walked briskly over to where Black was waiting. He ordered Black to open up the back of the transit and, as the doors creaked open, peered into the murky interior. He saw a mattress, a few items of clothing and a rumpled sleeping bag. He called Laura's name and, hearing no response, was about to turn away when the bag moved.

He swiftly pulled the bag out into the sunlight and laid it on the pavement. He ran the zip round the edge, and the figure of a small girl, her head inside a cushion cover, emerged. Urgently he tugged at the strings that held the mask in place. As he pulled it off he saw the girl's face, lobster-red and choking on the plaster gag. It took a few seconds to register that he knew the face: it was that of his own daughter.

One month later, at the High Court in Edinburgh, Black's statement to the police was read out: 'I wanted to keep her until I delivered a parcel . . . I only touched her a little. I wanted to keep her until I went somewhere like Blackpool where I could spend some time with her.'

For the prosecution Lord Fraser, the Lord Advocate, praised the 'commendable restraint' shown by Black's arresting officer. He did not explain that Laura's own father had found her, trussed and bound like a chicken. But he was at pains to stress how close the child had been to dying. 'The look on her face could only be described as absolute terror. She was suffused with heat. Left in that condition, she might have died within the hour.'

In the tiny interview room at Saughton Prison Robert Black ground out an emaciated handrolled cigarette in the tin ashtray. He had held it delicately, almost woman-like, at the end of his middle and index fingers.

There was a wealth of information about unsolved cases inside Black's head, of that I was now sure, just as I was certain that he had snatched many other children from the streets and parcelled them up inside his van. What he had said about the aborted attempt at an abduction in the village where he later snatched Laura, and the way he said it, suggested a well-rehearsed pattern of offending. But, equally, there were any number of unanswered questions about why the man offended in the way he did. Why, for example, had he aborted that attempt?

What was the fundamental reason for the violent abduction itself? It was hardly typical paedophiliac behaviour. Most conventional paedophiles – and Black clearly saw himself as a conventional paedophile – obtained their victims by an insidious process of seduction and guile. And, above all, what did Robert Black mean by his curious statement about his sexual fantasies, 'The girl needed to be unconscious or dead because I didn't want to hurt her'? He had said this to me on more than one occasion, but as yet I had been able to make no sense of it.

In search of answers I started by asking Black to take himself back to the morning of Saturday, 14 July, and the first girl he had considered abducting. Why had he stopped himself from snatching the first child?

BLACK: Too many houses about, people about. And this fellow, further back up the road working on his car . . .

RAY: Wouldn't the dog be a deterrent?

BLACK: No, I'm not afraid of dogs.

RAY: Right. Picture Laura now. Just picture her on the road. Put yourself back there . . . Right. Can you see her?

BLACK: I can picture the situation, yeah.

RAY: Right. What do you see?

BLACK: A girl. I can't remember if she was running or walking along the pavement. She had on a sort of T-shirt thing, light-coloured, and shorts.

RAY: What did you think when you saw her?

BLACK: (*Pause*) Let's go and have a look.

RAY: What do you mean?

BLACK: I suppose . . . (*Pause*) . . . Let's have a look and see if there's an opportunity.

RAY: So you followed her?

BLACK: I actually got the van, turned round, and she wasn't in sight then. I just drove in the direction she'd been going and I seen her up at the door . . . and I thought, 'That's it: no opportunity.'

I drove on a bit, found somewhere to turn round. I would have driven round the block and therefore missed seeing her again altogether, but there was something blocking the back street and I couldn't get through, so I had to turn round and come back the same way.

It was as I was coming back I seen that she was coming back down the path from the house and that's when I stopped.

I put my hand out around her neck and pulled her towards me. I lifted her up and put her in the van.

RAY: What did she do when you did that?

BLACK: She never done nothing until she was actually sitting in the van, and then she looked as if she was going to scream. I told her to be quiet . . . I started heading back and I seen this little piece of grass just set back off the road. I pulled in there and I lifted her out into the back of the van.

RAY: What were you thinking and feeling at that time?

BLACK: Well, I still had one delivery to do. I still had the delivery to do in Galashiels . . . And there might be somebody come right up to the van to take the parcel off me there. So I had to like get her into a position where she couldn't move or call out.

I turned her over on her face. I tied her arms behind her back. I turned her back over. I think I asked her her name then. She told me.

I found a sticky plaster, tore off a bit of that, asked her if she could breathe through her nose and she said er . . .

I told her to press her lips together, and I put the plaster over her mouth, and I took her shoes and socks off. I put a cushion cover over her head.

RAY: What sort of cushion cover was it?

BLACK: A small square one . . . I think I had three of them in the van: two of them had stuffing in and that one was empty.

RAY: So you had her hands tied behind her back. You had a cushion cover over her. You had her shoes and socks off. Then what did you do?

BLACK: I pulled her pants to one side and I had a look. I thought I'd just sort of stroked [her vagina] . . . but there was bruising on the inside – I don't know how.

RAY: I think you inserted your fingers.

BLACK: Well, I'm not conscious of having done that, you know . . .

RAY: But you must have done. How long did that go on for?

BLACK: From the time I picked her up until the time I was stopped – ten, fifteen minutes.

RAY: But how long did you sexually touch her?
BLACK: Five seconds.
RAY: Then what?
BLACK: I put her into the sleeping bag and . . . just slung it in the corner . . . Then I got back in and drove back through [the village] and got stopped . . .

Black was holding back, keeping to himself many of the details of the offence. Most paedophiles in similar positions do exactly the same. But there was something missing from the account – emotion. Although Black seemed prepared to discuss the bare outlines of his abduction and assault, much as he had with the two psychiatrists prior to his court appearance, he was suppressing any hint of his feelings about the offence. Within those feelings might lie the clue to his obsession with children. I tried a new tack to open up Black's emotions. What would have happened if the police had not stopped him in the village?

BLACK: When I'd done the delivery in Galashiels down the road, I would have assaulted Laura sexually. I would have untied her . . . I would have probably stripped her from the waist down, but I would have untied her and probably took the plaster off her mouth. And if she called out when I was assaulting her, then I might have put the gag back on.
RAY: What I'm finding amazing, and what I want to explore with you, is the two sides of you. When you got Laura you are saying very clearly that in your own thinking you are a paedophile who likes children, loves children, and yet the actual behaviour that you do is totally disruptive at both a physical and a psychological level. In a sense it's the murder of childhood. So what is actually going on? Do you find that an unconscious side of you takes over and bypasses your intellectual thinking? What actually happens?
BLACK: I don't know. When I tied up Laura I didn't want to actually harm her or hurt her.
RAY: But you devastated her. You created so much fear in her . . .
BLACK: Yeah, but I suppose you don't really think like that at the time, do you?

RAY: I think you do, yes.

BLACK: Well, not consciously anyway. I don't know: I've never really tried to analyse it, but I look at it, if you follow me, as not violent behaviour, although it is violating the child.

RAY: That's incredibly distorted thinking. How is abducting a little child in the street, tying her hands behind her back, putting tape over her mouth, putting a cushion cover over her head, sexually abusing her, putting her into a sleeping bag to the extent that she's going to die: how can that not be a violent act? How are you able in your mind to distance yourself, and disassociate yourself, from that behaviour?

BLACK: Violence to me is like (*makes a punching movement and a loud smacking noise*) . . .

RAY: Do you mean you didn't mean to harm her? . . . If she had died, it would not have been a deliberate act by you?

BLACK: (*Pause*) If anything had happened to her, like that, it would have been accidental. I said [at the time] it was only a possibility; if she had done, it would have been a pure accident.

RAY: Why can't you own up to the responsibility of what you did?

BLACK: I did . . . but, like, I was caught before I had really done anything to her.

RAY: You don't have a sense of what it was like for her, do you? The fear she would have experienced – taken away from those she loved . . . what were you thinking? What did it feel like to have control over that little girl and the terror she must have been in?

BLACK: I know it's (*long pause*) probably not true, but probably I was just about as scared as she was.

RAY: That's rubbish.

BLACK: Yeah . . . yeah. I don't know . . . how can I put it? I suppose when a child is in the van it's in my control. Like, from then on everything's got a sexual motive. But at the time with Laura (*pause*) I wasn't thinking about her at all . . . like, you know, what she must be feeling.

RAY: But what is the feeling you have? Is it excitement, fear, sadness, anger? If I give you a list of feelings, which ones are the closest?

BLACK: I know it's definitely not anger . . . Disappointment.

RAY: Disappointment at what?
BLACK: (*Pause*) That I'd allowed myself to go that far.

I didn't believe him. Robert Black's offending was too deliberate, too well rehearsed for that to be true. He was trying, as I had expected, to hoodwink me. He wanted me to believe that he was in some way a Jekyll-and-Hyde character and that the nice, pleasant, quietly spoken Dr Jekyll in front of me could only wring his hands in 'disappointment' at what Mr Hyde had done.

That would have, in large measure, absolved him of the need to take responsibility for his own actions. I was sure that he lost control at some point during his abductions, sure that some part of him overrode all the internal and external inhibitors that should have stopped him snatching and abusing little girls. But I was equally sure that part of his disappointment was simply regret that he had been caught. None the less I was prepared to allow him to develop this idea: I would use it in our interviews as a means of freeing up what would otherwise have caused a blockage in the flow of information. It might become a safe way for him to release what was inside him, though in the end I would have to bring him back to the reality of his own responsibility.

Listening to his answers, I became aware that he talked in implicitly plural terms: only one child had ever been known to be in the van. But Black had said, 'When a child is in the van . . . ,' which suggested that this was far from an isolated event.

There was one issue about which I was as yet very unsure. As the interview progressed, the paradox of Robert Black's obsessive behaviour emerged in ever-greater contrast. He clearly thought of himself as a genuine paedophile, a man who wrongly believed that he both genuinely loved children and simultaneously saw them as sexually available, but what he did to them could quite easily lead to their deaths. I had to look for an explanation.

A parallel fetish began to manifest itself. Black had already told Dr Baird, the prosecution psychologist, what he would have done to Laura if he had not been stopped and arrested.

> He told me ... he would have found a quiet lay-by and molested her, and when asked what he meant by this he told me he would have put things into her vagina 'to see how big she was'.
>
> He would have put his fingers in and also his penis. When asked about other objects, he agreed he might have put other objects into her vagina, and when asked for an example, he saw a pen with which I was writing ...

As the hours ticked by, I began to see a possible connection between this bizarre desire and the central paradox – the contradiction between his beliefs as a paedophile and the likely death of his victim, however 'accidental' he might claim it would have been. Of course, he could have been lying, spinning me an involved tale. But I didn't think so. This had an uncomfortable sense of truth about it.

I've worked with a number of paedophiles who have killed their victims. Some did so as a reaction to the child screaming or trying to disclose their abuse. Others fell into the category of men who are aroused by sadism and derive sexual satisfaction by inflicting violence, pain and even death.

Robert Black didn't fit within either category. He had not tried to kill Laura when she screamed, nor did he match the profile of a sadistic sex-killer: certainly he didn't possess any of the type of child-torture pornography I would have expected had he belonged to the sadistic abuser group.

The explanation seemed to lie within his initial words during one of our discussions about the abduction and assault of Laura: 'I wanted to kill her because I didn't want her to be hurt.' It was hard then to make any sense of the statement: hard until it was linked with his other controlling fetish.

He was obsessed with orifices, in particular girls' vaginas. He did not have simply a sexual motive but was driven partly by a bizarre need to find out how much a child's vagina could accommodate – fingers, pencils or other objects.

He had attempted quite frequently to see what his own anus and bowel were able to take by inserting a variety of objects into himself. Sometimes he had taken photographs of himself doing this. At one stage in the interview I began to suspect that he would have preferred to be born with a vagina rather than a penis. Certainly every mention of 'penis' or 'oral sex' brought a disdainful and disgusted expression, at both a verbal and a non-verbal level. It was as if he really didn't want to have a penis.

Of course, this insight, if that's what it was, didn't excuse or justify his behaviour. But it did give a clue to his fantasies, and it offered a tantalizing glimpse of the tangled web in his mind that made up the reasons for his offending. His obsessive need to explore the vaginal size of a little girl could only hurt the child, so he appeared to think: 'I do not want to hurt the child, therefore the child has to die so that I do not hurt her.' It was an extraordinary notion. Black himself, perhaps because we were at such an early stage in our relationship, would neither confirm nor deny it when I put it to him directly, though he did accept that as long as the child was unconscious his mind would be able to rationalize hurting her.

The session over, both of us stood, a little awkwardly, as the prison officers prepared to march Black back to his cell. I had found the meeting fascinating: Black had confirmed all that he had told me during our first two interviews and more besides. There were still a thousand questions running through my mind. They would have to wait for our next meeting. But as we parted in the cold prison corridor the man whose lonely and destructive urges were beginning, for the first time, to unravel turned back to me and asked: 'Am I evil or am I mad?'

3
A Kind of Madness

The flight from Edinburgh to Birmingham takes a little over an hour. As I left Saughton Prison at 6 p.m. that evening I knew I would be home and with my family by 8.30 at the latest.

Black's question haunted me throughout the journey – and for a long time afterwards – not because of the issues raised by the question but because he had asked it at all. I didn't believe Robert Black was either mad or evil. In any case, labels like that rarely help in understanding why a man commits offences. But there was something in the way he asked it: however much in our earliest sessions he may have been trying to influence my report, there was now a part of him that genuinely wanted to discover why he committed these offences, genuinely wanted help. And in the answer lay the key to controlling his obsessive desire to abuse young girls.

None the less, the issue of Black's sanity was one I was forced to confront. Legally he was bad, not mad: two psychiatric reports had stated unequivocally that Robert Black was clinically sane. Defence psychiatrist Andrew Zealley had found: 'He revealed no evidence of abnormal thought processes, is not suffering from a mood disorder such as depressive illness and . . . there is no evidence that he suffers from any organic brain disorder . . . I consider that this man is sane and fit to plead.'

But if, or when, his case made headlines, I knew it would be hard to match this technical medico-legal assessment with the more prosaic public opinion of an offender of Black's calibre. There is a quite understandable popular view that any man who does, or even wants to do, what Robert Black had done must quite simply be crazy. It is, after all, far from normal. It can be very difficult to explain to people that although what an offender has inflicted on his victim is not rational, and may even appear completely demented, the law applies a quite different set of standards.

In essence, for a man to be declared insane, and therefore unfit to plead, he must, at the time of the offence, have been suffering from some definable mental illness that affected his ability to know that what he was doing was wrong. Robert Black clearly knew exactly what he was doing and that it was illegal. His ability to recall even the tiniest of details, coupled with his careful preparations, left no room for doubt that he was legally competent to stand trial.

But, aside from the difficulty in bridging the yawning chasm between the narrow legal definition of sanity and the wider swell of public opinion, declaring Black sane had one other effect: it meant that he would not receive any compulsory psychiatric therapy to combat his obsession with young children. Lord Fraser's ringing speech at sentencing had forever identified Black as a danger to children, but it had not contained any requirement for pyschiatric counselling. Nor, in fairness, could it have: unlike their American counterparts, judges in Britain are not empowered to order such treatment as part of a penal sentence. So, while Lord Fraser would have forwarded to the Scottish Office a confidential recommendation for the number of years Black should stay in prison – a 'life sentence' never meaning what the words appears to signify – there was little prospect that the roots of his offending would be attacked during his incarceration.

At some point in the early years of the twenty-first century Robert Black might be released again on to the streets with no after-care, no follow-up and no official attempt at preventative therapy. If there was madness in his case, this surely was it.

I was by now becoming used to the wearying trek from the English Midlands to Edinburgh. The sessions with Robert Black were an emotional and financial drain on me, let alone on the time I needed to devote to other cases. But I felt that, in a way I had yet fully to understand, our meetings were important beyond the simple economics of an already overcrowded diary. Inside Black's mind a contradiction was seeking resolution: he genuinely wanted to understand what drove him to abduct and assault young girls but was simultaneously terrified of facing up to a destructive and unforgiving obsession.

I decided I would have to start at the beginning. Something – or, more likely, some things, for sex offenders are rarely the product of one traumatic experience – had clearly happened to Robert Black in his childhood to create the disturbed and dangerous offender he had become. Sex offenders are created, not born, but the process by which their aberrant thinking and behaviour are formed is complex and multi-causal. Behind Robert Black's obsession with young girls lay an elaborate web of events and experiences, some obviously traumatic, some seemingly anodyne or quotidian.

My task was to take this hesitant man back through this labyrinth. Because Black was reluctant, embarrassed, I wanted to use a special breathing technique, first to enable him to confront the feelings that dominated his offending and blocked the path of any therapy and, later, to explore his childhood. At our next meeting I suggested it. Black nodded his assent.

To start with, I told him how I saw the split between his overpowering need to interfere with young girls and the intellectual revulsion he experienced as soon as he had actually abused his victim. Then I deprived him of his physical and emotional 'crutches' – his tobacco and cigarette papers. There was to be no smoking, no escape from himself by the act of rolling a cigarette.

RAY: A lot of people know why they smoke, but it doesn't help them with knowing how to stop. In your case we know you have an obsession to look at and touch [young girls'] vaginas, and that your obsession to fill them up means that you were behaving in ways to fulfil your obsession, however much you didn't want to do it. Your feelings say, 'Do it,' your head says, 'Don't do it,' and at times your head isn't strong enough to overcome your feelings. Does that sound right?

BLACK: I don't know. I was never aware of my inner conflict or anything like that.

RAY: Are you saying your feelings and your head go together? Because you don't give me that impression.

BLACK: I don't know . . . (*sighs*) . . . I just don't know.

RAY: And you won't until you get in touch with those feelings. Look down and get in touch with your feelings. (*Pause*) Sad, isn't it?

BLACK: No, I was just thinking that I must be a cold fish if I can't find nothing there.

RAY: You can if you let yourself. Just breathe.

(*Very long pause as Black takes extended deep breaths*)

BLACK: What difference does it make?

RAY: It makes a big difference. What do you think about the parents of the children you abducted? What do you think about them?

BLACK: I haven't really thought about it.

RAY: No. Would you ever want to help them?

BLACK: If I could help, yeah.

(*Very long pause as Black breathes more deeply*)

RAY: What are you thinking?

BLACK: I don't know . . . I don't know if I can put a handle on this, like, mind and feelings.

RAY: No, I know. If you could, you wouldn't have done what you did. It's because you don't give in to what we might call empathy feelings that you're able to do it and carry on doing it. That's why it's so important to get in touch with this because whatever feeling rises up and allows you to do what you do, that's what we need. I want to know what it is. I want to know whether it's pain, anger or what sort of hurt it is.

BLACK: Lust.

RAY: Could you live with yourself if you had killed Laura, if Laura had died because of what you did?

(*Very long pause as Black takes extended deep breaths*)

BLACK: I don't know. I don't think so.

RAY: Could you allow your mind to get in touch with it? Could you allow your mind to think it about it?

BLACK: I couldn't even contemplate it, I don't think.

RAY: I mean, we'd look at Laura and say, 'God, that's hell for the little girl.' It's one of the most violent acts she could ever be in. She's going to die: that's what she is going to feel. (*Pause*) How would you like it if I did that to you? I mean, you're a little boy of six, and you're dragged off into a van, and you're tied up, and you're sexually abused, and you don't know what's going to happen to you.

BLACK: I'd be petrified, I suppose.

RAY: Absolutely, but you can't feel it, can you? You cannot feel what it was like for that little girl or her parents. (*Pause*) You couldn't cry for Laura, could you? You couldn't cry for her parents. Because you can't make yourself feel the pain of it. When did you last cry?

(*Very long pause, as Black breathes deeply*)

BLACK: Last week, I suppose.

RAY: Over what?

BLACK: Something I was reading.

RAY: Sentimentality?

BLACK: Yeah, something like that.

RAY: Yeah. You can cry over a bloody book, but you can't cry over what you do.

BLACK: Weird. Weird.

RAY: Maybe one way the whole story could come out is the moment you allow yourself to feel the pain of what you've caused and what you've done. Then probably you'd be able to share more . . . What are you thinking?

BLACK: I was just thinking that, like, at the time with Laura I wasn't thinking about her at all. Like, you know, what she must be thinking.

RAY: No, I know you weren't. You were just feeling what you were feeling. And that's what I believe happened with other children too. That's why you could do what you did. And, for the sake of everybody involved, I'd like to be able to explore it with you. How you do it: how would you do that? How did we create [such] a person in our society? Do you know anything about your natural mother? What was her name?

BLACK: Jessie Black. I was illegitimate. That's as far as it goes. I don't know whether it was pressure from her parents or whether she just didn't want me. I don't know. I know I was fostered when I was six months. (*Pause*) I suppose my mother wasn't in a position to hold on to me.

The moment he said this two thoughts raced through my head. They were twin reactions, based on the same foundations but reaching very different conclusions, and they were running in stereo.

The first was that Black's perception of his background matched the classic profile of almost every serial killer of children I had ever worked with or studied. All of these men had endured lonely and isolated childhoods during which they had felt unloved, uncared for, rejected. Fostering or adoption was a recurring theme in their early years, as were over-controlling 'carers' and harsh institutional homes. Physical violence and sexual abuse were reported time and time again in their early years. The story Robert Black told me of his early years matched every one of these reported indicators. Circumstances dictate largely why children develop into men who kill and kill again. Did that suggest he too was a serial killer? Was that what I would find as I delved further into his mind?

My other immediate response was that underlying everything Black said was a cloying self-pity, a deliberate shifting of the blame for his subsequent actions on to others. It would be temptingly easy to seize on his wretched childhood experiences as the sole cause of what Robert Black had become. In his mind he would want me to buy into just that as a way of minimizing his responsibility for his own actions. It was a fine line I would have to tread. Yet ultimately I believed – knew – that children with loving parents who are cherished and valued and grow up with a feeling of self-worth rarely, if ever, end up in prison cells serving life for the abduction and sexual assault of a six-year-old girl.

It had taken almost an hour to reach this point. We were both exhausted: probing the painful memories from which Black had been hiding for all his adult life was an extraordinarily draining process. I felt that, having breached the man's formidable mental barriers (albeit only partially), it was time to close down the breathing technique and explore the known facts about Black's childhood in a more conventional way.

I switched off the tape-recorder and took from my bag a standard Gracewell assessment form. Together we were going to complete the questionnaire: I would read out the categories and then record verbatim Black's responses. There is something curiously stark and inexpressibly sad about these assessment forms. In them lives – twisted, painful existences – are sliced neatly into analytical sections. For all the trauma described by the recorded responses the language is somehow cold and emotionally dead.

Part One of the Gracewell questionnaire registered a few basic personal facts about Robert Black – age, religion, criminal record and latest conviction: 47, none, lengthy and Laura Turnbull were the responses recorded. But over the page in Part Two the brief, almost taciturn, answers began to paint a revealing picture of Robert Black's earliest years.

In the section recording the details of his family members, Black first named his foster-parents, Margaret and Jack Tulip. On a scale of one to ten (with ten representing the optimum score) he awarded Margaret eight points for the quality of her relationship with him. (I was suspicious that this might be more wishful thinking than reality, since Black gave his natural mother a score of five out of ten for the same question.) But it was the questions about his male parents that began to make me even more uneasy. Black correctly recorded the fact that the name of his natural father had never been known – Jessie Black had resolutely refused to fill in that section of the birth certificate. None the less, there had been a father-figure in young Robert's life: Jack Tulip, Margaret's husband and the head of the strict Kinlochleven household. Black insisted that though he knew Mr Tulip was dead – had died, in fact, when Robert was five years old – he had no memory of his foster-father. Under the heading on the questionnaire 'Relationship to you' he simply stated: 'Never knew him'.

It became clear very quickly that Robert Black had, or said he had, absolutely no memory of anything before his first day at school when he reached the age of five. Most of us can recall isolated incidents of our pre-five childhood. We may not recall them accurately or particularly clearly, but we can remember something, some vague, impressionistic sense of who we were and who was around us in the home. Black had nothing of this: for him the early years were an empty black hole. It was as if something had blotted out completely every single memory until the day he went to the village school.

I kept asking him to try and think back. And he kept coming up with the same puzzled and puzzling response: there was nothing there. No memory at all. In my experience this type of total mental block was consistent with, though not, of course, unequivocal proof of, some early trauma. I suspected that something had happened, perhaps something involving Jack Tulip, that had so scarred young Robert's mind that he had simply erased it from his conscious memory – or, more likely, supressed it within the darker recesses of his mind. Exploring that memory gap, seeking out the elusive early trauma, could provide the key to the man Robert Black had become. But there were two major obstacles to pursuing such a clinically straightforward route.

The first was that I still had no clear idea of the extent of Black's offending. Exactly what sort of man was he? A traditional paedophile? A predatory abuser? Or a sadistic serial molester? In time I knew he would have to answer these questions. But I needed to answer them before searching for the traumatic pre-five experience that I suspected lurked somewhere in Black's subconscious.

The second hurdle was more practical. Whatever the precise nature of Black's sexual fixation, there was absolutely no doubt that he was an abuser. Working with any abuser required me to walk the tightrope between appearing sympathetic to the man's personal history and refusing to allow him to claim the role of victim.

All abusers seek some way of excusing or justifying what they have done. While it is often true that men who abuse children have themselves been victimized as youngsters, it is terribly dangerous to allow them to see themselves as victims rather than the perpetrators. Once a therapist lets this happen – and I've seen it happen many, many times – there is little or no prospect of getting the abuser to be honest about his offending and therefore no real chance of addressing the problem of controlling his behaviour.

With Robert Black that meant that I had to put aside, for the time being, my suspicions about his early childhood and to concentrate for a little while on assessing his accessible memories of childhood and subsequent career as an offender. As Black could remember something of his first day at school, I took that as a starting point. I switched the tape-recorder back on and returned to the questions on the form.

Black recalled this first day as traumatic: he cried on being taken to the small village elementary school by Margaret Tulip. In itself this was far from unusual – in fact, had young Robert Black *not* cried on his first day in class, I would have viewed his missing memories of infancy with even more unease. But then other small anecdotes from his Highland childhood, often seemingly innocuous individually, began to build into an uncomfortable pattern.

The first was Black's earliest sexual recollection: a memory of going into the hills with a young girl and the pair of them stripping off each other's clothes. Once again, the event itself could appear a common part of childhood – two youngsters playing 'I'll-show-you-mine-if-you-show-me-yours'. But Robert Black had an unusual level of recall for a forty-seven-year-old man looking back to an ostensibly innocent experience when he was five. Above all, he could recall the girl's name. On its own this was quite unsual: coupled with his apparent inability to remember anything at all of his pre-five life, it was an indication that the incident had some powerful and lingering impact.

And then there were his memories of Margaret Tulip. By his own account, Black's childhood in the Tulip household was a happy one. He described, first, typical boyish escapades and scrapes. But something prompted a darker recollection.

RAY: What are your memories?

BLACK: Just little things. I remember climbing a cliff, sort of thing, me and another boy, and I fell. It was a classic, you know: I just grabbed hold of a little tree to stop myself going down. Well, it was quite a long way down.

(*Black laughs at the memory*)

RAY: How old were you then?

BLACK: Anywhere between seven and ten. (*Long pause*) I can remember one Christmas I didn't get no Christmas presents because I'd been bad. I got one present from somebody that lived out of town. It was a football. That was the only present I got that year.

RAY: What had you done?

BLACK: I don't know what. I can't remember what I'd done. But she [Margaret Tulip] says, 'Santa Claus isn't coming this year to you.' And he didn't, apart from that one football. And then I went and lost it. I kicked it, and it bashed off a rock into the river. It was a proper leather football, you know? And I saved up for ages and ages . . . I can't remember how much I'd saved up, but we went to Fort William for an outing, a day trip or something like that, and I was going round all the shops trying to find myself another football . . .

The story was a sad vignette of a small boy growing up in a foster-home where love and affection seemed notable for their absence. To take him further into his childhood I turned the pages of the questionnaire to Section 5, 'Detailed Sexual History'. The first half-dozen answers were revealing.

Were you allowed to talk about sex with your parents?
No. I left at ten when she died.

Did your parents show each other physical affection?
Single parent [Black still had no viable memory of Jack Tulip].

Were your parents physically/verbally affectionate to you?
No. Can't remember.

Did you talk about sex with friends? If so, was it a subject of jokes and embarrassed comments?
Mostly.

Was it thought to be dirty?
It was taboo.

Did you ever play games with sexual content as a child?
Yes. On myself and with a toddler.

Reading over the answers, I detected the beginnings of a pattern. But, rather than approach directly what I sensed might be coming, I asked Black whether, as a child, he had suffered from nightmares.

> BLACK: I can remember having nightmares – I can't remember what age [I] was. It would always be the same thing. It was like a cellar situation with water in the cellar, and a monster – a big, hairy monster. I used to be locked in the house on my own, locked in as punishment. I got belted for climbing out of the window. She would remove my trousers and pants and get the belt. I'd probably get no more than six [smacks with the belt] at a time. And I had the fear that there was something under the bed. I used to sleep in my mother's bed. I can always remember her being old. I used to wet the bed and she used to belt me. There was a pot under the bed. But I couldn't go under the bed because of the monster. When mum went to the toilet I would see her with a cloth under her skirt, giving herself a wipe.

There was clearly a strong emotional problem somewhere in the relationship between young Robert Black and his elderly foster-mother. And something within that problem appeared to revolve around urine and excrement, which made what followed less of a surprise when Black began to talk again.

> BLACK: I used to push things into my anus. I was eight years old. What I'd like to know is what brought it on? Why? I thought [then] it was something I'd always done, you know?
>
> RAY: What was the first thing you can remember putting into yourself?
>
> BLACK: (*Pause*) It was a little piece of metal about that length probably [holds his fingers approximately 8 inches apart].
>
> RAY: About as long as a pen?
>
> BLACK: Yeah. I held the toilet roll and I . . . it had two little slots and a holder . . . I remember I used to think 'I'm going to do it this time, I'm going to do it this time' – and I never did. Shit on my hands and rub it all over. I never did, though. I always thought, like, 'You'll do it,' but I never did.

RAY: But you fantasized about rubbing shit all over yourself?
BLACK: Well, not so much rubbing it. Just shit in my hands and rubbing it in. I never thought of rubbing it all over myself.

The exchange seemed to confirm the inference I had drawn from my first interview with Black: that the man had a lifelong obsession with the orifices of the human body, an obsession that seemed to exclude the possibility of his coming to terms with his own penis. A section later on in the questionnaire cemented this theory that Black was somehow ashamed of the visible symbol of his masculinity. The section put forward a series of areas, physical and psychological, involving sex and asked the client to indicate whether he felt positive or negative towards each.

Towards the concepts of masturbation, foreplay, vaginal intercourse, orgasms reached without intercourse, erotic literature, pornography and sexual fantasy, Robert Black confirmed positive feelings. Towards only two categories did he indicate definite negative responses. One was homosexual anal intercourse. The other, tellingly, was his own genitals.

I was convinced I had picked up a trail. Questions aimed at revealing the history of the type of sexual activity in which Black had taken part since childhood followed. Each prompted revealing responses. Oral sex, masturbation, voyeurism, fetishism (children and bodily orifices), masochism in the form of anal pain, bondage to stop his victims escaping, indecent assault, indecent assault with a weapon and coprophilia – Robert Black confirmed he had carried out each and every one.

But, tucked away at the end of the section, questions 27 and 28 asked whether Black had ever enjoyed transvestism or sought to be a transsexual. Slowly he nodded. As to transvestism, he had sometimes dressed himself in little girls' clothes. And as to seeking out the life of a transsexual, Black simply recorded: 'Yes. I always wanted to dress up as a girl.'

By the end of the questionnaire I was certain that the man sitting in front of me had two overriding obsessions, aside from his evident paedophilia.

The first was an insuperable fetish about vaginas and anuses. This wasn't a simple liking for either or a mere issue of viewing them, experiencing them even, as sexually erotic parts of the body. There was something more obsessively analytical about it. He appeared to be tormented by a need to explore them as physical objects – to see how much they could hold.

The second, and in some ways corollary, force was a powerful yearning not to be what he was, a young boy growing into a man. He would far rather have been born a girl: certainly he did not want, much less like, his own penis.

But, however revealing these insights were, they were still a long way short of explaining how even such a disturbed young boy could end up as a violent abductor of little girls. There had to be more.

There was. As if he had breached one small barrier, Robert Black began to describe a catalogue of early sexual offending: a history of aberrant and dangerous sexual behaviour that began in Kinlochleven when he was just seven years old.

BLACK: There's something else I can remember. I used to go to Highland Dance classes, and I can remember spending most of the time lying on the floor looking up the girls' skirts.

RAY: How old would you have been then?

BLACK: Seven, eight: something in that area. Also, I remember pushing a push-chair for a neighbour. I took the baby into my house. She wasn't able to talk.

RAY: What age were you?

BLACK: Eight. Nine.

RAY: And whose baby was that?

BLACK: I can't remember . . . Obviously I knew the parent.

RAY: But did they know you had the baby?

BLACK: Oh, yeah.

RAY: You were meant to be taking the baby for a walk?

BLACK: Yeah. Looking after it.

RAY: And, without them knowing, what did you do?

BLACK: I took her home . . . (*Pause*) And I looked at her privates.

RAY: So she didn't have a nappy on?

BLACK: I can't remember.

RAY: But, whatever you did, you took it off?
BLACK: Mmm.
RAY: And you touched her?
BLACK: I don't think so, no. I think I just looked.

On balance, I suspected that the incident with the baby had involved a good deal more than mere voyeurism. Most offenders deliberately minimize the extent and effects of their abusive behaviour. But that, in a sense, was less important than the fact that Black was now beginning – slowly, hesitantly – to open up a fraction of the dark, hidden corners of his secret life. As he said, in some wonder: 'I've said to you things that I've never said to nobody else.'

The police had told me that by his early teens Black had been arrested for the first of a series of sexual offences. Next, I knew, I must lead him through the later years of his life with Margaret Tulip in Kinlochleven.

At first there seemed little of special interest to note other than the image of a lonely and somehow quite apart boy growing up without a real sense of family or security. Athletics sparked his interest, however. By his own account, young Robert Black was a proficient, if isolated, sportsman: football and track events seemed to be his natural strength – which made his declared perception of what was to follow rather pathetic. By the age of ten he had been at the peak of his sporting prowess and had entered the school's summer athletics competition. As he recalled: 'I was a natural athlete. Sprint, long jump, high jump: I knew I was going to win, and I was looking forward to the summer sports. Then my foster-mother died, and I was taken away. I wondered how good I could have been if someone had got hold of me.'

With Margaret Tulip's death young Robert Black was once more an orphan. The Taylors (Uncle John and Auntie Flo to Robert), family friends in the village, offered to take him in, but the social services refused, possibly because the Taylors already had four children of their own.

Robert Black was on the move again, away from the

Highlands, the village school and summer sports to Falkirk, where he attended a local primary school by day and lived at Redding Children's Home out of school hours. The home was mixed, with an almost equal complement of boys and girls (far from the norm in the summer of 1958). For Robert Black, already on an abberrant sexual course, the home became another front on his personal sexual battlefield. First came an invitation to learn about the mechanics of sexual intercourse. 'There was an older girl in that school. I was ten. She was going to introduce me to intercourse. She told me to creep along to the girls' dorm: her bed was just inside the door. I crept in, and when I arrived she was in bed with an older girl. I felt sorry.'

If, as he implied, Black experienced this incident as a rejection, it fitted the pattern of his new life within the home. 'When I first went into that home I changed from being outgoing to shy and withdrawn. I didn't tell my teacher my mother had died: how do you tell that your mother is dead?'

According to Black, he stopped inserting objects into his anus at Redding, though whether this was because of lack of privacy, diminished self-confidence or remission from his obsession was not clear. But this pause in his abberant sexuality could not hold indefinitely. By the following summer he had returned to abusing young girls. 'Me and two other boys went to a field with a girl the same age. We took her knickers off, lifted her skirt and all tried to put our penises in. Didn't really know what we were doing or how to go about it.' There was something in the way that Black described this encounter – a little too easily, perhaps – that made me want to question him further.

RAY: You went there thinking you were going to have sex?
BLACK: Yeah.
RAY: With a couple of girls or one girl?
BLACK: One girl.
RAY: You were with a group of boys, were you?
BLACK: Yeah, I think there was three boys.
RAY: And what did you do?
BLACK: I know we laid her down, took her knickers off and put them over her head . . . (*Black laughs*) I remember, right, I

laid them over her head, I don't know why. Like we could look at her but she wasn't allowed to look at us, sort of thing.

RAY: Right, and you attempted to have sex with her?

BLACK: Yeah. I'd say that.

RAY: But did you insert your penis into her vagina?

BLACK: No, I think I would have remembered that. (*Black laughs*) I can't even remember whether I had an erection or not.

RAY: But you touched her?

BLACK: Mmm.

RAY: And how old was she?

BLACK: She was round about the same age, maybe a year older or something like that.

RAY: And she wasn't consenting to this?

BLACK: Oh, I can't remember . . . I was forcing her, like, you know?

My suspicions seemed to be confirmed. Black was confessing to his first halting and technically inept attempted rape.

There was a terrible inevitability about it. For many years I have been concerned by the social services' policy of placing offending boys with victim girls – and then wondering why there is reabuse. The combination of offenders and victims causes immense problems. To anyone with half an eye to the young man's troubled past the incident should have given a warning signal. But this was the frequently brutal Scottish care system of the late 1950s: Robert Black was a nuisance and a troublemaker – sexually precocious, to be sure – but his offence did not warrant a referral to the police. Instead the Redding Children's Home arranged Black's transfer from the temptations of a mixed environment to the Dickensian and single-sex conditions of the Red House at Musselburgh.

It was now May of 1959. Once installed at Musselburgh Grammar for his education, and with the attic bedroom for his new home, Robert Black was to turn again to two dominating motifs of his Kinlochleven existence.

The first, and the less worrying, was sport. He threw himself into all sport with vigour, but to swimming he gave particular dedication and determination. Anyone seeking out young Robert Black in the years between 1959 and 1963 was most likely to find him at one of the many indoor and outdoor pools he haunted.

The second ghost from his past was less appealing. He began again to insert objects into his anus, a habit he had dropped while at Redding.

Perhaps it was a hangdog and flinching air that marked him out as a potential victim for abuse. Whatever the reason, by the age of thirteen Black had been targeted and groomed as the new boy in the life of an administrator at the home. From Robert's descriptions the man was what would be termed a 'non-predatory fixated paedophile'.

Unlike Black himself, who relied on speed and strength to seize his victims, the Home administrator 'seduced' one child at a time by worming his way into the boy's life. From there it was but a short step to unwelcome but hard-to-resist sexual attentions. He also used a current victim to seek out and prepare his successor.

This type of victim selection and grooming is not widely understood. The early part of the behaviour between the offender and the victim is one of testing. The offender is deciding who will be the best victim: which child is least likely to say anything. He will typically take the child whom he wants to abuse some way into his confidence. If the child breaks that confidence during the testing period, it is unlikely that anything will happen because no criminal offence has taken place. Some professionals may even claim that a fuss is being made over nothing. However, the offender knows that if the child does not say anything during the testing stage, he or she is unlikely to do so when the offender moves into the next stage: the hands-on abuse.

RAY: Were other boys being abused by the same man?

BLACK: Not at the same time, no. He liked them one at a time. His system was, from what I've been able to make out since and from what he told me at the time, when a boy was leaving – [a boy] he was abusing at the time – he asked them who he should go for next.

RAY: And what did he do to you?

BLACK: Make me put his penis in my mouth, touch him, you know. Funnily enough, I think that's the most revolting bit:

like, he puts it in my mouth. He did try to bugger me once, but he couldn't get an erection.

RAY: No? And how long did that go on for?

BLACK: It could have been anything between one and two years, I suppose.

Robert Black, convicted child molester, was finding it hard to discuss his own abuse. Certainly, he had not been able to talk to anyone at the home about it and must have kept it to himself as a dark and vicious secret for the next thirty-five years. Nor did the lack of actual penetration make the offence any less. One of the failings of the way in which the legal system deals with child abuse is its insistence on grading the levels of seriousness of different types of sexual offence. Inevitably, penetration – buggery – ranks highest.

What Robert told me simply reinforced my experience that this sliding scale of seriousness should not be used to determine the power of the offence. Enforced oral sex is one of the most difficult offences for the victim to come to terms with: we should never underestimate its effect on a young boy. It was hard not to feel sympathy for the adolescent Robert Black – alone, abandoned, disturbed and now sexually abused at a home that was intended to care for his welfare.

I had seen any number of similar cases, any number of men with almost identical histories. Abuse within the care system – and how often that phrase seems nothing more than a sick and cynical joke – is endemic even today. For that reason I find it hard to talk about 'care': it's totally the wrong word, it would appear, for Black and for many other children. At the time when Robert needed no rejection, at the time when he needed care and love and boundaries, he was further exploited.

Children in care – and there are, at any one time, at least 65,000 of them – are almost by definition some of the most vulnerable youngsters in Britain. Yet they are persistently treated not as valuable, if frequently disturbed, people but rather as an intractable headache for overworked management. In part this is a legacy of the way in which our legal system has traditionally viewed children – as objects belonging to a parent, a guardian or a local authority. This view originated from the first legal recognition of the status of minors effectively as chattels in the archaic and labyrinthine Court of Chancery.

Children in care today have little opportunity to voice concerns about their treatment or to tell someone they can trust about abuse at the hands of an adult in authority. How much more difficult, then, for an awkward and unconfident youth in Scotland at the turn of the 1950s?

Sitting opposite Robert Black in a bleak prison interview room, I recognized, if not a product of the care system, at least one of its many thousands of victims. I have worked with many men who have grown up and done what Black had done, who have themselves been abused and put into care, where further abuse went on. I have a sense that when that happens it is by no means clear whether the victim is able to develop his own core personality. Both they, and I as the therapist, are constantly struggling to find out who they really are. All the same, I needed to remind myself that while sympathy for Black's adolescent ordeal was not in itself out of place, many other abused adolescents did not grow up to be serial child molesters. Black's experience must not be allowed to cloud our professional relationship.

The dangerous side of Black's character was never far away, and it was to re-emerge shortly after he left the Red House in the summer of 1962. He had completed his basic studies at Musselburgh Grammar and had moved to Greenock to start work as a butcher's delivery boy. He was fifteen and living in a working boys' hostel, a halfway house between the confines of a care home and the wilderness of adult bedsitters.

BLACK: I know there was at least one incident . . . like, outside the hostel. There was one other boy and this little girl, in a hut somewhere in a field or something. It could have been a hen house, I don't know . . . like an old deserted hen house. I don't know who made the approaches. I know it wasn't me because I was called in afterwards, and it seemed she'd agreed, for a cigarette, to let us have a look.

RAY: Right. What did you do there?

BLACK: Well . . . (*Pause*) . . . The girl dropped her knickers and . . .

RAY: And how old was she?

BLACK: I don't know. She could have been anything from eight to eleven, I'd say. And I can remember when – you know, as I say, I never made the approach, I was called in like, 'You want to have a look here?', you know – and I can remember she sat down and laid her back across my knee and I just had a look and I think I touched her . . . I don't know. I can't remember for sure. And then she said, like, she was the boss position, she'd had enough. When she'd had her fag, that was it.

Put like that, a casual listener might be inclined to write the incident off as a piece of belated juvenile experimentation with no harm done. But the event was clearly part of a pattern of his life and fitted both with his obsession with under-age girls and with what he called touching their vaginas.

It appeared that there had been no complaint to the police, no follow-up after the incident. Again, that may make it appear less significant. But I knew from the official reports that at around that time in 1963 Black had been convicted of a sexual offence involving another young girl. Two similar crimes committed so close together are never insignificant. They tend to show a man in a continuum or cycle of offending.

The conviction was recorded at Greenock Juvenile Court on Tuesday, 25 June 1963. Robert Black, by then sixteen years old, was arraigned for lewd and libidinous behaviour and an assault on a seven-year-old girl. Court records from minor juvenile benches in the Lowland suburbs twenty years ago are scanty. I would have to prise the details from Black himself. When they came they would place in stark relief not simply the pre-pubescent nightmares Black endured in Kinlochleven but also the true nature of the man sitting across the bare prison-issue table.

RAY: Tell me what you did. I'm not going to interrupt this time. I'm just going to let you speak.

BLACK: Mmm . . . I was in the park at Greenock at the swings, and it was getting on towards twilight, and all the other kids had gone except for the one little girl. I asked her if she wanted to see, would she like to see, a kitten, and I knew where there was kittens and . . . I persuaded her to come with me. The funny thing was, on the way out of the park we passed a policeman who obviously knew me – I think I was going [around that time] to a youth club run by a police sergeant and the policeman knew me, and I thought about that. Just below the park there was, like, air-raid shelters, that type of building. I took her in there, and as she started to go in she realized it was dark inside, and she wanted to get out again: she started to cry. I think I clapped my hand over her mouth to stop her crying out, you know? I took her inside and I held her down on the ground with my hand round her throat and I was holding her down and . . . (*Pause*) . . . I must have half-strangled her or something because she was unconscious. It's one of the positions that hurts and . . . (*Pause*) I remember her, well . . . She stopped making a noise, like, you know . . . When she went quiet I took her knickers off and I lifted her up so as I was holding her behind her knees and her vagina was wide open and I just poked my finger in there once . . .

RAY: Hang on, let's not go too fast. Were you able to distinguish at that time whether she was unconscious or dead? Or what did you think?

BLACK: Well, I thought she was unconscious. So . . . I don't suppose I was positive but, like, you know . . .

RAY: Were you frightened she might be dead?

BLACK: It crossed my mind, yeah.

RAY: So, whether she was unconscious or dead, what did you do then? You took the pants off her, and then what did you do with her?

BLACK: I picked her up by the knees and she was hanging down . . . Her head wasn't touching the floor. Her skirt fell down and I could see the hole in her vagina was gaping, like it must have been well relaxed, and it was wide open and I put my finger straight in, all the way in. I took it out again, just the once, and I laid her down on the floor and masturbated. When I'd done that I put her knickers back on.

RAY: Where did you ejaculate?

BLACK: On the floor.

RAY: On the floor? So she was still unconscious at that time?

BLACK: Seemed to be, yeah.
RAY: But she was unconscious or dead?
BLACK: I don't know which.
RAY: You didn't know which, or it didn't matter, because you still carried on with the behaviour. What did you do when you stood over her?
BLACK: I masturbated.
RAY: Looking at her?
BLACK: Yeah.
RAY: So you masturbated as she was laid there on the floor, unconscious or dead, and her skirt up around her waist and her knickers were off?
BLACK: As I say, I put her knickers on, then I left her there and walked out and, like, the next day I was arrested.
RAY: Why would they only charge you with lewd and libidinous behaviour for what was clearly an attempted murder?
BLACK: Well, there was no intention to murder.
RAY: What does it feel like when you tell me you're in a dark place, in an air-raid shelter, with a little girl? How old was she?
BLACK: Seven, I think.
RAY: Seven. And you may have killed her. What does that feel like?
BLACK: What did it feel like? Well, I was scared. I didn't know, as you said, whether she was alive or dead.
RAY: And you were scared. But what did it feel as you were masturbating watching it? Very excited? You must have done.
BLACK: I must have done, but . . .
RAY: How long did you squeeze her throat for?
BLACK: A minute. Two minutes.
RAY: Did she struggle when you did that?
BLACK: I can't remember.
RAY: What do you think?
BLACK: I can't remember whether she was struggling or not.
RAY: What do you think? What's your guess?
BLACK: She may have been, I don't know.
RAY: Can you see her face?
BLACK: I can't picture her face. I think she had fair hair. That's about all I can remember. All I know is that from what I

managed to gather she was found wandering, like, crying and bleeding.

RAY: What I'm finding amazing, I suppose, is when we talked about Laura, and your fantasy concerning Laura, that in a sense it was like a re-enactment of what you just told me. I mean what is actually going on? Do you find that an unconscious side of you takes over, that bypasses intellectual thinking, or what?

BLACK: I don't know. I've always looked back on that first incident with revulsion, really. Like, you know, how could you do such a thing?

RAY: Yeah, yeah. But what I'm interested in is that it stayed there in your head and that you've had the image of it for a very long time. You may have struggled with it for a very long time – not wanting, but it kept coming into your head . . . It kept coming back.

BLACK: Yes. So it's been there.

RAY: Yes. Now I also know because the fantasy has been there that sometimes you have been masturbating about other things, that image still comes into your head and you don't like that. You didn't like it over the years, but it was there and you end up guilty and therefore feel bad. Am I right?

BLACK: Yeah.

RAY: And, as you masturbate, you connect those images with orgasm. Orgasm is the most powerful experience and internal feeling that you can have. But, connected to that orgasm and fantasy, was that behaviour. Right? It's okay, you can tell: don't worry about this.

BLACK: Well, I've always tried to block that image out.

RAY: I know you have. But you haven't always been able to, have you?

BLACK: Well, no. As I say it comes back again.

RAY: Yes, and it not only comes back, but at the time masturbation to the fantasy is something that's reinforcing the image. The way you've lived with that. No one has helped you. No one has talked to you. No one has helped you overcome that image . . . Today, here in this room, you can go back to that cellar, and there in your head is that child, just as real now as it was then. Right?

BLACK: Yes.

Black's words, neatly typed and orderly, do not describe what it actually felt like to hear this information. I had known about the offence, but I had not known its detail. Despite his saying that he felt revulsion, this did not come across in the way that he told the story. It was fresh, it was real and it was painful to hear. The way Black described it was so vivid that it took part of me with him.

I could see what he saw, smell what he smelt. I actually felt I was in the air-raid shelter. I could smell the dark, taste its musty smell. I could see the little girl unconscious, see her being picked up and placed over his arm. The image of the cruelty to which he was subjecting the child was itself a physical pain. It felt initially as if I had been stabbed with a knife. That image would never go away but would be compartmentalized within myself.

I was aware that my reactions could stop him from saying more. I had to walk that tightrope between allowing him to speak and encouraging him to exaggerate. At the same time I had to be careful not to let him believe that I was accepting his behaviour as normal. But the story also revealed something crucial about the type of offender I was working with.

I suspected that it was a composite story: a compound of the air-raid shelter incident with other more recent assaults or even killings. For the first time in my interviews with Black I became absolutely convinced that he was a man who not only could have killed Laura Turner but *would* have done so, given the opportunity. The account he gave – composite or not – was also so detailed, so graphic, that I was sure that this cellar offence had become his main sexual fantasy over the ensuing years. The crucial point was his response when the child collapsed, unconscious. Even when he thought she might be dead, he did not react.

I had worked with child killers who had tortured a child to death. I had worked with offenders who had killed a child as it tried to run and tell. In each case there had been an increasing level of violence as they sought to keep control of the victim. Some of these men had injured the child once they realized that it had died: they were in some way punishing the child for having died on them. Black's case exemplified neither of these familiar scenarios. Even though his victim was unconscious or dead, he carried on with the sexual element of his assault by molesting her and then masturbating. It pointed to a rare pattern of offending.

I began to wonder why he had described the offence to me so minutely. He must have realized that I had no way of knowing the details – details that took my understanding of him to a far deeper and more disturbing level – and yet he had offered them quite freely.

Some of the information helped me to develop his offending profile and establish his *modus operandi* for other assaults or murders. It seemed important that he did not leave any forensic traces in the cellar other than, presumably, his semen as he masturbated on to the floor. This would have been imperceptible when the police examined the crime scene. They would have looked, even in those days, for evidence of his sperm on the child's clothing or body: that would have been the normal pattern to expect. But Black had avoided this. Was it a conscious decision? Was the fact that he did not abuse the girl with his penis more evidence of calculating behaviour, or did it, rather, reflect a semi-conscious revulsion at his sexual organs?

It was too early to come to a conclusion. But the wealth of detail he had provided was vital in itself. This too matched the pattern of our sessions together. Each was a cat-and-mouse game: in each interview he would offer fresh information that would give me a new insight into the man. There was an element of game-playing in this, but it was a necessary part of working with Black. He would portion out little titbits, and I sensed that that this was a conscious policy.

One titbit, seemingly irrelevant, was both important and revealing. He made it clear that he was happy to be seen alone with a child by the policeman they passed on the way to the cellar. It was impossible to know whether this detail was fantasy, a composite or reality. And it did not matter which it was: the fact that he told me about the policeman was important. No detail in an account of a crime is irrelevant, even if the teller has no conscious awareness of the reason for its inclusion. The subconscious can take over and insert revealing clues. With the policeman in the park, it was as though Black was enjoying an inner sense of triumph: of being 'clever' enough to walk past a uniformed constable, hand in hand with a child he was about to abuse. Empirically true or not, in his mind he had put something over on those who would later investigate him.

From the moment when Black finished telling me this story, with all its complexities and subtexts, I knew that I was facing a killer of children. The account also made me angry. I had seen Robert Black's criminal record: I knew the punishment that Greenock Juvenile Court had imposed. How could he have been given a deferred sentence for such a serious assault – an attack in which he left his victim for dead? And why, given the obvious power and lasting effect of the offence in his fantasies, had nothing been done to help him?

None the less, we had achieved a breakthrough. I leant back against my chair, my mind simultaneously exhausted and racing. It had been a long day and a longer struggle. It was time to call a halt. I asked for a prison officer to escort Black back to his cell. I promised to return soon and pick up where we had left off.

But as I stepped into a taxi and headed across Edinburgh to the airport, two insistent questions ran through my mind. How many children had this man abused? And how many had he actually killed?

4
Ghosts in the Machine

These were questions that others had already begun to ask.

At the end of July 1990 detectives from ten police forces throughout England, Scotland, Ireland and Wales travelled to Edinburgh for an extraordinary conference. It was the largest gathering of senior investigating officers from so many regions that any participating force could recall. And so it should have been.

The meeting had a simple agenda: to discuss whether one man alone could have been responsible for the five unsolved murders, and an equal number of abductions of small girls, that were the collective responsibility of the assembled ten forces. There were other forces, other unsolved cases, but the five murders had been given the highest priority.

The man in question was Robert Black, then awaiting his day in court for the abduction and assault of Laura Turner.

The meeting's chairman was Hector Clark, Deputy Chief Constable of Lothian and Borders Police. Clark was the overall head of Britain's biggest ever computerized man-hunt – the search for the killer of Susan Maxwell and Caroline Hogg.

Among the detectives travelling to Edinburgh was Superintendent John Stainthorpe, one of West Yorkshire Police's most senior and experienced murder-squad investigators. Like Clark, he had a long-outstanding case to solve, the abduction and murder of Sarah Jayne Harper.

Four hundred miles away, Devon and Cornwall Police had issued travel warrants to their senior officers. Into their briefcases were pushed a handful of important files from the most famous British case of recent years, Genette Tate – missing, presumed dead.

In south London two senior detectives from Number 4 AMIP, one of the capital's eight specialist murder squads, prepared documents on the abduction and murder of fourteen-year-old Patsy Morris in June 1980.

Maxwell, Hogg, Harper, Tate, Morris: five young schoolgirls abducted and killed (although Genette Tate's body had never been found). There were others too who had been abducted but survived. Their names, along with the lower-priority murder cases, were added to the list of potential crimes committed by Robert Black.

All the detectives were aware that even the most infamous of domestic child killers – Ian Brady and Myra Hindley – had been convicted of only three murders. The ever-growing list that might be laid at Robert Black's door would confer on him the gruesome notoriety of being Britain's worst serial child murderer. They were aware too that it is often tempting to pin the blame for troublesome, unsolved cases on a convenient and unsympathetic scapegoat – especially when that scapegoat could already be facing a hefty prison sentence for similar offences.

If that knowledge urged caution, it could be counterbalanced by the depressing fact that, at any given moment, there were tens of thousands of children officially missing from home – potential victims of the man now on remand in HMP Saughton. Worse, from the detectives' point of view, there was little or no effective means of tracking these missing youngsters, some of whom were as young as six years old. Britain has no central register of absentee children, nowhere for detectives to turn for cross-reference reports. Instead when a parent reports the child missing – and police are regularly amazed by how often parents fail to report the disappearance of even very young children – the official note of their concern is unlikely to move far from the station where it was filed. Certainly, there is almost no prospect of its travelling automatically throughout the informal police network.

So among the detectives attending the conference were a number with cases of suspicious disappearances rather than evidence of abduction and murder. But suspicion, or even the traditional policeman's hunch, was not good enough for a case to be made against Robert Black.

Most child murderers – especially when the killing involves a sexual assault – know their victims. Despite the prominence given to campaigns such as 'Stranger Danger', the overwhelming body of sexually motivated homicides involves men who are, at the very least, acquaintances of the child. Most frequently the killer and his victim are related to one another. The circumstances of Laura Turner's abduction – and particularly the way in which Black snatched his victim off the street, then gagged and bound her so that she almost died – were so unusual that it was vital to be certain whether this trademark *modus operandi* matched the particulars of the unsolved cases.

Despite friction between the various police forces present at that meeting in Edinburgh, a decision was taken to focus on three murders and one attempted abduction. These would form the first tranche of prosecutions: if they succeeded, Black would become number-one suspect for the remaining cases. A swift calculation showed that there were at least seven relevant unsolved murders in Britain, four in Europe and dozens of abductions or assaults that were consigned, for the time being, to the back burner.

The first week of August is traditionally a time of celebration in Coldstream. The town straddles the border between England and Scotland; half of it is in one country and half in the other.

Just below Coldstream, on the English side of the notional frontier, is the village of Braxton. There in 1513 the battle of Flodden Field was fought, and the Earl of Surrey emerged victorious over King James V of Scotland. Every year, as part of Civic Week celebrations, the townspeople set out on foot and on horseback to recreate the part of the battle known as the Flodden Ride.

The summer of 1980 was no different from those that had gone before or those that would follow. In the weeks leading up to the Ride, Coldstream prepared for its annual seven-day carnival. If its festivities were a little less exuberant than Carnival in sunnier parts of the world, at least the weather was doing its best to create a pleasant atmosphere.

On Friday, 30 June, Susan Maxwell was looking forward to an afternoon's tennis with her schoolfriend Alison Raeburn. Susan was eleven years old, the eldest of the three children of Liz and Fordyce Maxwell. The couple had been journalists, at one time working in Edinburgh for the *Scotsman*, but had left the capital to farm in the beautiful Borders hills around Coldstream. Photographs of Susan show a plumpish, freckled girl, 4 feet 6 inches tall, with short, dark-brown hair. She was, though, somehow more mature than her years or her stature might suggest. She was the child of Liz's first marriage and had become a 'little mother' to her siblings.

The Maxwells had brought their children up carefully. Susan and her five-year-old sister Jacqueline both knew not to talk to strangers. Even little Tom, just three years old, was beginning to learn this important lesson. On Susan's previous excursions to the tennis courts either Liz or Fordyce had arranged to pick her up at the end of the match. This Friday, the last day of June in that beautiful summer, they had agreed to let Susan walk the two miles from the municipal courts to Crammond Hill Farm, the family home at Cornhill-on-Tweed.

> It was just an ordinary sort of day [Liz recalled years later]. Suzy wanted to play tennis. It was a super-hot afternoon and we were all in the garden. Suzy wanted to go into Coldstream on her bike, but we didn't want her to because we were frightened of the traffic. We asked her if she would be all right walking back on her own. It was the first time she had ever walked anywhere on her own at all. But we didn't really think there was anything dangerous about it because she knew people all along the way.

And it should not have been dangerous. Coldstream is a small town: Cornhill, the village where the Maxwells lived, even tinier. The Borders is an area where people know each other and look out for the local children. Strangers tend to be noticed and remarked upon very quickly. But that day some of the people Susan Maxwell knew along her route were, for no particular reason, not about – not that Liz or Fordyce knew that until later. 'There were people who would normally have been there, like the shepherd in the next field, for example, and just for some quirk they weren't there. Nobody saw her after a certain stage.'

That stage came at 4.30 that afternoon, when the small figure of Susan Maxwell carrying her Dunlop Alfa tennis racket with its distinctive white-painted handle and wearing a matching outfit of yellow towelling T-shirt and tennis shorts, was seen walking across the Coldstream Bridge. The road, the A697 arterial route from Coldstream to Newcastle, is the main highway across the Scottish border in the region. Just past the bridge a small stone monument, white-faced and bearing the red cross of St George, marks the spot where England begins. It is a busy road, popular with commercial traffic and with tourists, many of whom stop to take photographs of the small stone border marker. And there were many sightings of Susan that afternoon.

> It was surprising the number of people who had seen her [remembered Fordyce]. At least, up to a certain point in the road. There was a gap. It wasn't much more than about a minute, two minutes possibly, that they couldn't account for. She'd been seen [by a motorist] coming off the end of the bridge, and another car had come along two minutes later, or a minute later, or whatever, and there was no sign of her. So she was gone in the space of a minute and a half.

Liz Maxwell hadn't intended to drive into Coldstream to pick up her daughter, but as the long, hot afternoon wore on, she relented and set off for the tennis courts.

> She wasn't expecting me. But I thought, 'It's a very hot afternoon; after she's been playing tennis for an hour, she'll be hot and sticky and too tired to walk back.' So I put the wee ones in the car and we went over. And I thought I might meet her on the way across, but there was no sign of her. I went to the tennis courts: there was nobody there. I looked for her on the way back, and I came back and phoned the friend she was with. She

> said she had left Suzy on the outskirts of Coldstream. And I started to panic then.

At that point Liz and Fordyce dialled 999.

For fourteen long days Northumbria Police quartered the region. Cornhill itself is a small community of no more than 350 people, yet within two days of Susan's disappearance 200 volunteers had joined the police in their search.

That part of the Borders is rich in arable land and much of it is covered with large stretches of dense and forbidding woodland. For two weeks the search teams beat paths through field and forest over an area of 50 square miles. Fordyce Maxwell trod every mile with the search parties: every ditch, valley, wood, stream, even rubbish dumps. He and his fellow searchers looked everywhere for Susan. It served as a kind of desperate therapy, taking his mind off the worst speculation and imagining. Liz had less to divert her thoughts.

> That first night was probably the worst as darkness fell and she wasn't home – I mean, she'd never been away from home before. The police were out with the tracker dogs by that time, searching the banks of the river, but the thought of her being out in the dark was just the worst. I was just so eaten up with fear and panic . . . it's just impossible to describe. Where on earth could she be? Was she out somewhere outside? That night just seemed so long. We didn't really get much sleep for . . . well, for the next seven years, really.

But there were still the demands of a young family to cope with. Four days after Susan vanished it was Jacqueline's birthday. No one felt much like celebrating, not without Susan. It was, Liz said bluntly at the time, 'absolute torture', adding: 'If anyone has her, will they please let her go?'

The police meanwhile continued their efforts. A reconstruction was staged, using a girl who looked like Susan. She solemnly walked across Coldstream Bridge, her every movement recorded by banks of cameras and the detectives' comments scribbled in dozens of reporters' notebooks. Yet in spite of all the pleading, all the search parties, all the media coverage, there was no sign of Susan, or of anything she had been wearing that Friday afternoon, or even of the tennis racket, ball and blue plastic drinks flask she had carried.

On the evening of Jacqueline Maxwell's fifth birthday Northumbria Police held a public meeting in the village. The normally somnolent village hall was packed to overflowing as Chief Inspector Fred Stephenson once again appealed for witnesses to Susan's last walk across the bridge.

> Vehicles were parked in a lay-by. Lorries were parked. Someone, somewhere must have seen something. What happened to the racket or ball? Did she get into a car? Did someone see her get into a car? People don't just vanish.

Chief Inspector Stephenson was right. People, even small and vulnerable children, don't normally disappear without trace. Liz Maxwell had come to some sort of conclusion about her daughter's disappearance.. 'The only thing I can suggest is that somebody stopped and asked her directions – and grabbed her.'

It was to prove a startlingly accurate deduction – almost a premonition. But in July 1982 confirmation was still a decade away. All the Maxwells really knew then was that at some time, somewhere, Susan would be found. And no one was in any real doubt that when she was discovered she would be dead.

But for families of missing children the hardest part is not finally knowing, not being able to put the loss to rest, enduring the tiny, debilitating flicker of hope that eats away inside the stomach and chest even when the brain rationally insists that the child must be dead.

> It was bad enough to think that she was dead. But for her to be there alone, in a strange place, not knowing where she was, thinking that we must have forsaken her. I mean, her last thoughts must have been 'Why are my Mummy and Daddy not coming to get me? Is somebody not going to rescue me?' That's what has haunted me all this time.

The two-storey terraced house at 25 Beach Lane, Portobello, was always crowded. John and Annette Hogg had five children, some from a first marriage. The youngest, Caroline, was five years old.

The people of Portobello were, in the summer of 1983, enjoying a heatwave. It was the second year in a row that Scotland had been blessed with unusually good weather. Living just 100 yards from the seafront and a wide, sandy beach, the Hogg children made the most of their good fortune.

Friday, 8 July, had been a glorious day. In the late afternoon Caroline had been to a friend's party. Annette had dressed her in a lilac-and-white checked gingham dress from Littlewood's store; its cap lace sleeves reinforced the image of a special frock for a special occasion. Around Caroline's neck Annette had fastened a small silver locket. White ankle socks and a pair of party shoes completed the outfit.

Later the same evening, after the party was over and the children had eaten their tea, Annette Hogg took them to the bus-stop to wave their grandmother goodnight. The family returned home at 7 p.m., and Caroline asked permission to spend a few minutes playing on the swings in the park just up the road.

Annette agreed: it was quite usual for Caroline to run along the street, past Towerbank Primary School where she had been a pupil for three terms, to the playground facing the seafront. She had been well schooled by her parents not to talk to strangers and never to stray along the Promenade to the bright lights of the Fun City permanent fairground at the top end of the beach road. In any event it was only to be for a few minutes; it was going to be a last burst of play at the end of a beautiful summer's evening: Caroline had been told to come home after five minutes on the swings. Quickly she slipped off her party shoes and pushed a pair of pink trainers on her feet. Then she was out of the door and down the street.

At 7.15 Annette strolled towards the playground to pick up her daughter. She walked up Beach Lane on to the Promenade and turned right towards the swings. There was no sign of Caroline. Anxiously her mother began searching the area, but wherever she looked she couldn't find her daughter. At 7.50 p.m. she called the police station in Portobello High Street.

Lothian and Borders Police had a standard procedure for dealing with calls from distressed parents reporting a missing child. A woman police officer was immediately dispatched to 25 Beach Lane. She asked Annette and John the routine questions. What had they already done? How long had Caroline been gone? Had she ever gone away before? What did she look like, and what was she wearing?

Next the WPC walked around the immediate area herself, stopping off with friends and relatives to see if they had seen Caroline. When all this proved fruitless she called the police station and alerted her senior officers. The call was passed to Chief Inspector Brian Day. Portobello was a district station in the Leith Division: Day had been on duty since early afternoon and was due to sign off for the night. By 10 p.m. not only had he abandoned any plans for sleeping, but he had organized a new search of the area.

By midnight it was clear that Caroline Hogg's disappearance was not going to have an instantly happy ending. Day picked up the phone and dialled the home number of CID officer Superintendent Ronald Stalker. A third and much wider search was immediately put into operation, though not, according to Stalker, without some difficulty. 'It was not easy on a Friday night to reallocate men from other duties, but the response was extremely good. Then we roused everyone we could think of who could help.'

The searchers swarmed across the maze of disused buildings and construction sites in the streets adjacent to 25 Beach Lane. Along the Promenade from the playground, and just in front of Fun City fairground, Portobello swimming pool was a labyrinthine headache. The pool had long since been shut down, but its jungle of underground tunnels had to be searched, along with every one of the several hundred clothes lockers in the pool changing rooms. The teams searched under benches and behind cupboards, in the pool, along the beach and in the nearby stream.

One hundred and thirty officers combed and quartered the ground. By noon on Saturday many had worked a double shift and were bleary-eyed from lack of sleep. Dogs too had been brought in – all to no avail. At midday Superintendent Stalker admitted defeat: 'We had no idea where she was, so we decided to appeal to the public to help us to intensify the search.'

That appeal brought forward 1,000 new volunteers by Sunday morning. And it also produced witness sightings of Caroline Hogg's missing minutes. Several bystanders had noticed the 3-foot 6-inch-tall youngster, her blond hair tied in bunches with bobbles as she played on the swings. Then at 7.30 p.m., with the mist closing in from the sea, she had been seen on the Promenade: and she wasn't alone.

Witness sightings of Caroline that evening had one common characteristic. Each included an almost identical description of her companion. He was somewhere between thirty and forty years old, between 5 feet 8 inches and 5 feet 10 inches tall, and he had dark, perhaps collar-length hair. Two other points stand out. The man was unshaven with an estimated two or three days' stubble, and he was wearing glasses, heavy NHS-type frames with tinted glass.

Police photofits, released some weeks later, show a heavy-set man, jowly and evidently powerful. Twenty years on, and with the benefit of hindsight, they bore a remarkable resemblance to the man arrested in the Borders for the Laura Turner abduction. At 7.50 p.m. Caroline was seen by another witness. This time she was inside Fun City, climbing on the Toyland merry-go-round. A heavy-set man with dark hair, stubble and glasses was seen to pay her fare. It cost 15 pence. That was the last confirmed sighting of Caroline Hogg.

In the days that followed, Lothian and Borders Police stepped up their hunt. Thousands of volunteers turned up at the town hall to beat their way through the overgrown semi-rural paths and byways out on to the bleak hillsides. Many more thousands of statements were laboriously hand-written by weary officers.

Annette and John Hogg spoke only once in the glare of a phalanx of cameras. On Monday, 11 July, the police organized a press conference at the Leith Divisional station. Unlike Liz and Fordyce Maxwell, the couple (John Hogg was a plumber) had little or no experience of the media and found them harder to cope with. The press conference was torment. John said: 'We came here today hoping if someone sees this at home . . . just bring her back. If anyone knows anything at all, let the police know. Please, let her come home.' Annette, her face drawn and marked with tears, managed no more than a simple plea. 'If she is in anyone's house and she watches TV and could see us . . . Just come home. We really miss her. I really miss her.'

Leeds was a city that grew rich on the wool trade and then fell on hard times when the market forced the noisy looms into silence. In the 1980s the city was in a period of transition. The crumbling monuments to Victorian paternalism were gradually being torn down and replaced by architectural evidence of the yuppie generation: modern edifices of concrete and glass, cold in winter and greenhouses come summer.

Four miles south-west of Leeds city centre is the town of Morley. It is one of a number of once proud villages founded on textiles, coal and light engineering that have gradually been absorbed into the suburban sprawl that makes up Greater Leeds. But Morley has, at least, retained much of its original architecture. The streets fanning out from the town centre are a web of terraced stone houses, closely packed remnants of a working-class community. Perhaps surprisingly, the older Victorian and Edwardian-era homes fetch the lowest prices despite being well built and deceptively spacious.

Brunswick Place is just such a row, a small cluster of back-to-back two-storey buildings. Near by are a representative mix of light industrial premises and more low-cost old housing. At Number 1, Sarah Jayne Harper lived with her mother Jacki, nine-year-old sister Claire and brother David, five. The children's father did not share the little house: Terence and Jacki Harper had divorced in 1984, nine years after Sarah was born.

Sarah had been born on 15 August 1975, when Jacki was just sixteen. She had lived all her life in the streets around her home. Morley was the only place she knew, and if by 1986 she felt safe enough to play in nearby Peel or Ackroyd Street, her confidence was shared by any number of other ten-year-old girls from the neighbourhood.

At the top end of Peel Street, just 150 yards from the Harpers' home in Brunswick Place, is K & M Stores, a traditional corner shop selling everything from pop and crisps, through groceries, to beer and spirits. A few yards away is Jackson's fish-and-chip shop, representing the other staple requirement of any small northern community. Just around the corner in Ackroyd Street is a handful of small businesses. In March 1986 one of these was rented by Miles Buckley Spencer: his business was involved with the display of advertising posters.

Sarah knew these streets backwards. Every morning in term-time she and her sister Claire walked the few hundred yards to Peel Street Junior School. Most evenings the girls came home together: it was rare for Sarah to walk back alone. In Ackroyd Street, the other boundary of her small world, was the Salvation Army Citadel. Sarah was a keen member and played the cornet in the band.

Wednesday, 26 March, was a damp example of the dying northern winter: murky days and dark nights linger much longer in the north than in the softer south. But there was one thing to cheer up Sarah, her sister and brother. That Wednesday was a school holiday.

The Harpers spent the day as a family: Jacki took the children shopping and then on to see relatives in the area. Like many young families in the town, Jacki had not moved her children far away from their grandparents. Her own mother, Marlene Hopton, lived less than half a mile away. They were at home in Brunswick Place by 6.30 p.m. Jacki set about making the tea – bacon grills with chips and bread and butter.

Coronation Street is shown at 7.30 on Wednesday evenings. The familiar blowsy signature tune was just ending, shortly to be replaced on the rival BBC by *Dallas*, when Jacki asked

Sarah to run along to K & M Stores for a loaf of bread. She opened her purse and handed over £1. On her way out of the door Sarah picked up two empty lemonade bottles: they carried a deposit and would be worth 20 pence at the shop. Jacki said later: 'I'd used the last of the bread and asked someone if they'd go to the shop and fetch a loaf, and Sarah said: "I'll go, Mum. Can I take the dog?" I said, "No, you can't take the dog because you can't take the dog into the shop." And I gave her the money and she went off to the shop. And I never saw her again.'

The night had turned from damp to extremely wet. It was raining hard, and Sarah pulled the hood of her blue anorak over her head. She could have run to the shop blindfolded: she took the route she always used, along Brunswick Place and through the small alley (known universally as the 'snicket') into Peel Street. It took her less than five minutes. As she pushed open the shop door, she saw two faces she knew well. Sandra Jackson ran the nearby fish-and-chip shop: she was chatting with Kanchan Champaneri, the wife of the owner of K & M Stores.

Sarah asked for a loaf of white bread and two packets of crisps. She also handed over the two lemonade bottles. Mrs Champaneri put the food into a small white plastic bag and gave Sarah her change. As she left the shop it was exactly 8.05 p.m.

Near by, in Clough Street, Joanne Mitchell and Nicola Gregson were hanging about despite the heavy rain. They recognized the girl's slight, 4-foot frame, collar-length blond hair, anorak, pink corduroy skirt, white socks and brown shoes. They watched her walk away from the shop and set off back towards the 'snicket' and the safety of Brunswick Place.

By 8.15 Jacki Harper was becoming worried. She checked with K & M Stores to make sure her daughter had been there. When Mrs Champaneri confirmed that she had, Jacki set out in her car to search the neighbourhood. At a little before 9 p.m., Jacki Harper picked up the phone and dialled the police.

Detective Superintendent John Stainthorpe is a plain-speaking man, his natural Yorkshire bluntness honed by a thirty-five-year career in the police which had seen more than its fair share of murders. Stainthorpe had been in harness during most of the county's major murder inquiries: the serial killing sprees by Brady and Hindley and by Peter Sutcliffe had all happened during his tenure; all were on his patch.

Almost from the moment he interviewed Jacki Harper, Stainthorpe's sixth sense warned him that this was neither a minor and short-lived disappearance nor a simple, if unpleasant, case of a child being abducted and subsequently killed. Of Sarah's likely death he was in little doubt: he was sure that her body would eventually be found, broken and abandoned.

Experience suggested that it would be discovered close to the point where she was abducted. Most violent abusers or killers tend to concentrate their efforts on a territory close to where they or their victims live. Experience also suggested that the man who had plucked Sarah from Peel Street would either live or work locally and might well know the child. He could even be a relative.

There was something that raised his hackles though. Two days later he was able to pin it down. 'Quite frankly,' he told a news conference on Sunday, 30 March, 'the girl seems to have disappeared into thin air. There has not been one promising sighting at all since she left the shop.'

None the less the detective had already been implementing the procedures standard in such cases. Five hundred houses in the neighbourhood of Brunswick Place, Peel Street and Ackroyd Street had been searched, as had large tracts of the scrubby moorland surrounding Morley. Hundreds of volunteers turned up at the town hall in response to Stainthorpe's policy of pleading for assistance and publishing Sarah's photo. But the search, ever wider day by day, produced nothing – not a trace of the little girl or her clothing. As March turned into April and the weather brightened a little, Stainthorpe was forced to concede publicly his private belief that Sarah was dead rather than simply missing.

In the house at Brunswick Place too the same grim reality

was being faced. Police Constable Julie Eastwood had all but moved in with the Harpers since the night Sarah had vanished; Jacki's mother, Marlene Hopton was there too. And on Tuesday, 1 April, it was she who first voiced the family's fear:

> I am praying that she is not dead, but I am beginning to think the worst after so long. The longer it goes on the more hope diminishes. The last four days have been absolute hell. Jacki is doing her best to bear up. She has short spasms where she is normal and then crumbles and goes to pieces again.

Two days later Jacki Harper made her first appeal on television. If Marlene had been prepared to show that the family believed the worst, Jacki, heavily pregnant with her fourth child, was determined to fight on to the last:

> If she is dead, at least she cannot be hurt any more. But we do hope she is alive. I just feel so guilty for sending her out, but she had been so many times you just don't think. She would not go off with someone strange – not willingly, she wouldn't . . . I've always drilled it into her. Please, whoever has got her, please bring her home. I just want her back. Even if she is dead, just pick up the phone and tell us where the body is . . .

Among other cases of abduction being investigated by detectives in July 1990 was that of Teresa Ann Thornhill. Teresa lived less than five minutes' walk away from her school. A small, slight girl, who looked a good three years younger than her age, she lived in the suburban outskirts of Radford, Nottingham, and attended the local Forest Comprehensive School on Gregory Boulevard. In April 1988 she was fifteen years old and due, that summer, to leave the classroom for a promised job in a local bakery.

She was the younger of Brian and Ruby Thornhill's children. Her elder brother had already left home, so that Teresa was the only child in the household. Her looks often led those who didn't know her well to believe that she was still on the edge of the transition from youngster to teenager. 'Teresa,' her mother later recalled, 'has always been of slight build and not very tall.' Teresa herself was rather more blunt: 'I look young for my age. In April 1988, although I was fifteen years old, I looked about twelve. I was 4 feet 10 inches tall, slim, just developing a woman's figure. I had short, straight light-brown hair. I have a very pale complexion and did not wear any make-up at the time.'

Like most young women her age in that neighbourhood, Teresa Thornhill had a boyfriend, but it was not an exclusive relationship, and she spent time both with her girlfriends and with other young men from the area. Sunday, 28 April 1988, was a normal weekend in the Thornhill household. Teresa spent the morning helping around the house before setting out to see a schoolfriend in nearby Hyson Green. She crossed Alfreton Road and walked past the Clarence Hotel towards the junction with Birkin Avenue. At around 12 noon she noticed a blue Ford Transit van drive past her and up the street. Teresa thought nothing of it and spent a cheerful half-hour with her friend before going home for a traditional Sunday lunch.

At 3 p.m. that afternoon another friend called at the Thornhill house and suggested that Teresa and she should go to Wollaton Park for a walk with two local lads. Wollaton Park is an imposing swathe of formal gardens surrounding a stately-home-turned-museum. Its rolling acres sweep down from the historic walls towards Nottingham's busy main roads around it. In spring and summer the park is a popular place for families and young people to picnic, play or simply idle away a lazy afternoon.

The four friends stayed in Wollaton Park until around 6 p.m. Near by they caught a bus that took them close to the estate around which they lived. Two peeled off, leaving Teresa walking with Andrew Beeson, sixteen years old and a packer at a local clothing company. He said later:

> I continued to walk with Teresa. At about 7.10 p.m., just before the junction of Forster Street and Hartley Road, I saw a dark-blue Transit van waiting to pull out and turn in the direction of Radford Boulevard. The reason the van caught my

attention was because it had a large number of dents in the bonnet. At the traffic lights at Radford Boulevard Teresa and I went off in different directions. The reason I didn't walk with Teresa so near her home was because she had a boyfriend, and I didn't wish to be seen with her in case he got the wrong idea. We had planned to meet at the twitchel [small alleyway] which leads to Beckenham Road off Norton Street.

Andrew's circumspection meant that Teresa was out of his sight for a few minutes – the time it took him to take a slightly circuitous route around the streets. Teresa turned on to Radford Boulevard and almost immediately saw the blue Transit van she had noticed that morning. Afterwards she described what happened:

The van must have come up from behind us on Hartley Road. It turned left on to Radford Boulevard. It then turned first right on to Norton Street.

I crossed the road and walked on to Norton Street on the left-hand side of the road. It was then I really noticed the big blue van. I saw it travel from the end of the street towards me. It must have turned around at the end of the street and driven back towards me. It stopped a few yards in front of me on the opposite side of the road to me.

I saw the driver get out and open the bonnet of the engine. As I walked level with the van the man shouted, 'Oi,' to me. I looked towards him to make sure he was talking to me. I couldn't see anybody else about. I ignored him, looked away and carried on walking. Then he shouted, 'Can you fix engines?' I replied, 'No, I can't.'

I became worried and slightly quickened my pace and walked away. I didn't look back. When I walked on a few paces I suddenly felt the man grab me from behind. He grabbed me in a bear hug. I screamed and tried to struggle free. He picked me up and carried me across the road to the big blue van. I was still screaming and fighting to get away.

He then put his big hand over my mouth, covering my nose. With his hand over my face I felt as if I was going to pass out, so I bit him on his hand. This forced him to release his hand from my face. I then bit him on his arm and screamed again. He was

> still carrying me towards the van. I think it was at this point that I knocked his glasses off.
>
> As he held me, he opened the driver's door of the van and tried to bundle me inside. I fought him with all my strength and used . . . my feet to push backwards and stop him getting me inside. I think he said something like 'Get in, you bitch' as we were struggling.
>
> I remember being frightened for my life. I thought that once the man had me inside the van, I would never see my family again and they wouldn't see me. This made me struggle and fight to stay out of the van: I was fighting hard because I was fighting for my life.
>
> During the struggle I shouted for my mother even though I knew she wasn't anywhere about to help me. I just wanted my mother. I screamed.

Andrew Beeson heard the screaming as he walked past the bend in the road to where he was due to meet Teresa:

> I immediately recognized the voice as Teresa's. I ran towards the van, and I could see Teresa's feet kicking out from underneath the open door. As I approached I saw a man physically struggling with Teresa: he was trying to pull her into the van.

Andrew Beeson saved Teresa Thornhill's life that night. As he ran towards the Transit he yelled, 'Get off her, you fat fucking bastard.' It was enough. Teresa felt the man's hands relax, and she fell into the middle of the road. As Andrew reached her and held her safe, the blue Transit gunned into life and screeched away up the street, leaving dark tyre marks. Andrew was not able to make out the registration number.

As the meeting of detectives in Edinburgh drew to its close that July in 1990 – it was four years since Sarah Harper disappeared, seven since Caroline Hogg was snatched, eight since Susan Maxwell was abducted and two since Teresa Thornhill fought off her assailant – each force had learnt enough about Robert

Black's pattern of offending to make him a prime suspect in most of the cases they had brought with them.

Each was to go back to its division to re-examine the files, while Lothian and Borders Police tried to put together an outline of both Black's life and his criminal record. In particular, detectives investigating the Maxwell, Hogg and Harper cases set about checking Black's employment history and movements on the days when each of the children disappeared to see if they could build an unshakeable circumstantial case.

Ironically, as Lothian and Borders Police laboured, over the ensuing months, to piece together the jigsaw of his life, Robert Black was a stone's throw away in Saughton Prison. Other than admitting his guilt for the abduction in the Borders village, he had steadfastly refused to speak to any detective.

For the first time ever in his forty-three years, however, he had found that he could talk to someone about the dark, hidden corners of his life. It was now late November of 1990, two months after our first meetings. In the interim he had been moved from Edinburgh's Saughton Prison to the grim environs of HMP Peterhead, an hour's drive from the centre of Aberdeen.

As I climbed out of the small, box-like Shorts aircraft that plied the East Coast route, I reflected ruefully on the consequences of the move. For one thing, it was far more expensive – and no one was paying me to visit Robert Black. But there was a more immediate effect that was impossible to miss: the nauseating confusion of stenches that mingled in the air around the prison. All prisons have their own smell, a mixture of sweat, dirt, disinfectant and bodily odours. But Peterhead has two additional flavours: fish, from the giant Russian factory ships that dock near by, and the pungent, fruity fumes of a local pickle factory. It's the thing I always remember about going to Peterhead: the place quite literally takes your breath away.

Peterhead is a Victorian prison perched on an isolated hill overlooking the town and the North Sea. As the visitor turns off the main Peterhead-to-Aberdeen road, the first hint of the grim lock-up ahead is a bleak housing estate for the prison officers. The jail itself is surrounded by a tall wall hiding the old brick buildings that house the prisoners. Only a series of tiny windows covered with large iron bars – each the light source for a small cell – is visible.

Once Peterhead housed some of the most dangerous of Scottish prisoners, and it had a reputation to match – hostage-taking and rioting. When I first started to visit, in order to train the staff, it had an insecure future. But gradually its population changed. By the time Robert Black moved there from Saughton, the prison was already a major holding centre for sex offenders.

As we sat down opposite each other that November day, I wondered whether the two-month gap would have fractured our growing relationship. After a few minutes of inconsequential pleasantries (questions about Black's response to his new prison home) I was determined to pick up the sessions from where we had left off in Edinburgh: Black's first major abduction and sexual assault in an air-raid shelter that had almost led to his victim's death.

I introduced again the breathing technique that had previously proved partially successful in opening up the darker recesses of Black's mind, and he volunteered quite quickly the events that occurred immediately after he walked out of the air-raid shelter, leaving his victim for dead. 'I was picked up the next day and I think I had probation reports, psychiatric reports. I was on remand for about a month: two weeks for a probation report and two weeks for a psychiatry report.' If he knew what was in those reports, Robert Black wasn't saying. And yet those reports were, in their own way, vital stages in the dangerous course his life had taken: each highlighted the chaotic conditions within the penal system when it was faced with sexual offenders.

The psychiatric report was prepared first. In it the assistant psychiatrist assigned to interview Black reported that his subject had shown 'proper concern' for both his own actions and their effect on the victim. The document went on to suggest that the abduction and assault were an 'isolated incident' in the process of Black's emotional growth and that, since his personality was 'sound', he was quite likely to develop emotionally in a 'quite normal way'. Finally the assistant psychiatrist insisted there was no need for psychiatric intervention; Black would be more likely to develop normally 'in a family background'. Wearily, I recognized this type of report: I had seen it too often across the years. There was an initial feeling of anger too. I asked myself, 'When are we going to sort out the problem of psychiatry in criminal cases?'

There are some exceptional pyschiatrists who work within the criminal framework, but there are still too many reports written by people who have no forensic background or criminal understanding. I've had reports in front of me that say, 'This is a one-off, an isolated incident: he'll never do it again.' Yet in the report that I've subsequently written the man in question has admitted to many, many offences: he's been doing it for many, many years. And he is clearly intent on carrying on doing it.

If the psychiatric report was dangerously naïve, the report prepared by the Probation Service on 16 July 1963 was rather less sanguine. It detailed Black's actions prior to the air-raid shelter offence and suggested that he might well have a 'seriously disturbed personality requiring residential psychiatric care'. But it came as little surprise to me to see that, on 25 June 1963, Greenock Juvenile Court ignored the probation report and, on the basis of the warmly reassuring psychiatric assessment, deferred the case for a year pending a formal admonishment. For an offence of gross sexual violence against a seven-year-old girl Robert Black walked out of court a free man. Not a single paragraph was printed in any newspaper: the case was simply ignored.

Immediately after the trial Black returned to Grangemouth, lodging in Newlands Road. Far from controlling his aberrant sexuality – as the assistant psychiatrist had, presumably, hoped – his brush with the courts seemed to have instilled a sense of urgency in Black's obsession with children. He began repeatedly abusing the young daughter of the couple who owned the house in Newlands Road.

RAY: How old was she?
BLACK: Nine, ten, something like that.

RAY: What did you do with her?
BLACK: I don't know . . . I touched her a few times.
RAY: Do you remember her name?
BLACK: Carol-Ann. On some occasions she seemed, well . . . On other occasions she put up a bit of a fight. There was once I was actually in bed and she came into the bedroom and laid down on the bed beside me, you know, on top of the covers . . .
RAY: But that would be behaviour that you had programmed.
BLACK: Well, I'd never really invited her into the bedroom before.

I knew Carol-Ann would have a different version of the abuse she had endured. Although it was not reported to the police at the time – Black was simply sent packing from his lodgings – she later told investigators that he had repeatedly pushed his fingers into her vagina.

But there was a slightly different pattern in Black's abuse of Carol-Ann: he was crossing the line between the role of violent predatory abductor and attacker and the more common seductive approach adopted by most paedophiles. Nor was the girl the only victim of Black's new technique. He gradually told me that he formed what he saw as relationships with at least two young girls at this period in his life. Of course, what he called a 'relationship' was only a means of enabling him to abuse them, but it was a different pattern that I had to be aware of.

In one sense, Black was right: child sex abuse is not an incident but a type of relationship – a corrupting and violating relationship, but a relationship none the less. This is rooted in the fact that the child survives the abuse: the offender interprets the ways the child finds to survive as a justification of his actions. For example, the child may take money; the child may go back to the house many times; the child may even reach orgasm. But these adult signals are the consequences of forming a relationship with the child and turning it into an abusive relationship.

Then, when the police investigate, they encounter evidence of the child's apparent compliance with the abuse. When, or if, the case comes to court the defendant's lawyers will emphasize this evidence of a relationship. In doing so, they may describe the child as 'promiscuous'. Neither they nor the court seem able to understand that this 'promiscuity' is a direct result of the relationship formed by the offender so that he can abuse. Because of this I train the police to use evidence of *mens rea* – the abuser's intent. They must show that the relationship formed indicates an intent by the paedophile to dominate and control his victim. It should never be the defence that introduces the relationship into the court to defend the abuser: the prosecution should introduce it to prove how calculating was the offender.

Black's statement that he groomed his victims (in the classic pattern of the seductive paedophile) was evidence of the complexity of the man sitting opposite me. He told me that at the same time as he adopted this new approach he was still seeking out and assaulting small girls he didn't know – hadn't attempted to seduce – as he did his rounds as a delivery boy.

RAY: So you were forming with a couple of girls relationships that you then turned to sexual abuse. But the rest of the abuse on other girls – that was all strangers?

BLACK: Yeah.

RAY: Can you tell me what happened there?

BLACK: [If] there was a girl on her own in the flats when I was delivering, I'd like sit down and talk to her for a few minutes, like, you know, and try and touch her: sometimes succeeded, sometimes not.

RAY: And was that a daily occurrence?

BLACK: Not daily, like, but it happened fairly regular.

RAY: But you don't know how many children?

BLACK: No.

RAY: What's your guess?

BLACK: I'd say it should be in the thirties or forties.

RAY: Right. There could be more?

BLACK: Could be . . .

Thirty or forty children. I turned it over in my mind. Was this a true figure? It is not uncommon for paedophiles to abuse more than 200 children in their lifetime of offending, so the numbers to which Black was confessing were entirely possible. But, as with almost anything a sex offender tells me, it was impossible to be sure. There are two opposing issues potentially at work when a man is prepared to put a figure to the number of his victims. He could be still in partial denial: prepared to admit some of his guilt but not all. Equally, he could be giving me a vastly inflated number because he thinks that is what I want to hear.

I didn't think Robert Black was playing this game. While he gave every impression of finding our sessions helpful and important, getting information from him was like drawing teeth. He wasn't the type of offender readily to incriminate himself with fantastic stories simply to keep me going. But then, in a sense, I also felt that over nearly thirty years the exact number of his victims was irrelevant. Tying him down to precise statistics was never likely to help them. If Robert Black told me one day he had abused fifty rather than forty young girls in this period, I knew no one was going to start looking for the other ten victims.

In some ways that was an indictment of the value we place on children's lives. Each of Black's victims had had her life blighted. If it had been any other serious crime – armed robbery, drug smuggling, terrorism – such new intelligence would have been seized on even this long after the event. But with child abuse I knew that no police force, no social services department, would allocate a penny of its resources or a minute of its time to finding and helping the victims of those assaults.

It was not something I needed to pursue immediately. I filed it away at the back of my mind and returned to a more important question: what, if anything, brought this frenzy of abusing to a halt? According to Black, it stopped when he met 'my first and only love', a woman of his own age called Pamela.

RAY: How old were you then, with Pamela?
BLACK: I suppose I was about seventeen when I met her.

RAY: And that went on for how long?
BLACK: Until I was nineteen.
RAY: So that was a good period?
BLACK: Yeah.
RAY: So what happened with Pamela? It became sexual, didn't it?
BLACK: Yeah, eventually. Yeah.
RAY: And it was a good relationship, was it?
BLACK: Yeah, I thought so. Yeah.
RAY: And what went wrong?
BLACK: Well, I moved away [from Grangemouth], but the intention was to save up to get engaged.
RAY: Yeah?
BLACK: And she broke it off. She said she'd met someone else.
RAY: And as soon as she broke it off you went back to abusing again?
BLACK: It looks that way, yeah.

If I could put aside the horrific nature of his offending, there was an almost tangible sense of loss about Robert Black's early life. His natural mother abandoned him, and then his foster-parents died. He was clearly a little boy lost in the two care homes to which he was promptly sent on becoming an orphan: already an offender but still a child with a growing sense of rejection and isolation. In care he perceived himself to have been rejected by the girl his own age who had 'invited' him into her bed; and then his first real girlfriend as an adult abandoned their relationship for an apparently better prospect. Perhaps there was something in Black that destroyed a successful love affair with a woman his own age.

RAY: I don't understand why, as a person, you were unable to enter into a relationship with an adult woman because you're not unattractive: you're a normal man.
BLACK: Maybe because I've always thought of myself as ugly anyway.
RAY: Did you?
BLACK: Well, I never thought of myself as a good-looking bloke.
RAY: Did you find that sex with women was very different? I

mean, it didn't obviously deal with your paedophile feelings and your thinking towards girls. Having sex with an adult woman wasn't the same as touching a girl. So it didn't . . .

BLACK: No, I was just as interested in that.

RAY: You were?

BLACK: I suppose.

RAY: Are you interested in boys?

BLACK: No.

RAY: Or men?

BLACK: No.

RAY: So it was women or girls you didn't mind. But if you had a woman here or a girl here, you would obviously have chosen the girl?

BLACK: (*Pause*) I don't know what to say. I don't know . . . Maybe something that I'm . . . (*Pause*) I don't know if I give out vibes or whatever, you know, but personally, inside me, I've always felt I wanted to be married, have a family. And I tended to look at every relationship as a potential marriage. Whether I put out those sort of vibes or talked about it . . . it put the girls off, you know?

RAY: But you never got rejected by a girl. You don't get rejected by little girls, do you? You only get rejected by women.

BLACK: (*Pause*) I think that's a point. I never really gave myself that much chance of getting rejected by women.

RAY: But you didn't want to be. You didn't want to have the same experience you'd had with Pamela. You didn't want that to happen again, did you, because it hurt a lot?

BLACK: I carried the can a long time.

RAY: Do you still feel angry about that?

BLACK: Not angry, no. Sorry.

RAY: Sad? Do you think you'd have taken the course of your life as you've taken it if that had not happened?

BLACK: No, I don't think so.

RAY: You think you'd have led a different life?

BLACK: I think so.

RAY: And that's what you always wanted – marriage, children? Would you have been able not to abuse the children?

BLACK: I'll never be able to answer that because I'll never be in that position.

RAY: What do you think?

BLACK: I think probably, yeah, if I'd been able to [get married]. (*Pause*) But then again, I don't know: I can't answer that 100 per cent.

RAY: Because you're not sure.

BLACK: Because I'm not 100 per cent sure. I don't think I would have done. I couldn't swear to it, put it that way.

RAY: Can you really look back . . .? Are you saying that when you were with her you did not ever get involved with another child during that period? You didn't touch a child? Can you have a think about that very carefully?

BLACK: As far as I can remember no, never.

RAY: Were you still looking?

BLACK: At that time when I was living in Grangemouth there wasn't really an opportunity to look. I suppose it never occurred to me.

I was far from convinced either that through simple lack of opportunity Robert Black had managed to stop fantasizing about the abuse of young girls or that marriage and his own children would somehow magically have cured his paedophilia. I have seen any number of cases in which a man has married a woman with children and, whether he engineered the relationship deliberately or not, transferred his attentions from his new wife to the children in the family. It's a major problem for our society. Divorce and second or third marriages are becoming the norm: there is always going to be a small percentage of men who marry into existing families who do so to gain access to the children.

Whatever Black said to me I was convinced that the underlying paedophilia – his dominant obsession with young girls and with exploring the size of their vaginas – had not so simply gone away. At most it may have been in remission: but it must still have been there, just under the surface. To test this theory I began to probe simultaneously Black's most overt fantasies and the physical aspects of adult women that most repulsed him. Behind this investigation was the knowledge that, when first interviewed by the police during the Laura case, Black had indicated a fascination with a hairless woman's body: 'It's beautiful,' he had told the detectives. 'Why do men have to have horrible dangly bits?'

RAY: When were you first conscious of the female form, the girl with no hair? When were you conscious of that becoming important to you?

BLACK: Well, I don't know. I suppose once I realized that as girls got older they got hair, you know, probably in their early teens. I thought . . . I suppose being in the Boys' Home. Mind you, the incident with the girl in the home at Greenock: she had hair, ginger hair – not a lot of it, mind you. And that might have been the first time that I realized that girls got hair down there. But if I thought I didn't like it, I don't know.

RAY: If you were to place the perfect girl in that chair with you as a target, what would she be? How old would she be?

BLACK: Ten, eleven.

RAY: Ten or eleven years old. What would she be wearing? Picture her there in the chair, and look at the chair. Put her there.

BLACK: A dress or a skirt.

RAY: Short? Long? What sort of colour?

BLACK: It doesn't matter.

RAY: Hairstyle?

BLACK: It doesn't matter . . . as long as it suits her face, I suppose.

RAY: What sort of face would she have?

BLACK: Pretty.

RAY: A pretty face?

BLACK: But you don't see many ugly children, do you? Not really – except the ones you see on that TV advert.

RAY: Would she be happy? Sad? What would her face be?

BLACK: Happy.

RAY: Happy. What would her personality be?

BLACK: (*Pause*) Outgoing, friendly.

RAY: And would she be clean, tomboyish or dirty?

BLACK: Clean, I suppose.

RAY: When you put a girl like that in the chair – picture the girl – what do you think when you see a girl like that?

BLACK: (*Pause*) I suppose I wish I had a daughter that looked like that.

RAY: What else do you think?
BLACK: Somebody I can . . . like . . . cuddle, you know.
RAY: What else do you think?
BLACK: (*Long pause*) I suppose . . . I would imagine her sitting there without any underwear on. Maybe have a look and see without her knowing about it.
RAY: That's what the target is: she has a skirt on but no pants?
BLACK: Yeah.
RAY: What are you wanting to do with her and to her?
BLACK: (*Long pause*) I'm just happy to look.
RAY: But what would you want to do with her if she was in this room now? You're on your own with her: what would you be thinking about? What would you like to do?
BLACK: (*Pause*) I'd like to touch her, fondle her.
RAY: Right. Where?
BLACK: Privates.
RAY: What's the word for those?
BLACK: Fanny, I suppose.
RAY: What is the clinical word?
BLACK: Vagina.

This attempt to change the language Black used may seem priggish, but it is an important first stage in the process of generating change in an offender. When, for example, an abuser describes an incident as 'only a blow job' the therapist has to change the way he speaks about it. 'Blow job', or even the more clinical alternative, 'oral sex', does not describe the abusive nature of the offence. The words have a tendency to anaesthetize and distance the offender from the abuse.

The use of plain words is important for the therapist too. The non-descriptive terms form a language that has meaning in a quite different context. Oral sex is part of human sexuality. It is about giving and loving; it is about vulnerablity and trust; it is an expression of giving and receiving sexuality. Putting a penis into a child's mouth is not oral sex: it is an assault with a sexual element. If the therapist does not change the abuser's language, it can allow the development of a macho group of offenders who fail to confront the true nature of what they have inflicted on their victims, which makes change even more difficult.

RAY: What else would you like to do?
BLACK: (*Pause*) That's about it, really.
RAY: What else would you like to do? What would you be thinking about doing?
BLACK: If that's about it, how could there be a lot else?
RAY: Well, because the way you said it implied there was something else. 'That was about it, really' can mean that there's something else.
BLACK: I'm quite happy holding and touching her.
RAY: Do you want to insert your fingers into her?
BLACK: (*Pause*) It would depend. She might be . . . too small.
RAY: How would you know that?
BLACK: I'd look, feel.
RAY: Yeah. Besides what you're thinking, what would you feel when you see that little girl? What would your feelings be?
BLACK: Affection.
RAY: Affection? What else?
BLACK: Maybe a bit of revulsion, like 'Why are you doing this?'
RAY: Yeah: what else?
BLACK: (*Very long pause*) Contentment, I suppose.
RAY: Tell me what you believe, as a paedophile, about children?
BLACK: (*Pause*) I . . . difficult. It's . . .
RAY: What should the age of consent be?
BLACK: Somebody once said to me that their motto was 'When they're big enough, they're old enough'. I tended to agree with that.
RAY: So what do you believe about children?
BLACK: I suppose in my mind the ideal situation would be (*pause*) a child that was completely willing and eager.
RAY: How old?
BLACK: I used to think round about (*pause*) . . . Well, the ones I used to think most about were round about ten years old.
RAY: Yeah. But they couldn't give consent, could they?
BLACK: No, but . . . (*pause*) Not legal consent, if you know what I mean, but (*pause*) I'm just trying to put myself in the situation where . . . one would . . . actually enjoy it.

RAY: So you never met a girl who enjoyed it?
BLACK: Not really, no.

How often had I heard offenders use such distorted thinking to justify their offending? Somehow they believed, or allowed themselves to believe, that a young child could give meaningful and informed consent to a violation of his or her body. Throughout the 1960s and 1970s volumes of material – some of it purporting to be academic research – had supported these beliefs. Paedophile liberation groups, all crying the new slogan of 'consensual, transgenerational sex', had established themselves worldwide. One American organization, the René Guyon Society, coined the motto 'Sex before eight or else it's too late'.

One of the tragedies of child sex abuse is that few people understand that the sex offender develops distorted thinking to facilitate his 'belief' that the child wants, and enjoys, sex with him. It was ironic that Black, who had good reason to clutch at this fig leaf of 'consensual' sex with children, seemed to show some insight into the truth: that children do not enjoy being abused.

At the end of 1966, when Robert Black was nineteen, the sawmill he was working for in Grangemouth won a contract in Kinlochleven. Black was offered the opportunity to return to the small Highland town where he had spent much of his boyhood. He accepted. He moved in with a local couple, acquaintances from the old days. But their life had moved on: they now had a six-year-old daughter. Black divided his spare time between the local bars and babysitting the girl while her parents enjoyed a night out.

What followed was, perhaps, inevitable. On 30 December he began to abuse the girl, following his now established ritual of forcing his fingers into her vagina. The abuse carried on for the best part of a month before the girl told her parents, and they told the police. One night, as Robert Black stood drinking in the corner of his favourite bar, detectives from Oban arrived to arrest him. He surrendered without a fight.

He was charged with three counts of indecent assault. There is on file no record of his plea – guilty or innocent – but on 22 March 1967 Oban Sheriff's Court found the allegations proved and sentenced him to twelve months' Borstal training.

It was a measure of how little the penal system understood men like Robert Black that for this, his second conviction for sexual offences against children, the court did not require a new psychiatric report. Black was simply sent away to be punished. It was as if the problem he evidently had – his obsession with young girls and exploring the size of their vaginas – could in some way be cured by locking him up in a strict, military-style camp with other wayward youth. He had no counselling, no psychiatric intervention – nothing, in fact, that might break up the emerging pattern of his offending. And at the end of his sentence he moved, untreated and unhelped, from Polmont-by-Falkirk Borstal to the halfway house of a probation hostel.

What made this societal complacency worse – and so typical – was a relationship he formed inside the hostel. He was befriended by another young inmate who appears to have been a rapist – or, at least, a would-be rapist. Together they planned a series of sexual attacks on adult women. If Black's description of his intended victims was accurate, and I had no way of checking, it was another example of the complexity of his sexual problems.

Whatever a therapist thinks he has discovered about an offender, however accurate he believes his profile of the man to be, there can always be crossover in any offending. Some seemingly heterosexual paedophiles will switch from abusing girls to abusing boys. So it was quite possible that Black, particularly in the company of a rapist targeting adult women, could shift his focus, albeit briefly, from pre-pubescent girls to older victims.

And in this small corner of Black's history was, perhaps, the clearest example of the need for some form of intensive counselling. Here was a confirmed paedophile, a young man who had been locked up with a substantial record of extreme sexual offences, who had effectively been consigned to the care of a slightly older offender with his own aberrant sexuality. Is it any real surprise that Robert Black emerged with his distorted thinking intact – and rather better equipped to put it into practice?

It was a pattern I have seen over and over again. The official ignorance or complacency (it can be hard to determine where one ends and the other begins) that allowed Robert Black to emerge from the penal system marginally more dangerous than when he entered it did not end when he left Borstal and the probation hostel. Day after day we free men like Robert Black, – some less dangerous, some more – from prison or youth offender institutions. We release them back into the community with their aberrant sexual behaviour untreated but their anger and abilities considerably enhanced. We never seem to learn. Assessment of adolescent sex offenders is clearly needed: young sex offenders are more likely to grow into more serious offenders rather than grow out of the problem.

This is one of the key differences between sexual offending and other more regular criminal behaviour. With other areas of crime – burglary, car theft, violence – most young offenders outgrow their pattern. The needs and demands of adulthood seem gradually to make their presence felt. With sexual offending the reverse is likely to be true. And, once again, this difference highlights a cruel and frustrating irony. This government, like most before it, claims to be tough on reducing adolescent crime. Promises to fund new and harsh secure accommodation have been made. Yet adolescent crime is coming down; community projects are being shown to work, and existing secure units are only three-quarters full.

What has created a different perception has been a handful of high-profile cases of individuals offending extensively while on bail and of other young offenders being given so-called 'holidays'. Rather than suggesting that these may have been isolated mistakes, a right-wing government has placated an enraged Middle England with ill-considered promises of counter-productive punishment centres – effectively new Borstals. This is a decision based upon politics and media grandstanding and has thrown into sharp focus the fact that governments are more interested in maintaining political advantage than in listening to the advice of professionals. If we put into effective community programmes the money now wasted on locking up a small number of young offenders, we, as a society, could look forward to promising results. If that money were put towards adolescent sex-offender projects, we might see fewer Robert Blacks developing.

It was in the spring of 1968 that Robert Black emerged from Polmont-by-Falkirk Borstal to team up with his new-found friend to target and rape women. There is no independent corroboration of Black's brief account of this period, no way of knowing whether the victims of this campaign were genuinely adults or when, in character, Black returned to attacking young girls. The only aspect of his account that seems plausible is that Black never physically raped any of the women targeted during this period: he was content to watch his friend and accomplice carry out the physical assaults. His voyeurism had already begun to emerge as a motif in its own right within Black's distorted sexuality.

It was mid-afternoon, time for Black to return to his cell on the wing, no longer segregated because most prisoners in Peterhead were now sex offenders. I was left with two stark thoughts as I packed away the small cassette recorder that had registered each of Black's new confessions.

The first was that, in the year during which he had been in Borstal, a clear and crucial opportunity had been missed to attack the roots of the man's dangerous behaviour. The second was that Robert Black still harboured hopes of getting out of prison.

> BLACK: I ain't got a lot to cope with – it's just being locked up twenty-three hours a day in here. B Hall, that I'm in just now, has all the sex offenders. An officer said to me this week, like, 'You come off strict observation [and] you'll be down that end of the hall' (*points to the opposite end of the wing*). He says, 'You won't be bothered down there.' But I don't know

how much freedom I'll have, like, you know, whether I'll be able to go on a work party. I don't know.

RAY: What are you feeling about realizing that you're spending your life here in prison?

BLACK: (*Pause*) What I hope for is that . . . like, I hope some time in the future I'll be able to look for a release date rather than spend my whole life here.

5
The Price of Failure

In the drab and functional offices of police forces throughout England and Scotland at least three senior detectives were working to ensure that Black's ambitions would never be realized. AMIPs were then a relatively new invention. Created three years earlier, the acronym stood for 'Area Major Investigation Pool'. There were eight throughout London, each covering a sizeable portion of the capital. The AMIPs were designed to be working murder squads, though inevitably other crimes – serial rape or major abductions – were loaded on to their shoulders.

In a room off the main office of Number 4 AMIP in Croydon, Detective Superintendent Russ Allen was both co-ordinating the Metropolitan Police response to the location of a major child abuser on its territory and checking Black's apparent *modus operandi* against the circumstances of unsolved child murders in London.

Allen was an SIO (Senior Investigating Officer) and, as such, was in charge of dozens of overlapping investigations. On average an SIO could expect to handle upwards of thirty murder cases every year, no small burden with only a small permanent staff of trained junior officers and the right to commandeer whichever local detectives were available as each investigation progressed. An intelligent and sensitive man, if startlingly blunt at times, Allen was a far cry from the stereotypical plodding career detective. His ability had been recognized by senior management at New Scotland Yard, and when the Metropolitan Police needed a safe pair of hands to coordinate the teams of provincial police who descended on Black's Stamford Hill flat in the wake of his arrest, Allen was given the job. He quickly came to two conclusions about Robert Black.

The first was that this was a terribly dangerous man. In fact, I don't think I've ever come across anyone so mean – someone that could do this sort of thing to children. He's perverted beyond anyone's wildest dreams.

The second was that this man should never be released on to the streets again because I would fear for the children wherever he is.

I must confess I would love to see the death penalty in existence for this individual, but, failing that, he should never be let loose again.

Two hundred miles away, in the divisional station at Holbeck, Leeds, Allen's opposite number in West Yorkshire Police was reviewing the Sarah Harper file with a growing sense of excitement and unease. Detective Superintendent John Stainthorpe had headed the investigation into the girl's disappearance and watched all his officers' efforts come to nothing. It was simultaneously frustrating and worrying: it indicated either that they were dealing with an extremely cunning offender or that they were simply looking in the wrong places. It gave Stainthorpe no pleasure to conclude that the latter was probably nearer the mark.

West Yorkshire Police is a unique force. Its geographical area encompasses some of the country's most dramatically beautiful rural communities, from the Brontë villages in the west to *The Last of the Summer Wine* territory in the south, and some of the most squalid urban conditions anywhere in Britain. The ghetto legacy of the Industrial Revolution lingers, mean and bitter, in the streets of Leeds, Bradford, Halifax and Huddersfield. To join the problems bred in the bleak and miserable rookeries of post-industrial Yorkshire – prostitution, petty theft and child exploitation – had come drug warfare and the peculiarly disorganized crime associated with West Indian 'posses'. As a force, West Yorkshire Police had endured a spectacularly swift learning curve. The nemesis of the old style, heavily reliant on large and aggressively inclined beat officers, had come with the advent of Peter Sutcliffe, the so-called 'Yorkshire Ripper'. Sutcliffe and, most particularly, West Yorkshire

Police's failure to catch him had required the force to reassess its methods of crime detection. A coruscating official inquiry report into the failure had merely added momentum.

John Stainthorpe is short, burly and, invariably, to the point. A pugnacious jaw-line sets off an impressive baldness. A detective for thirty-five years, he conveys with ease an unwillingness to suffer fools gladly, if at all. But Stainthorpe had learnt the primary lesson of the Sutcliffe fiasco – an enquiry so bungled that West Yorkshire Police had interviewed the man more than once without noticing his evident suitability as an prime suspect. That failure had been due largely to the traditional police system for recording and plotting major inquiries, which relied on a manual system of card indices both to register relevant new information about suspects and to note subsequent action taken or results yielded.

In an investigation lasting several years, and encompassing many victims, the chief product is a forest of paper. Somewhere in that forest may be planted the tree that is the key to solving the case – but how to find one tree in such an expanse of woodland? Sutcliffe was eventually caught, purely by chance, two years before Susan Maxwell was abducted. The official inquiry that followed his conviction suggested strongly that in such cases manual systems should be abandoned in favour of the new computer technology that, at the press of a button on a terminal, could allow vital information to be logged, acted upon and updated in a matter of seconds.

Sarah Harper's disappearance had been a computerized enquiry from day one, which made John Stainthorpe's task relatively simple. It certainly made it immeasurably easier than the job now facing the officers under Hector Clark's supervision in Edinburgh.

Clark, a career officer in the north-east, had, by 1982, risen to the rank of Assistant Chief Constable with Northumbria Police. A year later he had been transferred to Edinburgh as Deputy Chief Constable of Lothian and Borders Police and, when Caroline Hogg went missing, had been given the job of coordinating the hunt for her and Susan Maxwell. Although the two inquiries were linked – the same man was being sought in both cases – only the Hogg investigation had been carried out on a computer, using old (and now obsolete) software. The Maxwell inquiry had been entirely a paper system.

During the mid-1980s pressure had mounted within the ranks of Clark's own team to computerize Maxwell. At first he had resisted, but when Sarah Harper's case was added to the joint inquiry the Home Office had forced his hand. The cost and time required to 'back-convert' the Maxwell files was daunting. By 1986 the investigation had generated seven and a half tons of paper. Coordinated on a card-index system were 15,000 statements, 20,000 vehicle registration numbers and 65,000 individual names and addresses.

Worse, there was no point in simply dumping all this information on to the Hogg computerized database. Not merely had this method proved unsuccessful in progressing the enquiry, but its computers were incompatible with (they could not 'talk to') those on which West Yorkshire Police had recorded the Harper investigation. A method had to be found to convert the records into comprehensible form.

Four days before Robert Black was caught with Laura Turner in the back of his Transit van, the mammoth task had ended. All the salient details of the Maxwell case were on a computer database that was compatible with the Hogg and Maxwell cases.

Hector Clark set his men to work. Even with the new technology, it was a daunting task to re-examine such long-cold cases.

They found Susan Maxwell on Friday, 13 August 1982.

> 'We had been making a last-ditch appeal on *The Jimmy Young Show,*' recalls Fordyce. 'The nearest [radio] studio was down at Alnwick, and we were driving back with one of the policemen. We stopped at Alnwick police station, and there was a message there for the policeman. He never said a lot about it to us on the way back, and we drove from Alnwick to Cornhill. He never

put the radio on in the car. The radio was never on. And when we got back there was another senior policeman waiting at the farm.'

It had been fourteen days since Suzy Maxwell had disappeared. Fourteen days – and, worst of all, nights – for Fordyce and Liz and the large extended family that kept them, Jacqueline and Tom afloat and somehow sane. And fourteen days as well in which they had come to know, and trust deeply, the officers from Northumbria Police who were with them all the time. The most senior officer on the case was now waiting for them at the farm. His precise words have stuck indelibly in Liz's mind.

> He said that Staffordshire Police had found a child at Uttoxeter. And we asked where that was: I couldn't really think where it was. I just thought, 'Why is he telling us this? What's that got to do with Suzy?' Because I knew it wasn't anywhere near us. But he said they'd found a little girl. And I remember he wouldn't use the word 'dead'. He just said: 'This little girl is not alive.' And that was when the sort of coldness just spread right through me, and I thought: 'This is what we've been waiting for.'

Susan Maxwell's body had been found in a shallow ditch in a copse beside a lay-by at the edge of the A518 road at Loxley, two miles outside Uttoxeter. The distance between the lay-by and the bridge at Coldstream from where she had been abducted was 250 miles.

Liz and Fordyce Maxwell are a bright, warm and articulate couple. Perhaps as befits journalists, they have learned to channel their feelings into words that best sum up the terrible sadness that blighted their lives that summer. They respond openly to questions, patiently repeating the story they have told countless times. Rarely does an interviewer ask them anything new. Rarely is there anything new to say.

None the less there are times when detectable pain slides into the dignified quiet of Fordyce's voice, times when the lines of sorrow etched into both his and Liz's face are blanketed for a few seconds by a kind of bewilderment. Then his speech becomes even slower and more gentle.

> The man who found her thought it was a doll at first, the lad who was coming through the copse. He thought it was a large doll, lying there. That's quite a horrible thing to think about.

Liz too has recurring thoughts about that lay-by that simply won't dissipate as the years go by.

> One of the worst aspects for me was that she'd been lying dead in the open for a fortnight . . . exposed to animals and things. I mean, just the thought that she didn't even have a dignified burial. She was a child who had lived quite a sheltered life. She had only known kindness. I just couldn't imagine the sort of person who would take a child, a terrified child, away from her parents and abuse her and throw her away as if she was just a worthless piece of rubbish. This would be something so alien to her that she would know how wrong it was. I think I sort of tell myself that she died of fright: and that is a horrible thing to die of. But it may have been the least of the ills.

It was never established how Susan Maxwell died. The summer heatwave had done its work. By the time her body was found in the lay-by beside a road 250 miles away from her home, family and friends, it was too badly decomposed for the pathologist to identify the cause of death. The police were sure it was Susan only after checking her school dental records. Equally, it was impossible to determine whether she had been sexually assaulted – and therefore to be certain what type of offender to look for. The police could only assume a sexual motive because whoever had abducted and killed Susan had carefully removed her underpants, then replaced her tennis shorts on the body. The pants themselves were missing.

What began that summer as an unpleasant, if not especially unusual, child-murder investigation rapidly became an albatross around the neck of Northumbria and Staffordshire Police.

Murder is a unique crime in that about 94 per cent of cases

are solved and solved quickly. Most murder-squad detectives estimate forty-eight hours as the maximum time between discovering a body and charging a suspect. Any longer and they realize they have a 'sticker' on their hands – an inquiry that is likely to drag on for months or sometimes years.

Equally there are patterns into which murder falls. Statistically women are most likely to be murdered by their husbands or lovers, and those men quite frequently telephone the police to tell them what they have done. Men – young men especially – are most vulnerable in social settings: nightclubs, discos or football games. Above all, there are only two real motives (political terrorism aside) for the murder of an adult: sex in all its forms and variations, and money.

With children the patterns are different, yet just as clear. If a child has been murdered and there is no evidence of sexual interference, detectives look first at his or her immediate family. When sex has apparently been a motive the statistics point the police away from the family and towards someone who is known to, or knows of, the victim. Most children are murdered by adults living close to their victim's home. It is relatively rare for a stranger to kill a child whom he or she does not know and who lives in a different part of the country. Rare, but not unknown.

So when detectives from Northumbria and Staffordshire upgraded the Susan Maxwell case from an abduction to a murder, they looked first, quite naturally and properly, in their own territories. Known sex offenders were researched by contacting the Local Intelligence Officers (LIOs) of each division within their force areas. LIOs are the eyes and ears of the police. Each force is divided into a series of geographical regions called divisions. Each division has an LIO whose job is to monitor, record and make available intelligence on suspects or those with a criminal record for a wide range of offences living on his or her patch. Most LIOs keep files on local sex offenders, although there is no legal requirement to do so. Sometimes – increasingly as forces update themselves – these records are held on a Local Intelligence computer. Otherwise the traditional card index is the key to the files.

In Northumbria, where Susan was snatched, and in Staffordshire, where her body was dumped, detectives checked the movements and alibis of known sex offenders, while uniformed officers trudged patiently from house to house and set up roadside exercises aimed at jogging the memory of anyone who had been near either location on either day. But all to no avail.

They found Caroline Hogg's body on Monday, 18 July 1983.

She had been dumped at the edge of a lay-by on the A444 Burton-on-Trent to Nuneaton Road at Twycross in Leicestershire. Like Susan's, her body was badly decomposed, the result of ten days' exposure to the glorious summer weather. Like Susan too, she had been abandoned almost 250 miles away from her home. And Twycross was less than 50 miles from Loxley. Two girls had been spirited away from their homes hundreds of miles away and dumped in lay-bys at the side of busy roads in the English Midlands so badly decomposed that it was impossible to tell how they had died.

Like Susan before her, whoever had murdered Caroline had also taken her clothing: the little girl lay completely naked at the side of the road. But though the weather had done its worst, the pathologist was able to give detectives one chilling piece of additional information. Whoever had snatched Caroline Hogg, and however he had subsequently killed her, he had not dumped her body immediately. There was forensic evidence to suggest that after she died her body had been kept for between two and three days in an enclosed space, probably the boot of a car or the back of a van.

There is no such thing as an irrelevant piece of forensic evidence garnered from the body of a victim. This new fact alone highlighted behavioural aspects of the murderer. It made it highly unlikely that he or she was killed in a rush of passion or as an unintended consequence of a crime that had in some way spiralled out of conscious control. The mere fact that the murderer had apparently held on to the child's body for several days suggested either someone who was fixated on the death of a child or someone who was calculating enough to inure himself or herself to the presence of a dead five-year-old girl in the vehicle.

When Hector Clark had been placed in overall charge of the joint Maxwell/Hogg inquiry he had decided to target known sex offenders in the respective geographical regions where the children had been abducted and later found.

> I decided to look at people with a certain type of sexual need with associated convictions. But these were the most serious type [of offender]. If you decided to look at everyone that had a conviction for indecent assault, for example, it would bring too many people into the arena. So we looked at people who had murdered, indecently assaulted or abducted young children, living within a certain area and within certain age parameters.

Since the night Caroline had disappeared Lothian and Borders Police had been swamped with help from the public. During the ten days when she was listed as missing, more than 2,000 volunteers combed the countryside around her home.

Once the body was found the public offered clues and sightings in abundance. Some were used to draw up photofit pictures of the man seen with Caroline at the funfair, artists' impressions that would ultimately prove startlingly accurate. Others offered tantalizing fragments of potentially vital information. Each had to be followed up.

And so it was that Lothian and Borders Police painstakingly traced the owners of 15,000 Ford Cortinas in search of just such a car that, a witness claimed, had been involved in a road accident in the Borders that night. The operation yielded little success. Two sets of foreign tourists, suspected of having innocently captured the scene of the abduction on film or video, were chased halfway across Europe. Nightly news bulletins were issued to the press, radio and television about the progress made in tracking down the footage. Finally the vital film and video footage turned out to be unrelated to the promenade and funfair at Portobello.

But the police kept trying. Each and every lead was logged and, eventually, followed up. It was a Herculean task. To help the process Clark began to use computer technology. So impressed was he by its capabilities that he was interviewed by ITN for its main television news bulletin shortly after taking charge.

> In the past [he told the interviewer] what we've had is a manual index of vehicles and people, and they're subject to misplacing, misfiling and loss. Now the computer just doesn't allow this. And we shouldn't overlook something which perhaps has happened in the past.

There were many who took this to be a reference to the failings of West Yorkshire Police during the Sutcliffe inquiry. Certainly, Clark's early days in charge of the joint investigation were graced by headlines that announced that he had promised not to allow the same mistakes as had been made in the Sutcliffe case to occur in the Maxwell/Hogg murder investigations.

Of Annette and John Hogg there was not a sign. The couple retreated into their grief: they did not, perhaps could not, face the ordeal of another press conference.

In Cornhill-on-Tweed Liz and Fordyce Maxwell knew what the couple were enduring.

> I couldn't accept that Suzy was dead for a long, long time [recalls Liz]. I would say that for about eighteen months I still refused to believe she was dead because we'd never seen her again and we didn't see the body. We weren't allowed to see the body, and we'd last seen this healthy, happy, laughing child go away. It was very difficult to understand that we weren't going to see her again, and I just kept looking for her, and imagined that I saw her, and thought that when I went to bed at night it had just been a nightmare and it would be OK when we woke again. And I read things about her, and it was almost like being detached: it was like looking at it being a third party. I could see the name 'Susan Maxwell', but it didn't feel as if it was our Suzy: it felt as if it was someone else.

There is almost tangible support between Liz and Fordyce Maxwell. Both have aged quickly over the past ten years, but they have aged into a quiet, gentle sadness that has kept them together and enabled them to offer Jacqueline and Tom the most normal childhood possible, given the circumstances.

However close a couple have been, a tragedy of such depth provokes different responses in each just at a time when unity is the strength needed simply to put one foot in front of another. And so it proved for the Maxwells. If Liz spent more than a year in what, had she consulted one, a psychiatrist would have diagnosed as 'denial', Fordyce was quickly broken by reality.

> I think we reacted quite differently. I think I half expected the worst right from the beginning, and I accepted much more quickly that Suzy was dead. I'm not sure which way was right. It was just the way it happened that I accepted it much more quickly, and I got rid of an amazing amount of grief very quickly and came to terms with it, whereas Liz, during the fortnight between finding Suzy and the funeral, was amazingly strong.
>
> The result was that after the funeral Liz suffered much more than I did. I mean, I still suffered, but because I'd come to terms with it I seemed to cope better and get on a more even keel more quickly, whereas Liz had been so strong for the whole month that Suzy was missing, dead and buried that there was an amazing backlash, and it took her an awful long time to come to terms with it.
>
> It always sticks in my mind that it was after six months things started to improve again, and I started taking an interest in other cases. And you would get stories where, after a tragedy, a couple has split up. And I can understand that. We'd been very close before, and I think we've become even closer over the years, but in those six months I could quite understand how a couple could just say, 'Look we can't cope with this: we're going to destroy each other.'

Their differing ways of handling Suzy's death and their markedly different pace of emotional recovery fuelled the corrosive power of their daughter's death. Liz found she needed Fordyce to react in the same way as she did and was frustrated by his apparent reluctance to do so.

> I think I was driving Fordyce crazy, well, and myself really, because I kept wanting to talk about it and go over it and say, 'But if we had done this . . .' and 'But why, why, why?' And Fordyce was more pragmatic and said, 'It has happened. There's no point in torturing yourself by going over this.' But I just couldn't help myself. It was just two different ways of coping, and mine was really quite destructive. But there really wasn't an awful lot I could do.
>
> When we heard about Caroline Hogg we realized immediately there was a connection. And I knew that this mother, this family, was going through what we had been going through.

And then there was the guilt. Liz had quickly discovered the two words most commonly used by parents caught up in this sort of tragedy: 'if only'.

> There's a sense of guilt within me: very much so. I wasn't there where I was needed at the time I was needed. And I'll never get over that. If I had gone and fetched her, Suzy would still be with us, and I'll never forgive myself for that. I know it wasn't really my fault: I mean, a million times she could have come back that way and been all right. But it happened that she wasn't, and if I had done something differently, she would have been OK.

But, argues Fordyce, you can only go so far with your 'if only'.

> If only we'd never moved back to the Borders. If only Suzy hadn't been allowed to play tennis. If only she'd taken her bike. If only someone had given her a lift. A lot of people recognized her [on the road between Coldstream and Cornhill]. A lot of people who knew her said, 'Oh, there's Suzy.' And, you think, if any of them had just stopped and said, 'Do you want a lift?' . . . There are so many 'ifs'. You can go over the 'ifs' until you go crazy.

The police investigation, all the while, was getting nowhere. Despite the man-hours, the leads, the potential suspects and now the computers, Hector Clark was no nearer catching the man who had abducted and killed Susan Maxwell and Caroline Hogg.

> Once you realize that your offender isn't within the area in close proximity to the scene of the abductions, you do have difficulty. Once you exhaust enquiries in and around the scene of the abductions, and in and around the areas where the bodies were found, there isn't an awful lot more you can do.
>
> You do look at people with previous convictions for that sort of offence. You do look at suggestions from members of the public or police officers as to the identity of the offender. You do carry out house-to-house enquiries. You do look to trace the drivers of certain vehicles who were seen in and around either the point of abduction or the point of deposition.
>
> But I always said that, to get to the bottom, once we had exhausted all our lines of enquiries the best chance of catching the man responsible was if he struck again. My biggest hope, however, was that he would be caught before he went too far and killed a girl.

They found Sarah Harper's body in the River Trent at Wilford on the outskirts of Nottingham. It was Monday, 19 April 1986: nineteen days since she had disappeared from the errand she had volunteered to go on for her mother. Jacki recalled:

> I was at my sister's house. I'd spent the weeks since Sarah disappeared at home, and I was going round the bend: it was like being in prison with the constant barrage of press at the door. I had to get out, so I left a message with the police that I had gone to my sister's in Huddersfield. And that's where the policeman came to find me.
>
> All he could say was 'Would you like to make a cup of tea?' And all I kept saying was 'Will you tell me what you have to tell me?' I knew why they were there – it was obvious. But he wouldn't tell me: he just kept going on about this bloody cup of

tea. All I wanted him to say was 'Yes, we've found her.' I would have liked to him to say, 'Yes, we've found her and she's a bit the worse for wear, but she's alive.' But inside I knew that she wasn't. I had realized that the morning after she disappeared. I knew inside she was dead: I knew I was never going to see her alive again.

Jacki Harper stands a little over five feet tall. A wiry and deceptively soft woman with an aggressive burst of very short blonde hair, her tough, no-nonsense approach to police, press and public since Sarah's abduction has led to whispered insinuations of a callous hardness about her daughter's case. But there is more, much more, to Jacki Harper than those who are tolerant enough to form a first impression can see. She lives now no more than 10 miles away from Morley and the shabby backstreets around Brunswick Place. Her council house in Heckmondwike is clean and warm and shared with a solid and cheerful fiancé, his children and Sarah's sisters and brother. A selection of cats and a white rat called Percy complete the household.

With her slight frame and boyish appearance, Jacki Harper doesn't look her thirty-five years. But she has lived them: adult life has not been kind to her: Sarah's death and the collapse of two marriages have left their mark. Tough-talking Jacki – she has been known to throw journalists off her doorstep with a few well-chosen expletives – is a shell: inside lives a woman who has found an accommodation with grief.

I just get on with my life. I don't have the time to hang about waiting for things to happen. I've got children to look after; I've got a family to bring up; I've got a home to run; and I've got my life to get on with. And I refuse to let this ruin my life any more than it already has done. Only other mothers who have gone through the same thing can understand what this means. Because you couldn't imagine the pain and the hurt.

I'd seen previous cases on the news and thought that I could understand. But nothing comes close to the pain and the hurt and the longing – the longing afterwards, years afterwards – that you feel. The pain doesn't go away. You stop crying, you stop screaming and you get back to a normal life, but the pain's there and there's something missing, and it's always going to be missing and the pain's always going to be there.

When I analyse it, it's not really Sarah that I cry for – it's myself, which is really selfish. But we're human beings, and human beings are selfish, and I cry because I miss her.

For all his bluster and Yorkshire bluntness, John Stainthorpe recognizes such naked, vulnerable emotion for what it is and respects it. From the moment when Nottingham Police found Sarah's body he made it his business to ensure that Jacki Harper had all the support and care his team could offer.

There is a dilemma that frequently faces detectives leading a murder inquiry: how much of the available forensic evidence should be passed on to the victim's family? When the body dissected on the pathologist's table is that of a child, that decision is among the hardest an officer can ever make. The post-mortem revealed four major points of interest: all would eventually emerge in court, and three were sure to cause Jacki great distress. Gradually Stainthorpe led her to the revelations.

The first was that Sarah had been sexually abused. There is no such thing as a non-violent sexual assault – at least, not from a child's perspective – but this attack had been particularly brutal. It was as if Sarah's assailant had violently explored both her vagina and her anus. There would, Stainthorpe noted grimly, have been a lot of blood spilt.

The next was the cause of death. Although the pathologist recorded asphyxia, this was asphyxia with a twist. The evidence of the post-mortem suggested that Sarah had been bound and gagged until she lost consciousness. But she had died of drowning. Whoever had abducted and assaulted her had tossed her body into the river still breathing. But first he had removed her light-blue cotton anorak, pale-pink corduroy skirt, white knee socks and brown slip-on shoes.

Finally the position of the corpse in the river had suggested that it had drifted downstream. Stainthorpe ordered forensic tests to be carried out on the water in Sarah's stomach and lungs. With the assistance of the local water authority he was able to show that she had been dumped not in the River Trent at Wilford, where her body was found, but in the River Soar, just off the A453 road at Ratcliffe-on-Soar. The time would have been around midnight on the day she had been abducted.

While the pathologist completed his grisly task, Stainthorpe's officers had been out on the streets around Morley seeking sightings of strangers, obscure but unusual incidents, anything that stuck in the minds of the men, women and children who lived in houses around Sarah Harper's home. One officer recalls:

> It's a back-street area of Morley. It's only frequented by people who live and work there. It's not a place where one would expect a potential child abductor to start looking for victims. So we knew from the outset that the man we were looking for had obviously been to that part of Morley for some reason.

Because of the similarities between the cases, Sarah's murder was linked with those of Susan Maxwell and Caroline Hogg, and West Yorkshire Police began working not only with their opposite numbers in Nottinghamshire but also with the other four forces under Hector Clark's overall command.

If the pattern of their experience was anything to go by, locally based inquiries would take up an enormous amount of time and yield very little. Still, Stainthorpe had no option: he had to try every avenue. And for once the pattern was broken: the routine house-to-house enquiries produced a wealth of strong and potentially vital leads.

> There were a number of unidentified vehicles parked near to Sarah's home during the material time, one of which was a white Transit van. At the time this vehicle was of no more importance than the others except that it was parked directly outside Sarah's house.

Then we had people who had seen a man we thought might be the killer. They all gave a similar picture of the man at various places in the immediate vicinity at various times during that evening. The first was around 6.30 p.m. in a street very near to Sarah's house. An hour later someone who appeared to be the same man was seen getting into the white Transit van outside her home. The witness who saw this had a good look at the man. At 8.00 p.m, just as Sarah would be walking up the street towards the shop to buy the bread, there was a final sighting of the man inside the shop itself. The witness who saw this was able to help us produce an artist's impression of the man.

The resulting photofit shows a man with a solid face and gold-rimmed glasses. Unkempt fair hair seems to be verging on incipient baldness. It was a picture that would ultimately prove uncannily accurate. Stainthorpe religiously distributed this and all other relevant information to every police force in Britain. He had already asked the Local Intelligence Officers within every division of West Yorkshire Police to scour their records for possible suspects. Now he began the exhausting process of taking this needle-in-a-haystack search nationwide.

On 18 June 1986 the following letter was sent to all Chief Constables in England and Wales (Scotland and Northern Ireland are covered by different procedures):

Dear Sir:-

Murder of Sarah Harper (10 years), 1 Brunswick Place, Morley.

In connection with the investigation, all suspects currently known or identified to West Yorkshire or Nottingham Police aged between 17 and 70 years are having their movements traced between 7.30 p.m. and midnight on Wednesday, 26 March 1986.

If they cannot be satisfactorily alibied, then their clothing, homes and vehicles are being examined for Sarah's head hair, fibres from her clothing . . . bloodstains and fingerprints.

> Despite the intensive enquiries already made, the identity of the offender is not known and in particular the area in which he resides. Therefore I am obliged to enlist the aid of every police force to help in detecting this murder.
>
> I am mindful of the burden my request places on your resources. However, it is a most serious and distressing investigation and I should be obliged, having regard to your own force commitments, that if it is possible to initiate similar lines of enquiry as outlined above, then these should be initiated within your force, however limited.
>
> Details of persons should be forwarded to the incident room at Holbeck, Leeds, after they have been checked and eliminated for inclusion in the computerized enquiry system, which will then be cross-checked with the nominal index [manual paper records] of the murders of both Susan Maxwell and Caroline Hogg.

To ram home the importance of the request, Stainthorpe had commissioned a police video of the relevant sections of the investigation, including details of the Transit van and the artist's impression. He included it with the letter to chief constables and asked that it be shown 'to all members of your force during briefing parades'.

Stainthorpe's team was, as his memo had noted, working on computer. And the incident room at Holbeck was stuffed not with the usual obsolete equipment that gathers dust in provincial forces across Britain but with the latest technology available in the country. So well had West Yorkshire Police learned the lessons of the coruscating 'Sutcliffe Enquiry Report' that it had persuaded the Home Office to donate the newest and most expensive system for large-scale investigations – HOLMES.

HOLMES is a powerful tool, a software package that has now become standard throughout the British police force. The acronym – clearly one dreamt up more to convey a hint of 221b Baker Street than to supply descriptive accuracy – was derived from 'Home Office Large Major Enquiry System', and the equipment was worth at least £300,000. It was designed to speed up, and make more efficient, the processing of the raw data which is the lifeblood of major crime enquiries.

Its efficiency was only slightly impaired by the inability of Lothian and Borders Police computers to communicate with it and by a lingering failure to transfer the Susan Maxwell files on to any form of computer. None the less in Holbeck HOLMES did its work. Very shortly Stainthorpe was able to be confident that both the face captured in the photofit, and the white Transit van its owner drove, belonged to the man who had abducted and killed Sarah Harper.

And the computer speedily processed the information on sex offenders known to LIOs within West Yorkshire Police. HOLMES informed detectives that the prime suspect was not a locally based paedophile. Stainthorpe realized he would have to depend on the LIOs in other forces to check the sex-offender files and deliver him the name he sought. 'If Robert Black had been brought to my attention then, I have no doubt that he would have been charged with the murder of Sarah Harper within the week. We had the evidence there: all that was missing was the name.'

But Black's name was never sent to Stainthorpe. Despite his convictions for sexually assaulting young girls, despite a criminal record that highlighted him as a paedophile living in London but clocking up driving offences all over the country, Black's name was stuck somewhere in someone's filing cabinet. For all the liaison between the forces under Hector Clark's overall command, for all the man-hours expended in detective work and house-to-house searches, no one pulled out Black's name from the Local Intelligence files. Hector Clark was later to explain that Robert Black's record was not serious enough to bring him into the enquiry.

As he closed the Black file during October 1990 John Stainthorpe was convinced of two things above all. The first was that Robert Black was a prime suspect for the murder of Sarah Harper. The second was that a terrible mistake had been made in missing him four years earlier.

> We had checked out a lot of suspects at that time – several thousand people with convictions for indecency who had access to a vehicle similar to the unidentified one in Morley, people who were not as well qualified as Robert Black. Black was exactly what we were looking for. He had all the convictions, the vehicle. He drove a van around the country on a regular basis. He fitted the description: in 1986 he looked identical to our artist's impression. He was the ideal suspect: why he was never put in the system I just do not know.

There was an almost tangible sense of weary frustration about John Stainthorpe as he recalled this failure. The next step, he knew, would be to research Black's movements on the day that Sarah Harper was abducted, abused and killed. And since there was little doubt that the same man had also killed Susan Maxwell and Caroline Hogg, Hector Clark's officers would need to know what Black had been doing on the days when they were murdered in the summers of 1982 and 1983. After so long, it was going to be a monumental task.

As the police in England and Scotland gradually progressed their enquiries, in Peterhead Prison Robert Black was inching through the lonely and wasteful years of the 1970s.

The police knew that we were meeting regularly: given Black's incarceration, it would have been impossible, in any event, to keep our meetings secret. Any information garnered during our sessions, however would almost certainly have been inadmissible as evidence in criminal trial, given the strictures of the 1986 Police and Criminal Evidence Act, under which all English and Welsh forces operate.

It is hard for those outside the law's rarefied atmosphere to understand the barriers erected to prevent what would seem a simple outcome based on common sense. Judges halt trials on technical grounds or rule key evidence inadmissible. Tape-recordings of alleged killers obtained by stealth or trickery are routinely barred from evidence. Yet to the general public, reading the details of a 'confession' in the morning newspaper, their exclusion seems to be a denial of natural justice rather than its vigorous protection.

A typical case concerned a man who was alleged to have raped a seven-year-old girl. It transpired that he had learning difficulties, but the police interviewed him without a social worker or a mental health worker present. At his subsequent trial the judge ruled all the information gained during the interview inadmissible.

The tragedy of such cases is that the public do not understand how this can happen. They ask, understandably, 'Where is justice for the victim?'

My main concern was to develop Black to the point where he could face up to what he was and what he had done. It's generally an enormously difficult process, but when the spectre of the courts hangs over every word, it becomes impossible. There is simply no mileage for a sex offender like Robert Black in admitting the extent of his crimes – all that would bring him is an extra sentence. And yet it was important – vital – that the knowledge and information sealed up inside him be released. Vital for him, but even more vital for the families of his victims. I had come to realize that he must have been responsible for a large number of offences against children – perhaps for many murders.

The parents of those children – even the children themselves, when they had survived – would need to know something of the man who did this to their lives. Unless these cases went to court there was no chance of their ever hearing the information they needed.

It was a conundrum, and one with which I had often wrestled. Rarely, though, had it seemed as important as the mental chess games I had to play with Robert Black in the stark surroundings of HMP Peterhead.

On impulse I asked Black if he would agree to his words being published in some form. Black gave the idea some thought and began to discuss the way in which he would be presented by the media if he were ever tried for murdering a child.

BLACK: I wouldn't be looked at as a man: I'd be looked at as a monster.

RAY: You don't look like a monster.

BLACK: I know that. Don't feel like a monster.

RAY: The stereotypical view of a sex offender is that he is either a man in a dirty raincoat with funny glasses or he's a 6-foot werewolf monster. And while people believe that, children are left vulnerable.

BLACK: Yeah . . . Ninety per cent of abuse is by people that the children know, that they wouldn't class as a stranger.

RAY: Absolutely. But a lot of those men are really strangers. They just stop being strangers – in the child's eyes – two seconds after meeting the child. Because the child's perception of a stranger is actually a monster . . .

I was impressed, though not surprised, by the grasp Black had of the very real gap in public understanding of how sex offenders look. I've worked with many men who abuse children, many men who kill children. And I know that societal stereotypes of offenders who look like monsters are not true.

By talking to Robert Black, in a way no one had bothered to do throughout his life, I found he was willing to help me demythologize sex offenders, help me combat the distorted and dangerous image the public has of a man who could abduct and abuse young children.

I pushed a piece of prison notepaper across the desk to Black and told him to write down, in his own words, something that would allow our sessions together to be made public. Black paused and drew the pad towards him. Slowly, in isolated capital letters, he blocked out the following message: 'I GIVE PERMISSION TO RAY WYRE TO TELL MY STORY LEARNED DURING THERAPY BOTH IN EDINBURGH AND IN PETERHEAD.'

Having signed the piece of paper, he left it where it lay and turned back to me, and to the painful process of exploring his own mind.

RAY: How do you see yourself? Do you see yourself as ruthless, calculating? What do you see yourself as?

BLACK: I don't know. Contradictory.

RAY: Absolutely.

BLACK: Like, for instance, when I'm at work, when I'm in the van, I'm always trying to keep things tidy. Whereas at home in my room everything's thrown every which way, and now and again I get mucked in and tidy it up.

RAY: Do you see that as two parts of you? Do you see that there's this tidy Robert and there's this couldn't-care-less, let-it-all-hang-out sort of Robert? If you were to divide yourself up, would you have one side here as the caring, loving, kind, responsible Robert and this other world of yours – I use the term 'destroyer' because sex abuse is the destruction of childhood – that cold part of you that you want to deny, you want to cover up? What percentage of you is this abuser? What percentage is that of you?

BLACK: About 15 or 20 per cent maybe.

RAY: So 20 per cent of you is that abusing Robert, whom for most of the time – 80 per cent of your life – you have control over. You're able to go to the pub, able to talk to me, able to be OK, able to be normal. And that 20 per cent you've hidden from everybody.

BLACK: I'm ashamed of it, really.

RAY: But even 20 per cent of one's life every year is an awful lot of abuse. Even if it were only 2 or 3 per cent, if you only had 2 or 3 per cent madness of behaviour, there's still a dilemma. Because you look at yourself and you think, 'I'm all right. I don't mean to do it: I didn't want to do it.' And yet you did it. What came into your mind when I said that?

BLACK: I'm just thinking that paedophiles in general don't think it's wrong.

RAY: Yes, but most paedophiles also say they don't hurt children: yet your behaviour hurt children. Paedophiles would say about people like you that you don't represent paedophilia. So even paedophiles would have problems with you. Something has happened that changed your direction. You pretended to abduct when you were a teenager, but you didn't have the wherewithal to carry it through. You didn't have a van, you didn't have anything. Something happened to you after Borstal. I know you made a vow that you were not going to get caught again: that was very powerful.

BLACK: It's not that I'm not going to get caught again. I'm not going to do anything to get myself sent back to prison.

RAY: But you said yourself that you were doing things that got you sent back to prison.

BLACK: Yeah. But a certain promise wore off.

RAY: So you went down to London. Then what happened? What was your lifestyle? What did you do – because you were still into paedophilia, weren't you?

BLACK: I had a lot of various jobs . . . There was God knows how many. Because, like, I wasn't very good at getting up in the mornings, so I kept losing jobs for bad time-keeping. Eventually I got a job as a life-guard in the swimming pool that was just five minutes' walk from where I was living. It was a six-month trial period: you know, you were on probation. It was a council job, working in the swimming pool, and at the end of the six months it was the same old story again: bad time-keeping.

RAY: And you lost it?

BLACK: Yeah.

RAY: So you got another job in a swimming pool?

BLACK: Mmm . . . Well, in between I had a few other jobs, and one summer I'd seen an advert in the paper for a job in an open-air pool. So I applied for that, and I got it, and I worked there the whole summer season. And it was coming near the end of the season. I applied to a different council for a job at Hornsey Road.

RAY: Baths?

BLACK: Yeah. And I worked there for a few years.

RAY: Did you find that period fed your fantasy – because, obviously, you were seeing lots of girls in the swimming pool?

BLACK: Yeah, in a way I suppose it did. I didn't go for the job specifically for that reason. I went because I liked the job.

RAY: You like swimming?

BLACK: Yeah. Plus it was shifts, so at least every other week I didn't have to get up early.

RAY: Did you do anything when they gave you access to those girls, like looking at them changing or anything like that?

BLACK: No. When it was open to the public I didn't have access to the female changing rooms. The pool had underwater lights, and you could go down under the pool, like. Lift out the lights and you could look in and watch them swimming sometimes.

RAY: And you used to do that?

BLACK: Yeah, sometimes. I wasn't the only one though. (*Black laughed loudly*)

I strongly suspected that Black's overwhelming paedophilia would not have been so easily controlled during this period. I already knew from an earlier session that the man's obsession with orifices had led him to break into the baths during the early hours of the morning: on these occasions Black would swim up and down the pool with a long-handled broom forced into his own anus. If he were capable of taking the one obsession to such extremes, I doubted the twin-drive of his paedophilia would be satisfied by mere voyeurism. And, sure enough, Black began to admit to a revealing incident.

BLACK: Some girl complained that I was touching her up in the pool.

RAY: And were you?

BLACK: I was playing with the girl in the pool, but if I touched her at all, it wasn't in an intentional way because there was more than her there: there was a crowd of kids, like, boys and girls.

RAY: How old was she?

BLACK: I think she were ten or eleven at the time. She looked a bit older, I think. I think her actual age was ten.

RAY: You are aroused to girls, though. So you could accidentally do things under the water that . . .

BLACK: Well, there was nothing intended.

RAY: Right.

BLACK: Anyway, they came and took me up the police station. They found out soon enough that I had a record for sexual offences.

RAY: When was that?

BLACK: It has to be before '76. Or maybe early '76.

RAY: Did they do you for it?

BLACK: No. (*Pause*) They told me I should hand in my notice. The police told them [to accept it] or they'd see I got the sack. So I went back and explained it to the manager that I had a past. (*Pause*) And he said not to worry about it. And then he came down later on and says, 'I've got to accept your resignation' – like, two weeks' notice or something. I couldn't believe it.

This story, a vignette of Robert Black's early life in London, was telling. It was also vital. Listening to it made me genuinely angry – not simply and self-indulgently angry at Black's actions but angry at the failure to see them as important. Why was this offence not recorded? Why wasn't Black at least cautioned? Of course, no one knew at the time that the combined strengths of at least six police forces would one day be searching for Robert Black. But it shouldn't have been difficult to understand that he might be a significant abuser. What happened in those swimming baths was a criminal offence.

I also suspected that Black's version of events might be a sanitized version of the truth. But moving him towards facing the reality of what he had done was a slow process: I decided to try a different tack. I knew that when Black's flat had been raided the police removed large quantities of child pornography. It was now time to press Black on the nature of the material and what effect it had had on his offending.

BLACK: I didn't find out about that until . . . (*Pause*). It was after 1976, so I was getting on for thirty. There was a place I used to go to where I first discovered the child pornography: a shop down near King's Cross in London. It didn't have a name – it was just like a shop front. You went in and there was, like, old books lined up, but if you wanted to get something else, you went in the back. They used to give you half price on what you brought back.

RAY: That was all child pornography?

BLACK: It wasn't to start with, when I first started going to the shop, you know . . . It was just a chance remark I made one day.

RAY: So normally you went there to get ordinary pornography?

BLACK: Yeah, it started off that way.

RAY: Well, what was the chance remark?

BLACK: I said, had he any, like, teenage sex magazines? And he said, 'No. I've got these.' And he hauled them out and they were called *Lollitots*.

Without realizing it, Black had given away important information about his distorted sexuality. Paedophilia goes hand in hand with child pornography. Almost every paedophile collects it obsessively. But, like every other category of erotic or obscene material, child pornography has subcategories catering for specialized perversions, from sado-masochism to coprophilia. By studying the type of material he bought – and, by implication, masturbated to – I would gain a useful snapshot of the direction of his fantasies.

The titles *Teenage Sex* and *Lollitots* are familiar to anyone who has spent even a short time studying the peculiar *demi-monde* of child-pornography production.

Teenage Sex is a glossy, full-colour magazine featuring predominantly adult models posing as adolescents. It is produced by one of the world's biggest commercial publishers of pornography. This company, Rodox/Color Climax, is based in a quiet light-industrial area of Copenhagen. Behind expensively quiet, pneumatic glass doors, the (mainly) women employees carry cardboard boxes stuffed with explicit hard-core magazines and videos to and from a warehouse. The warehouse itself is vast: a giant aircraft hangar of a building stacked high with the company's produce. Fork-lift trucks shift pornography by the pallet-load from one zone to another.

If nothing else, Rodox/Color Climax is a model of Scandinavian efficiency, a commercial success story for nearly thirty years. The premises are clean to the point of sterility; employees have full pension rights and sickness benefits and a sparklingly clean canteen. The company, founded in the mid-1960s, when Denmark began to legalize all forms of pornography production, pays the Danish government regular and substantial tax bills. Its founder and owner, Peter Theander, likes to think of his creation as the 'Rolls-Royce of pornography'. Certainly, the magazines and videos have high production standards: lighting, costume and continuity are *de rigueur* at Rodox/Color Climax. But the material itself is still hard-core pornography, however much it attempts to mimic art. *Teenage Sex* is one of the company's longest-running and most successful series of magazines.

The women featured in it – in the throes of apparent orgasm while being buggered, vaginally penetrated or, most frequently, receiving the male 'actor's' sperm full in the face – are all above the age of consent, in Denmark at least. But they are presented as much younger than they really are: *Teenage Sex* purports to portray adolescent girls on the cusp of womanhood. All too frequently these adult women are required to shave off tell-tale pubic hair to reinforce the desired image. It came as no surprise that Robert Black should have sought out the series.

For all its gory gynaecology, *Teenage Sex* is not child pornography. It is what police have come to term 'pseudo-child pornography' – an indication of the consumer's sexual drive but not conclusive evidence of paedophilia. And Rodox/Color Climax makes much of this distinction. The English 'Old Etonian' who writes much of the text to accompany the photographs (he uses the pseudonym 'Rupert James') claims that he will walk out of the company the day child pornography passes across his desk.

Yet Rodox/Color Climax was responsible for producing the most widely traded of all commercial child pornography, a series of films (later transferred to video) with the brand-name 'Lolita'. Only after a decade of official sanction of commercial child-pornography production – ten years during which the Danish government placed only one restriction on the production of material involving children: that no Danish youngsters were abused to make it – did the company call a halt to the 'Lolita' films. But by then Pandora's Box was open. Not only had the films been sold, quite literally, around the world but others had seen the success of 'Lolita', success based on unashamed commercial exploitation of young children, and had decided to copy it.

One of those was an expatriate Englishman living in Florida. Eric Cross was himself a paedophile who routinely abused young girls and 'traded' them with other paedophiles for access to their own victims. From this classic paedophilia grew the cottage industry he called *Lollitots.* When US agents finally arrested Cross there had been dozens of issues of the magazine and its sister imprints *Sweet Patti* and *Sweet Linda.* Printed in Denmark, they featured the children abused by Cross himself and photographs sent in by other active paedophiles. Some of the victims were as young as five years old. All were photographed naked, most while enduring sexual abuse. Full penetration of vagina or anus, urination and young children doused in their abusers' sperm were the order of the day at *Lollitots.* This, then, was the child pornography offered to Black by his local dealer. By his own account, it was to prove a fateful purchase.

BLACK: I think I went red. I took them, and I couldn't get out of there quick enough.

RAY: And that was the start of looking at child pornography?

BLACK: Yeah, it was the first time I knew it existed.

RAY: Did you find ordinary pornography – whatever ordinary means – just wasn't as good as the child pornography? Or were you into everything?

BLACK: No, No . . . Once I discovered the child pornography, I didn't buy so much of the ordinary stuff. It didn't seem to matter how many magazines I had: I was always willing to buy more.

The inventory of child pornography seized from Robert Black's attic room at 7 West Bank, was a sizeable cross-section of all the commercially produced child-sex magazines, films and videos. The list, drawn up on 24 July 1990 by Constable Max Downie of Lothian and Borders Police, totalled 110 magazines and fifty-eight films or videos.

EXHIBIT: blue suitcase containing 110 child porn books, 5 scrap books & a quantity of loose photos. Also within this package I examined . . . 4 child porn super 8 tapes, 5 empty boxes.

Of the contents of this package I affixed labels of identification to:-

1 child porn movie – *Pre-Teen Sex*
1 child porn movie – *Three Lesbian Lolitas*
1 child porn movie – *Incest/Little Red Riding Hood*

1 child porn movie – *Pre-Teen Trio*
1 child porn movie – *Lover Boys*
1 child porn movie – *Little Ones In Love* (empty box)
1 child porn movie – *Lesbian Lolita* (empty box)
1 child porn movie – *Lolita's Examination* (empty box)
1 child porn movie – *Child Love* (empty box)

There were other film spools or boxes, many others, with titles such as *Masturbating Lolita* or *Lolita's Auntie*, and a large quantity of unnamed child-pornography videos. Many of the titles were from Rodox/Color Climax's infamous 'Lolita' series. That Black collected them was hardly surprising: but their presence in his home, and in such quantity, confirmed the extent of his paedophilia, the distorted thinking and beliefs about children that perpetuated the abuse he inflicted upon them.

Even the advertising on the boxes of the 'Lolita' films presents problems. For example, the blurb for *Lolita* 4 reads: 'Many of us wonder what little girls of eleven think about sex: this film gives you the answer. No one told them what to do; they just go about it in their own special and exciting way.' Now, this is nonsense. Of course someone told them what to do. In every child-pornography film an adult directs the children's every move. The tragedy of this type of material is that even to make it requires the sexual abuse of a child. Then the whole debate about its availability gets somehow reduced to an overly simple 'cause and effect' argument.

I don't say that because Robert Black read these magazines or saw these films he went out and committed sexual crimes. That's too simplistic. But he needed distorted thinking and beliefs to maintain his abuse. And what each advert did, let alone each film, was to confirm what he believed about little girls. And when people read these words and see what Black has done, I hope that they will condemn the fact that this material is produced in the first place and that he was able to collect it over so many years.

He had not bought it all in this country. On the lined A4 pad I had given him he blocked out terse statements, detailing trips abroad to buy new films and magazines.

My choice of holiday destination was partly determined by my sexual interest in children. Initially to Denmark and Holland (Amsterdam). At the time of my arrest I was saving for a trip to Bangkok, Thailand. Countries which had liberal pornography laws, especially access to child pornography, was also a deciding factor . . . Going on holiday to the USA, not wanting my pornography collection to be discovered, I placed it in 'Left Luggage' at King's Cross [railway station].

BLACK: How I didn't get picked up I'll never know.

RAY: Yeah. And look at the effect of it on your life.

BLACK: Well, the funny thing was when I had it there, I used to keep it all together in a locked suitcase, usually stuck on top of a wardrobe. And I'd go for weeks without opening the case.

RAY: Hmm. [I found this claim hard to believe.] Did you find that your own fantasy life which had been created was better? Or was it that pornography wasn't really giving you the same fantasy that you had in your head? Because you were obsessed with orifices, weren't you?

BLACK: Well, I'd started splicing a lot of the films I had together. And what I was doing was cutting out all the bits where there was no visible vaginas.

RAY: Right.

BLACK: Like, if it was oral sex, it was left out. I don't know whether it made me worse or made me better. I don't know.

RAY: Well, it didn't stop you abusing, did it? In fact, the reality must have been better, otherwise you wouldn't have gone out and abused in the way that you did.

All that Black told me about his obsessive collecting of child pornography fitted a pattern I had become used to seeing. I was sick of the sterile debates and governmental inaction over the issue.

Pornography, especially child pornography, depicts not a world of loving, trusting and caring relationships but a world of abandonment, rejection and betrayal. Adult pornography gives a misleading snapshot of female sexuality. It suggests that women are available to fulfil male fantasies: it portrays men as the dominant partners, the sexual 'doers' and women as the sexually 'done unto'. The apotheosis of this mysognistic perspective is what the pornography industry describes as the 'cum shot', where the man (or men) ejaculates over a woman's face or body.

In the real world women are rarely comfortable with this male fantasy, yet that is the powerful image of sexuality that pornography promotes as lifelike. This is not a universally accepted view. There are those who argue either that these images are mere harmless fantasy or that they accurately reflect some women's sexual fantasies. Even if that were true, it does not apply to child pornography. The misleading images of children being subjected to what amounts to sexual assaults cannot be justified. And yet we do little to protect them from it.

Black's admission that he was, at the time when he was arrested, planning to travel to Thailand (where, I had to assume, he planned to abuse young children), typified our country's extraordinarily relaxed attitude to sexual tourism. Third-world countries like Thailand have long suffered from foreign paedophiles molesting their children (and their women) while on holiday. Some enterprising Western companies have even set up package tours for the sexually driven holiday-maker. Abusing a child in Bangkok is as illegal as it is in Britain. Yet our government, unlike those of Germany and Australia, refuses to prosecute paedophiles who are expelled from foreign countries for child abuse. Worse, we do little to monitor these men when they are sent home.

Britain is a net exporter of paedophiles. We do not recognize that all children, wherever they are in the world, have the right to be protected. I cannot believe this is a difficult concept to grasp. But even if it proves too much for our xenophobic government, the sex-tourism trade brings its dangers back to Britain. Aside from the obvious truth that a paedophile who abuses abroad is also likely to abuse at home, Australian police, for example, have become aware of their nationals contracting HIV through abusing children in Thailand. They then infect their victims in Australia. The same applies to Britain.

Child sex abuse is about not only the murder of childhood but also the murder of children.

As he closed the file on Sarah Harper's murder in his office at Holbeck police station, John Stainthorpe had come to two conclusions. The first was an unshakeable conviction that Robert Black had abducted and killed Sarah – he knew enough now of Black's movements on the night of her disappearance and over the ensuing days and weeks. It was a good feeling to be sure that, at last, he could charge someone with Sarah's death. His other conclusion was far less comforting. If his researches into Robert Black's life and career had revealed one thing to John Stainthorpe, it was that there had been a terrible failure in the police hunt for the killer of Susan Maxwell, Caroline Hogg and Sarah Harper – a terrible failure with a terrible price.

6

Into That Darkness

The version of Robert Black's life that Stainthorpe found, eventually, on file in the National Identification Bureau (NIB) was remarkably revealing. The NIB superseded the old Criminal Record Office (CRO) in the mid-1980s. But, despite its new title, it fulfils precisely the same function. Armed with the name and date of birth of a known offender, police from all over Britain can obtain details of all his or her recorded criminal convictions.

Robert Black had two separate entries in the old CRO system. File SCRO 7041/63 recorded all his charges in Scotland, while File CRO 18439/67D detailed his brushes with the law in England.

The Scottish record showed, in addition to the early convictions for lewd and libidinous practices in 1963 and indecent assault in 1967, that on 11 August 1968 Black had been charged in Glasgow. The record read: 'Found with intent to commit theft by housebreaking', but the outcome showed that the case had not been proceeded with. The English CRO file was much longer. Within four years of arriving in London Black had begun to accumulate a record for petty offences.

The first was heard at North London Magistrates' Court on 22 September 1972. It was the series of theft and motoring offences that had earned him respectively a two-year probation order, a conditional discharge and fines totalling £45.

Stainthorpe turned from the simple digest of Black's convictions to check this first English court appearance more closely. CRO Form 74 listed the offence in greater detail. It recorded that Black had been arrested at 1.40 p.m. on 26 August 1982 and had appeared in court two days later. Against the section marked 'Offences (briefly)', arresting officer PC 356 'N' Robertson had listed 'Taking a conveyance' and 'Going equipped to steal' – charges slightly different from those Black ultimately faced. In the section marked 'Method' Robertson had helpfully noted the circumstances of the offence: 'Had set of keys to steal Ford Zephyr and allowed himself to be carried in the car whilst knowing it was stolen.' Robertson also recorded that Black admitted a second similar offence.

The remainder of the form detailed Black's antecedents, employment and appearance. It showed he was – in August 1972, at least – a wood machinist; that he had light-brown receding hair and was already balding; that he had a faint scar on his right cheek, an inch-long scar on his right thigh and another scar inside his left foot. He was known to frequent the Horse and Groom pub in Stoke Newington, close to his home address at 7 West Bank, Stamford Hill.

But in the section provided for details of previous criminal record numbers or information there was a conspicuous blank. In 1972, when Robert Black first came to the notice of the police in England, no one connected him with the Robert Black who had a previous criminal record for sexual offences against children. It was, Stainthorpe reflected grimly, a costly but not untypical lapse.

He turned the page to examine the next entry on Black's English CRO file. On 5 May 1979 he had been fined £100 and ordered to pay £40 compensation to a man he had assaulted in the street. The fine had been imposed by Highbury Common Magistrates' Court, a busy bench in a less than salubrious district of north London. Again, Stainthorpe reached for the detailed CRO Form 74. In addition to registering his previous conviction, the form revealed that Black had kicked his (adult) victim in the face, causing cuts and bruising. The offence was apparently no more than a minor breach of Section 47 of the Offences Against the Person Act. But arresting officer PC467G Vincent Rosser recorded one prophetic and vital line of information on the bottom of the form: 'This man is a delivery driver and spends much of his time in other parts of the country.'

That Black had passed his driving test in 1976 and joined the delivery firm of Poster Dispatch and Storage Stainthorpe already knew. But here on CRO Form 47 was the line that should have connected Robert Black, itinerant van driver and sexual abuser of children, with the Maxwell, Hogg and Harper enquiries. The police had been seeking out exactly this type of man – Stainthorpe himself had asked all forces to research their records for convicted paedophiles who travelled the country. And here, sitting in the heart of NIB, was the information he needed. Not for the first time, Stainthorpe reflected that the system of storing and accessing crime intelligence was, as he bluntly put it, a joke.

Black's remaining record reinforced the point. Four separate appearances between 1979 and 1986 at magistrates' or sheriffs' courts at Teeside, Lancaster and Dumfries, four separate convictions for speeding. Stainthorpe recalled later.

> He was travelling up and down the country and was, frankly, the ideal suspect. We checked out many thousands of people who were not as well qualified as Robert Black historically speaking and conviction-wise.
>
> I had dedicated teams who went to crime intelligence offices and ensured that what we were looking for was done. Some other forces did the same for us. South Yorkshire Police formed a dedicated team; I believe Derbyshire formed a small team. Certainly, quite a few forces between West Yorkshire and the south had their own dedicated teams pulling out people with convictions such as Black had and bringing them to our attention.
>
> We looked at them; we prioritized them and we checked them out. Now Black would have been Grade A, make no mistake about that. Black was an absolute cracker of a suspect: how he was missed I just don't know.

The process of checking out a suspect is a laborious and painstaking task. The suspect's movements over the relevant hours, days and weeks all need to be ascertained, verified and then cross-referenced with any witness sightings already on the police files. Normally, of course, the work is done relatively soon after a child is abducted or a body found. For Stainthorpe and the other five forces involved in the joint Maxwell, Hogg and Harper enquiries, the task was doubly difficult: they had to reconstruct Black's movements at precise times on specific days up to eight years earlier.

The first job was to establish details of Black's employment record from the time he ceased working at the swimming pool in north London. Very quickly it became clear that he had drifted through a number of mundane temporary jobs until he passed his driving test in 1976.

Almost as soon as he received his full licence Black started work as a delivery driver for Poster Dispatch and Storage. The company had been founded in the 1950s and had gradually expanded as the poster-delivery business grew. When Black joined it as a driver it was based in Goodwin Street, London, but had contracts to deliver all over Britain. The posters it delivered were large and glossy. Most were destined to be glued to giant advertising hoardings in towns and cities across the country.

A company with a product to advertise would first contract a mainstream advertising agency – frequently Saatchi and Saatchi or Collett Dickenson Pearce. The agency would design an entire campaign: part of the campaign would, typically, involve large outdoor posters. The next stage in the chain would be a contract between the advertising agency and a company that specialized in leasing sites from a variety of contractors to display the posters. Many of the campaigns used truly vast poster images – up to ninety-six individual sheets could be used to make up the big picture displayed on a hoarding for between four and six weeks at a time. The leasing company would then agree with the advertising agency that it should appoint subcontractors to distribute the posters around the country. PDS was one of the subcontractors responsible for warehousing the posters and then circulating them to a network of agents, whose job was to ensure that they were displayed in the right places at the right time.

Because advertising campaigns, and particularly those relying on outdoor promotion rather than highly expensive television commercials, are by their very nature transient, these agents receive large numbers of posters from a number of different sources every working day. This in turn necessitates a strict system for recording just what has been delivered and when. Most outdoor contracting agencies keep a logbook that records the date, campaign title, size and quantity of posters received in each individual delivery. Aside from the very real need to keep track of thousands of individual sheets of paper coming into their depots daily, the system also offers contractors a safeguard against a claim by the advertising agency that their posters have not been properly displayed.

The joint-enquiry police swiftly learned the basics of the outdoor advertising industry. By late 1990 they were ready to act: teams contacted every known contractor throughout Britain, searched their premises and seized all their poster records. Having missed Robert Black for eight years, the detectives were not about to let any record of his deliveries slip through their fingers. Because Black worked for PDS for so long – he was away from the company only briefly during 1986 – much police attention was devoted to its records. The first information to emerge detailed precisely how PDS operated.

Almost as soon as the company was contracted by one of the major specialized agencies it would receive a 'drop list' of all the outdoor-advertising contractors who were to receive posters for the particular campaign at issue. The list also specified the quantity of posters to be delivered and the date by which they had to be dropped off. Meanwhile the posters themselves were being made up by firms of commercial printers. They in turn handed over large multiple packages to PDS. At the warehouse in Goodwin Street these large packs were split into smaller bundles: each would quickly be loaded into vans and their delivery organized on a series of geographical 'runs'. Each run was of a different length and duration: as a result there was a complicated bonus system for each, a system that required the driver's name to be recorded each time he took the route.

PDS operated at least five major runs throughout Britain. The Scottish run took in southern towns such as Luton and Northampton before dropping posters in cities in the Midlands,

Yorkshire and the North-east and then on through the Borders to Edinburgh, Dundee and Glasgow. The return route generally swept down the west coast of England. There was simultaneously a shorter run taking in some of the same Midlands cities as well as Manchester and Liverpool. It, like the East Anglia route, which ran from Southend to Ipswich, Norwich and on to Cambridge, was one of the shorter trips for PDS drivers. Although the bonuses were much smaller, these short journeys – and particularly the narrow London run – were much sought after by the company's drivers: they had no great desire to be away from their families for days and nights at a time. The Scottish run and the South Coast run, which, with a route stretching from Plymouth and Exeter in the west to Brighton in the east, rivalled it for duration, became the fiefdom of a relatively small number of drivers.

Many of the drivers lived in the London suburbs. Because the capital's traffic frequently turned the journey to the provinces into a frustrating endurance test, the practice grew up of setting off from base at night. This meant that many of the deliveries were made after hours, and PDS negotiated an agreement that provided drivers with special keys to the yards, delivery boxes or security areas of the contractors. The contractors, however, still carefully recorded the time when the posters should have been received and the time at which they were actually dropped off. It was a system that would ultimately prove vital in the search for evidence against Robert Black.

Aside from the run records, PDS had another method of keeping track of its drivers' movements. Every driver was issued with a petrol agency card. Each tankful of fuel was paid for on these cards: each transaction also recorded the precise time, date and location the card had been used.

In July 1982 Concord Posterlink, a specialist poster advertising company based in Regent Street, London, was handling a contract for Kestrel Lager. The brand was owned and then heavily promoted by the Scottish and Newcastle Beer Company. The advertising campaign for Kestrel involved a large number of outdoor sites across the length and breadth of Britain. Site contractors were told to book hoarding space, and PDS was given the job of delivering the posters to them.

On Thursday, 29 July 1982, Robert Black climbed into a white Ford Transit van owned by PDS and already packed with posters for delivery on the Scottish run. No petrol receipts exist for 1982: PDS policy was to destroy them after seven years, and the detectives arrived months after all records had been shredded. But by careful reconstruction of his deliveries they pieced together Black's route. He left London, travelling up the M1 and M6 towards the Scottish border on the west side of the country. He dropped off a quantity of posters at agents for the hoarding company, Mills and Allen, in Glasgow before heading east towards Edinburgh. At some point between 5 p.m. on Thursday, 29 July, and the same time on Friday, 30 July, Black delivered to premises in Edinburgh, Newcastle and Leeds. The route matched both his own previous pattern and sightings of a white Transit van recorded in the Susan Maxwell enquiry files.

Gillian Drummond was travelling from Coldstream to Cornhill on that Friday afternoon. At around 4.15 p.m. she saw a large white van with 'Transit' picked out in chrome on the front grille. It was parked at the right-hand side of the main road across Coldstream Bridge just on the English side of the border. Within fifteen minutes Susan Maxwell would have walked across the bridge towards it.

At 9.30 the next morning there was another sighting of an identical white Transit van. Frank Dale was driving from Uttoxeter towards Stafford when he saw the van in a lay-by on the A518 at Loxley. Near the van he saw a heavily built man, about 5 feet 8 inches tall, with sandy-coloured receding hair. The man was walking up and down the lay-by with a mug in his hand. Thirteen days later Susan Maxwell's body was found in the little group of trees beside the same lay-by.

In the summer of 1982, at the conclusion of a Scottish run, PDS drivers were entitled to claim a bonus payment of £88.50. On Friday, 6 August 1982, Black submitted his claim and was paid for delivering posters on that route between 29 July and 4

August. The PDS record book shows that no other driver made a similar Scottish run during that period.

On its own, the Maxwell evidence was far from conclusive: proof that Black had been in the general vicinity at the relevant time and a handful of sightings of a van similar to the one he was known to have used do not amount to a watertight case. But as the checks progressed on the Hogg and Harper murders the detectives began to see a pattern emerging.

PDS's 1983 petrol receipts were, thankfully, intact. These, coupled with the delivery evidence from a number of the company's clients, allowed a clear picture of Black's movements to be pieced together. On Thursday, 7 July 1983, a grey Ford Transit, registration plate PHX 922Y, pulled into the Collingtree Service Station at Wootton, near Northampton. The driver paid for a tankful of petrol with BP Agency Card No. 009. Later that day the same driver bought petrol for the van using the same BP card from the Grand Dale Service Station at North Ferriby, near Hull. BP Agency Card No. 009 was issued in the name of Robert Black. PDS records show that on that day he alone was the driver of the grey Ford Transit: he was bound north on another Scottish run. From Hull he travelled on to Gateshead near Newcastle, dropping off his load of posters at Mills and Allen's premises on the Team Valley Trading Estate. Between 3 p.m. and 6 p.m. he bought more petrol, this time from the Belford Service Station 15 miles south of Berwick-on-Tweed. The road goes in one direction only: to the border and on into Scotland.

The next record of Black's movements is in Glasgow. He dropped off a consignment of posters at two companies in the city between close of business that Friday and 9 a.m. the following Monday morning. To get from Berwick-on-Tweed to Glasgow almost inevitably requires driving through the outskirts of Edinburgh. Four miles east of Edinburgh city centre, on the likeliest route to Glasgow, lies Portobello. At 7 p.m. Caroline Hogg stepped out of the front door of her house and walked the few hundred yards to the playground at the waterfront.

As the detectives pieced together this seven-year-old jigsaw, two pieces of evidence glared at them. The first was that, as with Susan Maxwell a year earlier, there were sightings of a van identical to Black's near the playground at exactly the time Caroline walked into it. The other was that the artist's impression of the scruffy bearded man who paid for her 15-pence roundabout ride bore more than a passing resemblance to Robert Black.

From Glasgow he drove on to Carlisle and then Stafford, making deliveries at each location. He was back in his attic room in Stamford Hill by Saturday, 9 July. BP card records showed Black buying petrol at appropriate stages along the route. Then, for two days, there were no agency petrol slips from card 009. A swift check at PDS told the detectives that Black had earned two rest days. And then, on Tuesday, 12 July, he climbed back into the grey Ford Transit, filling its tank in London *en route* to Manchester for one of the smaller runs.

By now the detectives had gathered not only documentation from the petrol slips and PDS record books but a sizeable number of anecdotal stories about Robert Black from his fellow drivers. Some were able to describe his most usual routes north, together with the short cuts he preferred as a means of avoiding heavy traffic. Black probably travelled across country rather than taking the direct motorway link routes between London and Manchester. According to at least one of his colleagues, Robert Black generally liked to cut up through Leicestershire: at some point he usually took the A444 north.

The post-mortem on Caroline Hogg's remains indicated that her body had been kept in a vehicle for several days after her death. The forensic examination also suggested that the body had been dumped in the lay-by on the A444 road near Twycross on 12 July, the day Black would have driven past it on his way to Manchester.

A swift check on the PDS delivery records revealed a vital piece of corroborative evidence: at some time during working hours on 12 July Black pulled his Transit van into the yard of a billposting company called Rushdawn Ltd. He dropped off a bundle of posters promoting the Fiat's new Uno small car. Rushdawn's premises were in King Street, Bedworth. Exactly

11.4 miles away was the lay-by in which Caroline Hogg's body was laid that same day.

There was a tangible sense of excitement among the detectives handling the research: here at last was incontrovertible circumstantial evidence placing Black near both the point of abduction and the place where the body was dumped. It took only a swift check of the computerized enquiry records to reveal that a Transit van matching Robert Black's vehicle had been seen by a witness in that lay-by on that day.

Taken alone, the Susan Maxwell evidence would never have stood up in court; on its own merits, the Caroline Hogg research might have been strong enough – although still circumstantial – to justify a case being laid against Robert Black. But, taken together, both cases acquired a new strength: Black might argue that his presence near each of the locations was mere coincidence, but how much coincidence would a jury be prepared to swallow? The weight of evidence was slowly tilting against him.

Impressive as the detectives' research had been, it was to be the cross-checks between the PDS records and West Yorkshire Police's computerized enquiry system that finally sealed the case.

The first link in the chain came with the discovery that Black made frequent deliveries to a company called Miles Spencer in Ackroyd Street, Morley. He had been the regular delivery driver to the company's premises for several years and had become used to parking his van in the yard and sleeping in it overnight. Miles Spencer's yard is just 150 yards from K & M Stores, the shop where Sarah Harper bought a loaf of bread and packets of crisps on Wednesday, 26 March 1986. Yet at the time none of the firm's staff had thought to mention Black to the police.

John Stainthorpe called Jacki Harper: in which particular place was Sarah in the habit of playing at night? The answer came back: Ackroyd Street was a favourite. Sarah and her sister Claire were frequently to be found 'laiking out' in Miles Spencer's yard. A cross-check on PDS records for that Wednesday revealed that Black had been rostered to deliver posters advertising Pedigree Chum dogfood and the latest Fiat Regatta saloon car. The companies listed as recipients of the rolled paper bundles were in Nottingham, York, Leeds, Brighouse and Lincoln. One of the Leeds addresses was shown as Miles Spencer's yard in Ackroyd Street, Morley. Painstakingly Stainthorpe and his team fitted together Black's movements on the night.

> We discovered that Black arrived at Miles Spencer's yard around 6 p.m. He made a delivery of posters which was recorded in the firm's log as being received after hours.
>
> I believe that Black spent a lot of time wandering round this area looking for potential victims: he'd been coming here on a regular basis for about eight years. I think it's likely he knew where Sarah lived: he may even have known Sarah personally.
>
> At 6.30 p.m. that night Black was seen on foot in the streets around Brunswick Place. At that time his van was still parked up in Spencer's yard. I think he was already on the prowl for a victim.
>
> The next sighting of Black put him directly outside Sarah's house at 7.30 p.m. He had moved the van by then and was seen getting into it. The witness who saw him had a very good look and gave a description which exactly matches Black. At that time Sarah was still inside the house. But Black's presence outside strengthened my feeling that he knew where Sarah lived.
>
> At 8 p.m. there had been a final sighting of Robert Black. A witness saw him in K & M Stores. This was within five minutes of Sarah's disappearance, and I believe that he saw Sarah in the shop – he may well have been in there at the same time – and when she left he grabbed her as she walked back home through the 'snicket'.
>
> It would only take a few seconds for a man of Black's size, coupled with Sarah's frail build, to drag her to his van. The whole thing would take only a few seconds, and he would be away with her very quickly.

The witness sightings, backed by firm evidence of Black's delivery to Miles Spencer that same evening, were strong circumstantial evidence. But more important information was soon to emerge from the petrol agency vouchers of BP Card No. 009.

The series of dockets found in PDS files proved beyond

doubt the time Black had been in the Leeds area. By 5 p.m. he had delivered bundles of posters to two other companies in Armley and in Kirkstall, both small districts close to the city centre. Then, just after 5 p.m., he bought 10 gallons of petrol using his agency card from a filling station in Kirkstall. It was this simple transaction, coupled with the purchase that followed it, that sealed the case in Stainthorpe's mind.

The 10 gallons should have been enough to see him through to the outskirts of London on his return journey. PDS records had shown that the route for this trip had taken him from home to Leicester and on to Hull on the east coast before he drove into Leeds. But at around midnight that same Wednesday evening Black pulled in to Grandale Service Station on the A63 at North Ferriby. Here he filled the Transit with another 9.5 gallons of petrol.

The purchase seemed, at first glance, to make no sense. North Ferriby is close to the Humber Bridge, a few miles outside Hull. What had persuaded him to return to an area where he had already delivered? There were no more posters, so it could hardly be a business trip. And, then again, the distance from Morley to Hull was just 70 miles. Even the solid and tank-like Transit van could not swallow more than 9 gallons in just 70 miles. But there had been a witness sighting of a blue Transit van identical to the one he was using beside the B6450 road, off Junction 24 of the M1 near Nottingham. The witness had insisted that he had passed the van at 9.15 p.m. that Wednesday night.

The distance between Grand Dale Filling Station and the point where the van was seen was 93 miles. To test a theory, Stainthorpe instructed two of his officers to hire a van identical to Black's, fill it with 10 gallons of petrol at Kirkstall and then, in a precise reconstruction of the movements he suspected Black had made, drive first to Morley, then to Nottingham. He declared:

> At 8 p.m. precisely the officers left Brunswick Place and drove to the point on the B6540 where Black's vehicle was seen parked

up. The officers kept within the speed limits and arrived at the point at 9.15 p.m., the identical time stated by our witness.

Scientific evidence had already indicated that Sarah died within five hours of consuming her last meal, which was at 7.30 p.m. that night. It seemed certain that she had been put into the river, unconscious, between 10 p.m. and 11 p.m. The officers then drove their police van directly to the filling station at Grand Dale and refilled their tank. The journey took one and a half hours. And the amount of petrol they had to put into the tank was very, very close to the amount obtained by Black that night: there was just 2.4 litres in it.

To me it was ample corroboration of the route Black must have taken. He could never have used the amount of petrol he clearly had done by simply driving from Morley to Hull. And there was no need for him to go back there in any case. I believe the only reason he went back to Hull was in order to create some kind of alibi for himself, should he ever become a suspect for Sarah's murder. He would then be able to claim to police that he was never near Nottingham that night but went to Hull. He would have used the petrol receipt to support his claim.

But the PDS records, the petrol dockets and the trail of witness sightings were enough. Given this circumstantial evidence alone, Stainthorpe knew he had enough to convict Black of the abduction and murder of Sarah Jayne Harper. But added to the almost identical circumstantial evidence from the Maxwell and Hogg cases, even the normally cautious Crown Prosecution Service was forced to concede a very high probability of conviction. But there was still one more case to be added.

By April 1988, when Teresa Thornhill met and fought off her would-be abductor in Radford, Nottingham, PDS had undergone a substantial change. In 1986, and then again in 1987, the company had been sold to new owners. Its proprietors were now former employees Raymond Baker and Alan Hetherington.

Around the time of the first take-over Black had been sacked for poor time-keeping. But in 1987 the firm re-instated him as a regular driver. Within a year there would be yet more upheaval. Hetherington bought out Baker, and all the drivers were required to become self-employed 'freelance' operators: all PDS did was to supply vehicles filled with posters and a list of destinations for the drivers. By April 1988 Robert Black was listed as the regular driver of a blue Ford Transit, registration number D748 RAR, and as the holder of petrol agency card number 005.

On Saturday, 23 April 1998, Black set out on a run that was to take him from London to Warrington then on to Brough in Cumbria before crossing the top of England to Gateshead and back, via Nottingham, to Stamford Hill. At the start of his journey he filled the Transit's tank at a petrol station in Hornsey, north London. Of all the dozens of PDS drivers, casual or full-time, only Robert Black used his agency card to buy fuel that weekend.

Early on Sunday, 24 April, he completed his delivery in Warrington, filled up again with fuel and headed for Brough. He dropped off his posters and drove across country to Gateshead. Records held at the Mills and Allen depot there show that the posters, advertising Trebor Mints and Stones Bitter were off-loaded on the Sunday afternoon. Similar records from the company's Nottingham yard indicate a delivery there early that evening. Whether by coincidence or by design, Black was in the area of Radford precisely when Teresa Ann Thornhill met her attacker.

It seemed an almost perfect match: circumstance for circumstance. And, to add to this evidence, the detectives found a security video, recorded automatically by the NatWest bank adjacent to the point at which Teresa's abductor attempted to push her into his van. It showed a dark-blue Ford Transit, parked exactly as Teresa and Andrew Beeson had described. It even caught, in the distance, the last few seconds the youngsters had walked together before separating. Frustratingly, the picture framing cut off the van's registration number, but there was no doubt that it was the same make and model used by Robert Black that day.

Teresa Thornhill, still haunted by memories of what could have been her last few minutes alive, turned out to be a remarkably good witness. She had given a description of her attacker that was almost a photofit picture of Robert Black in April 1988. So accurate was it that she had been able to describe the type of tinted spectacles he was wearing. Six pairs of glasses were found in Robert Black's flat at 7 West Bank, Stamford Hill. Two pairs matched the artists' impressions of those worn by the man sought during the Hogg and Harper cases. A third pair was identical to those described by Teresa Ann Thornhill.

The complex process of checking and cross-referencing the Maxwell, Hogg, Harper and Thornhill enquiries, and then matching them against Black's known movements, had taken almost a year. By the autumn of 1991 Hector Clark, still head of the joint enquiry, was beginning to feel confident of being able to charge Black. But one aspect of the case was still outstanding. In any murder enquiry the position and location of the body, when found, can provide vital clues in the search for a killer.

In the joint enquiry the problem was not that there was a lack of clues but rather that one clearly enormous clue still needed unwrapping. Susan Maxwell, Caroline Hogg and Sarah Harper were abducted from areas of Britain that are far apart. Yet their bodies were found a short distance from the village of Donisthorpe, an obscure community in a relatively small region of the English Midlands. In each case the child was far away from her home.

This in itself was unique. No other child murderer, since records were first collated after the Second World War, had ever transported his victims' bodies so far away from the point of abduction. But, coupled with the proximity between the corpses – the police took to calling the area where all three were found the 'Midlands Triangle' – the tell-tale *modus operandi* cried out for some explanation. Inevitably there was one, and it was simple in the extreme.

Donisthorpe is a rural village close to the border between north Leicestershire and south Staffordshire. Ten miles away is the larger village of Melbourne; slightly closer lies Burton-on-

Trent. The area, though still agricultural, is scarred by a latticework of small but heavily used A roads. Detectives began searching Black's background for a connection. When they found it, it was located not in the Midlands but in London.

Katherine Forrester Rayson had been more, far more, than simply a landlady. In the absence of any family she adopted the role of surrogate mother to the lonely and isolated young man who had taken up residence in her attic. Robert Black might spend his evenings playing darts and drinking beer in the local pubs with Edward Rayson, but it was his wife who came closest to Black.

The Rayson family was large and slightly nebulous. Among their children it was John who formed a close and lasting friendship with his mother's strange lodger. In 1971 John married a local girl, Angeline Coral Compton, and the couple set up home together within a short drive of Stamford Hill. But seven years later they moved north to the village of Shenstone in Staffordshire.

For two years John lost contact with Robert Black. Then, in February 1980, he and Angeline moved to a larger house at Yoxall, near Burton-on-Trent. Angeline was pregnant: in April she gave birth to twin boys, Christopher and James. Shortly after their birth Robert Black resumed contact with his old friend and began visiting the family on a regular basis. But soon the house in Yoxall proved too small for their needs. On 12 September they moved no more than a handful of miles to a larger and more comfortable address on the other side of Burton-on-Trent. 'The Hawthorns' is a large, white-painted house set back from a quiet street called Acresford Road. Half a mile further on, Acresford Road runs into the A444. The Raysons' new home was set squarely in the middle of the village of Donisthorpe.

Robert Black began visiting 'The Hawthorns' almost immediately. On average he would turn up ten times a year, sometimes with Edward and Katherine Rayson but more often while on his travels delivering posters. Sometimes he stayed overnight; sometimes too he turned up to find John and Angeline weren't at home. As often as not, he would simply bed down in the back of his van, which he parked in their drive. Black was a welcome family friend at 'The Hawthorns'. He and John would talk long and hard together. On occasion they discussed the best routes around the country: as a driver, Black knew dozens of short cuts and ways to bypass the traffic. On one occasion he told John Rayson that to get to the M1 from Donisthorpe he always took a short cut via the A444 and then turned on to the A5 before joining the motorway at junction 18.

It was a seemingly innocent remark and one that had little significance for John Rayson. Certainly, he never made the connection between his childhood friend's encyclopaedic knowledge of the road network, and his preference for the A444, with the discovery of Caroline Hogg's body in a lay-by beside the road – not, at least, until much later.

> Black's friends and their relatives in the Midlands didn't tell us about him [says Hector Clark]. They now say they wish they had, but they didn't. In truth, they had no firm evidence to support what they felt. But one or two of them now wish they had told us what they felt about him.

On 24 September 1986, almost six months after Sarah Harper was abducted, John and Angeline Rayson moved house again. Their new home was at 1 Stable Court, Beech Avenue, in the village of Melbourne. Once again, Robert Black was a frequent visitor.

The Rayson family connection was circumstantial evidence strong enough to explain the 'Midlands Triangle' and enough to cement the case against Robert Black. It would not be the last time that a Rayson connection was significant in the investigation into Black's offences. But for now it was enough.

On Tuesday, 10 March 1992 – twenty months after he was arrested with Laura Turner trussed and bound in the back of his van – Robert Black was formally charged with murder. A spokesman for the Crown Prosecution Service announced:

> Summonses have been issued today by Newcastle-upon-Tyne magistrates' court. The summonses are in respect of the kidnap and murder of Susan Maxwell in July and August 1982; the unlawful imprisonment and murder of Caroline Hogg in July 1983; the kidnap and murder of Sarah Harper in March and April 1986; and the kidnap of Teresa Thornhill in April 1988.

But for the families of his victims it was all too late. Liz and Fordyce Maxwell had been warned from the day after Black was arrested in the Borders that he might turn out to be the man who killed their daughter. But eight years had dragged by since Suzy was taken – eight years that had taken their toll not just on her mother and father but on Jacqueline and Tom as well.

> I think it has become less important to us for someone to be arrested as the years have gone past [says Liz]. In the first year there was so much police activity, and you kept thinking that they were going to catch this person. And you wondered what he would be like.
>
> As the years go past, you try to settle into some sort of life again, and you realize that it doesn't really matter. It's not going to change anything: even if he was hanged, it wouldn't be justice or revenge. It would make no difference to us. All that matters to us is that we haven't got Suzy.
>
> Although I'm very pleased that this person is going to be removed from society and is not going to be able to kill anyone else, it really occupies my mind very little.
>
> At the beginning I thought that I might go into court with a gun or a knife, and I wouldn't wait for justice to be done – I'd administer my own. Then I realized that it wouldn't work. I'd shoot the wrong person and be in trouble, or it would just be a disaster. But even if there were still capital punishment, it still wouldn't be sufficient punishment because you cannot judge him and Suzy: you cannot equate their lives.

For all that she does not like to think about Robert Black, Liz Maxwell is still not able to push him or his crimes too far from her mind. Fordyce, naturally quieter and even calmer than his normally gentle wife, is aware that their joint lack of desire for revenge may seem odd or incomprehensible.

> What we've tried to do, the way we tried to cope right from the beginning, was to work very hard. We worked fairly hard as it was, and we tended to work even harder.
>
> We concentrated on Tom and Jacqueline and tried to give them as normal a life as possible. Liz always reckoned that it wasn't going to destroy the rest of the family, that our life wasn't going to be absolutely ruined by this person.
>
> And the way we came to terms with it was to more or less put that part of it to the back of our minds. Revenge didn't really come into it. The worst part has always been right from the very beginning: the worst part was that Suzy was dead.

Sitting on comfortable sofas in their normal household on a standard Saturday morning – Tom rushing off to a football game and Jacqueline not yet risen – it would be easy to believe that the Maxwell family had at last found a way of coping with the loss of Suzy. But the pain of her loss is suppressed, not excised. Just below the surface – rising up randomly, unexpectedly – Suzy's death lingers, a bitter-sweet memory shrouded in sorrow. It is a spectre that will never leave – that Liz would probably never want to leave.

> The wound is still there. It's not so raw and immediately painful, but it's still there, and you never forget what caused it.
>
> It's just a very big gap in your life, and I don't think it lessens as years go past because all you can imagine is what she is missing. And her little sister – who's now her big sister – is sixteen, and we can see that would have been the way that Suzy would have gone and what a nice young woman she would have grown into.
>
> Although we're the ones who suffered the loss, Suzy is the one who lost everything. She lost her life and all that goes with it: the fun of being a teenager and school friends and dances and boyfriends and her first job. These are the things, which stretch into years and years ahead, that Suzy's been deprived of. We've

got this immediate pain and we've got this gap, but Suzy's the one that has lost everything.

I think the time of year she disappeared is very evocative. You know, the harvest and the smells and sounds of summer. I can begin to feel my stomach beginning to heave again because my sensibilities are so heightened at that time.

All these things must have subconsciously registered, and they come round again. Like Christmas and birthdays and special occasions or just when the family's together. You just sort of feel this dull ache, and the black days can hit you without warning.

Nearly 200 miles away, in her council house in Heckmondwike, Jacki Harper pulls herself deeper into the floral armchair that seems in danger of swallowing her slight frame and faces up to the same emotions.

When I was told they'd arrested Robert Black for Sarah's death I think I felt relieved. Firstly because then I could put a face and a name to him, and I could stop suspecting people that were talking to me, wondering, 'Am I talking to my daughter's murderer?' And, secondly, relieved because he would not be able to do it again.

I don't feel anger so much as an ache. I don't feel any hate, and I don't feel any pity, and I don't feel sorry for him. Just an ache that I've lost something.

I knew I had to go to the trial. I had to know what he'd done. I never saw my daughter's body, and I get people saying, 'Well, maybe you shouldn't. You should remember her as she was.'

But that's very difficult to come to terms with: never seeing her. I don't know what he did – I've a vague outline, but I don't know what he did. I can only imagine – and the reality can't be any worse than the imagining.

While Hector Clark, John Stainthorpe and dozens of their senior officers laboured to tie together the threads of Robert Black's life, our sessions in Peterhead Prison were digging ever deeper into his mind.

It was late March 1992. As I was once again waved through the heavy security doors at Peterhead, I wondered how the decision to charge Black with the murders of Susan Maxwell, Caroline Hogg and Sarah Harper would affect our relationship.

Would the man now clam up completely, fearing that anything he said might be passed on to the police? Or would his need for help in understanding the desires deep inside him overcome his natural caution?

The more Robert and I worked together, the more he admitted his responsibility for a lifetime of offending. But, however far we burrowed into the depths of Black's existence, there were still insurmountable barriers to anything close to complete honesty.

It had been very clear from our earliest meetings that he would find it nearly impossible to admit that he had killed. To face up to this crime – especially to the killing of little children – is the hardest thing anyone could ever do. Robert Black's complicated, tortured feelings about young girls merely erected a further barrier.

He was willing to talk about abduction and attempted abduction, though he was not ready to accept the fear he must have aroused in his victims. In the case of Laura Turner he still professed to believe that his actions would not have led to her death, despite the very clear evidence at her trial that she was within forty minutes of suffocating inside his sleeping bag.

RAY: What are you feeling about realizing that you're spending your life here in prison?

BLACK: What I hope for is that, like, I hope some time in future I'll be able to look for a release date rather than spend my whole life here.

RAY: What will happen now that you've been charged with Maxwell, Hogg and Harper?

BLACK: Being charged don't worry me that much. But if there's some quirk of fate and I get found guilty, then I'd be worried.

RAY: What would you feel like then?

BLACK: Miserable. But it's impossible to feel more miserable than I do at the moment.

RAY: Could you live with yourself if you had killed Susan? If Susan had died because of what you did?

BLACK: (*Pause*) I don't know. I don't think so.

RAY: Could you allow your mind to get in touch with it? Could you allow your mind to think it?

BLACK: I couldn't even contemplate it, I don't think.

RAY: But you didn't want Laura to die, did you?

BLACK: No.

RAY: You didn't want the girl in the cellar to die, did you? But the ones we know about could have died, and when I ask you what you feel, you don't know. You say you're a cold fish.

BLACK: I can't find nothing there (*indicates his heart*).

RAY: No. And that's why I've always been able to believe that you did this to Susan, Caroline and Sarah.

I'm trying to help you talk because I need to know how you did what you did. If you did things that led, say, to the death of Susan, would you have a need to share with her parents that she wasn't sadistically abused before she died?

BLACK: I can see what you're getting at, yeah.

RAY: So you can see how important that could be and how that all lies within your power.

BLACK: Yeah, if I was guilty. Yeah.

RAY: But as we said earlier, how do you know that you're not blocking it out?

BLACK: Have I done anything at all? Like, is there anything there? Maybe there's nothing at all.

RAY: Maybe there's nothing but the coincidences. But just the way you have abused, and your life story, and the availability to you of those girls make it all highly probable.

BLACK: See, I've only seen one piece of evidence that the police have shown me. It was a petrol agency slip, you know, for getting petrol. And as far as I'm concerned, that could have been tampered with. A seven changed to an eight, or a three changed to an eight, or something like that. (*Pause*) And then again, I could have been in these places on those dates but, like, at what time of day?

RAY: But even if you weren't an abuser, even if you weren't an abductor, and even if you weren't a paedophile, you would be a suspect in this case. And yet you're all of those things as well, and you've done those things in addition to what else they've got. And I suppose, from my point of view, when people start to query content about a petrol coupon that's what I call offender denial.

BLACK: What I've seen was a photocopy. Maybe the original looked like that, I don't know.

RAY: You never let me have confidence that you didn't do it.

BLACK: Sorry about that.

RAY: That's OK. That's why I want to get in touch with feelings and we're going to have to work out how we can do that.

I don't know what the police have got. But even if they didn't have evidence against you; even if no one else was involved and only the two of us were left in this world, I would think that you, for whatever reason, abducted those girls. The MO is the same.

BLACK: I hoped maybe you'd stop believing it. I thought maybe I could convince you otherwise.

RAY: What do you think the verdict will be?

BLACK: I haven't a clue. I hope for justice, that's all. It's supposed to be the fairest justice system in the world. There was one question they asked me, down in Leeds, for the Sarah Harper case. They were very aggressive with me.

RAY: Did it work?

BLACK: No, I was on 'No comment' all the way through.

RAY: What was the question?

BLACK: They said they'd put out an appeal for anyone who'd been in the area at that time to come forward and [they said] 'The reason you didn't come forward was that you were guilty of it.'

RAY: You said, 'No comment.'

BLACK: Yeah. But I can't alter the reports. The girl went missing round about eight o'clock at night. The reason I didn't come forward was that I was in Leeds – in that part of Leeds. They say they can tell me what time I was there and everything. After I'd done Leeds I had to go on to Hull: I filled up in Hull around about eleven o'clock at night, or midnight or something like that.

RAY: Where was the body dropped?

BLACK: In Leicestershire some place [or] Nottingham. It was found near the River Trent or something.

RAY: When were you there?

BLACK: I don't know, do I? But what he's [the detective] saying is, he's saying I filled up in Leeds. I put about ten gallons in. Then I filled up again coming out of Hull – I put another ten gallons in. And no way between Leeds and Hull, and coming back out of Hull and filling up, should you use ten gallons of fuel, as I was told.

RAY: She wasn't dead when she was put in the water?

BLACK: That's something else he said. I don't know. Anyway, his theory was [that] I drove from Leeds into Nottinghamshire, Leicestershire, whatever, and then drove back up to Hull, filled up with petrol. And he says, 'We've timed it and it all ties in.' Where he's wrong, you see? I left Leeds from the other end, out on the A64 towards York, and when I got outside York, rather than go in – because I've been into York at eight o'clock at night, and it's been jam-packed with traffic – I stopped in a lay-by and had a kip. I can't remember for sure, but it's possible I left the engine running and the heater running. Because it was March . . .

As an alibi, even as an explanation for the extra fuel consumption, it was a thin and flimsy story. But I realized that Black was highly unlikely ever to admit to any of the murders: to do so would earn him notoriety equal to that of Myra Hindley and Ian Brady. It would also ensure that he never again stepped outside the walls of a prison – and preventing that seemed his prime concern.

Playing a hunch, I asked him about the abduction of Teresa Thornhill in Nottingham. Sure enough, he was prepared to admit the attempted kidnapping.

BLACK: I don't know what possessed me in Nottingham, like, you know, in broad daylight in the middle of the day . . .

RAY: Maybe you wanted to be caught. Maybe it had gone too far. Maybe you were worried about going totally out of control. Tell me the circumstances.

BLACK: She was with a boy. I thought she looked about eleven or twelve.

RAY: So what did you do?

BLACK: They split up. I think I was just off a continuation of Radford Boulevard. There were warehouses or a factory or something like that.

RAY: Right. You saw a boy and a girl walking together, then they separated. What did you do?

BLACK: I turned up a side street, and, as it happened, the girl turned up the side street as well. I pulled up and stopped just inside the street, and I got out and lifted the bonnet. I asked her if she'd do me a favour and asked her to help, asked her if she'd press the accelerator and I'd check something under the bonnet. And she done that, and as I came back round her she went to go away. I grabbed her and tried to get her into the vehicle. She struggled and then, I don't know, the boy must have come round the block because he was coming down towards us, shouting, and I let her go.

RAY: And what was in your thinking? What were you going to do?

BLACK: Well, get her into the van and then, like, drive somewhere, a lay-by somewhere.

RAY: Put her in the back of the van? Then what?

BLACK: Assault her.

RAY: Exactly the same as with Laura?

BLACK: I don't know. It would depend . . . like, was she going to struggle?

RAY: Well, Laura didn't struggle, but you still did all that to her.

BLACK: Yeah, but the reason for that was I still had a delivery to do.

RAY: So how long could you have kept her in the van?

BLACK: Well, I don't know.

RAY: We've got to find out what's going on in you at the point that you have a child who you've total control over. That's what we've been trying to understand. Because your behaviour when you have the child in your control becomes different to the behaviour when you're thinking and you're fantasizing. So you fantasize about sexually touching, having an obsession with putting your finger into the child's vagina – that's the behaviour that you want to do for some reason, but that doesn't appear to be what happens.

BLACK: I don't know what makes me do it. As I said, my intention with Laura was once I'd done the delivery . . .

RAY: We already have your intentions there, in the sense of what would have happened.

BLACK: How can you say you know what would have happened?

RAY: We do know. We do know that she would have died. What will you do about the Nottingham case?

BLACK: I don't know. I'll see what the lawyers have got to say. I'll wait and see. Because I asked the lawyer and he says, 'If you were to tell me that you were guilty, I couldn't stand up in court and plead that you were not guilty.' That's the way the law is.

RAY: What did you feel after Nottingham?

BLACK: I called myself all kinds of idiot.

RAY: Idiot? Did you feel bad?

BLACK: Yes, for attempting what I do.

RAY: Right. And then how long after that feeling did you stay in control and not do anything like that?

BLACK: I don't know. When was Nottingham? '88? I'd say that it wouldn't have mattered if the next day I'd seen a nice little girl of ten or nine or something like that. If she had been in a short skirt with socks up to here or something like that, I'd probably have thought, 'Cor, good lassie, that.'

It is hard to overstate how important this information seemed. Black was confessing to one of the substantive offences he had been charged with. And yet he appeared to be implying that he might plead not guilty. And the horror of what he had tried to do was immense. Even afterwards, the plain words printed out seemed somehow unable to describe the terrible ordeal he had put Teresa Thornhill through.

As an interviewer, I had to try to feel what she must have felt: otherwise, information that needed to be put to Black might easily be lost, given the cold, calculating way he talked about the offence. In some ways the very expressions he used, 'lassie' and 'idiot', were part of the problem that I had in holding on to the reality of the vicious offence we were discussing. Had Andrew Beeson not come back, Black might well have got away with Teresa. Quite possibly, she would have become another sad statistic.

The other feeling – and one that is hard to explain – was what I found myself thinking about Teresa. I knew I would probably never meet her: but in a strange way I felt close to her. I felt that she was so nearly one of Black's victims, and I knew that even 'attempted' behaviour has horrific effects on the victim. Cases studies of attempted rape have shown that the long-term effects can be even more serious than if full rape had actually taken place. They emphasize that it is not the degree of sexual contact that causes problems but the control and threats used at the time.

Teresa would know – or would at least suspect – how close she came to being abducted and killed. I felt an overwhelming sadness because I knew people would not understand her: because she had survived they would probably minimize the impact of this offence upon her. All this ran through my mind as Black described the attempted abduction.*

The session was nearly over. It was time for me to catch the flight from Aberdeen to Birmingham. I had been seeing Black for more than eighteen months, a year and a half spent finding a narrow and fearful path through the darkness in his mind. And yet, despite all our work together, Robert Black was still unable to admit the enormity of his crimes.

I was now almost totally convinced that he had killed Susan, Caroline and Sarah. But the most I had been able to get from him were 'non-denial denials': statements like 'If a man were to admit those crimes, he would never be released again.' I thought that breaking the intimate and personal rapport that governed our meetings might produce the best chance – perhaps the last chance – of a change of attitude.

At the close of that session I decided to try it. I told him I'd had enough. I said, 'That's it,' and I got up and moved away from him towards the door. And he screamed at me, 'If you were a Catholic priest and I was the most devout Catholic that ever lived, I still couldn't tell you that I killed them.'

I knew for certain then. It wasn't a confession – he couldn't even have given that to a priest. But he knew, and I knew, that he had murdered those three young girls.

* Two years later my fears would be borne out when Hector Clark published a book about his involvement in the hunt for Robert Black. In it he said of Teresa Thornhill that at least she 'still lives, unaffected, in Nottingham'.

7
Unquiet Graves

The city of Bradford is, in truth, still a small mill town that has outgrown its borders. The streets in its centre, many still cobbled and decaying, have been rudely dissected by modern three-lane expressways and bypasses. At the heart of this urban squalor sits the central police headquarters for the city and its rural hinterland.

In the summer of 1986, less than three months into the Sarah Harper enquiry, the building became the nerve centre of a new initiative. The grandly named Child Murder Bureau was backed by the Home Office as a means of drawing together all unsolved cases of child abduction and suspicious death since 1973 that might be related to the Maxwell, Harper and Hogg cases and, thereafter, of ensuring complete computer compatibility of all relevant enquiries. Its existence was, in its way, typical of the fragmented and divisive nature of British policing. The Child Murder Bureau concentrated, because of the sex of the three victims, on cases involving girls under the age of sixteen.

At the same time a team of officers from Derbyshire Police established a parallel operation using the acronym CATCHEM – Central Analytical Team Collating Homicide Expertise and Management. CATCHEM, based at Ripley in Derbyshire, operated a brand-new database into which were entered details of all murders of females up to the age of twenty-one and males up to the age of sixteen since 1953. The computer meticulously recorded even the most minute detail of *modus operandi*, from obvious clues to the tiniest of scars left on the body. New cases too were registered: every force with a relevant homicide was asked to fill in a form containing 230 separate questions.

CATCHEM was the brainchild of Derbyshire's Assistant Chief Constable, Don Dovaston: it grew out of a desperate sickness caused by sifting laboriously through hundreds of case notes in the course of investigating a series of murders of schoolgirls. There had, he felt, to be a better way.

> The computer's first task is to see if there are any other crimes that might be associated – maybe a series of offences. It advises on these cases, perhaps asking for further information. Investigation should not be based on the gut feeling of a particular officer: it has got to be more professional – and CATCHEM is.
>
> If it is successful the computer can begin to paint the offender's picture. It will specify gender, age group, the area where the murderer is most likely to live, whether they have previous convictions, what these are most likely to be – and more.

From the outset CATCHEM was funded by Derbyshire Police with the hope that in the future its computerized service could be used as the model for a national profiling scheme. But in 1986 such a scheme was a long way off, and the database remained resolutely a locally managed initiative.

Three years later, in London, detectives from 2AMIP – the murder squad based at Arbor Square in the East End – began a similarly exhaustive task but this time focusing exclusively on boys as victims. The AMIP team's involvement grew out of the discovery of a homosexual paedophile ring that had severely abused, and sometimes killed, its young victims. 'Operation Orchid', as the enquiry was code-named, set out to establish just how many boys had been sexually assaulted or murdered and how many men were part of the ring of abusers.

At the time I had no involvement with 'Orchid'. But in the middle of my interviews with Robert Black I was approached by 2AMIP and asked to listen to some tapes they had recorded. The tapes were of interviews with two paedophiles who were confessing their involvement, Arthur Smith and Leslie Bailey. The police wanted me to assess the information on tapes and write a report that might be sent to the Crown Prosecution Service.

By the time the tapes arrived it was December of 1992, and I was facing a deadline. The police wanted my report just after

New Year. I spent Christmas at home, but as soon as the immediate festivities were over I flew to County Donegal, in Ireland for a conference. It had been years since I had taken any sort of holiday, and I would have liked simply to sit on the tallest sea cliffs in Europe, absorbing the immense beauty of Ireland. Instead, while my colleagues walked the cliffs, I sat in the hotel alone and listended to recordings of pain, tragedy and man's inhumanity to children. I listened to 156 hours of taped interviews with the two men, describing how little boys were abducted, sexually abused and killed. They talked about Jason Swift, Mark Tildesley and Barry Lewis – all major unsolved cases of sexual murder of young boys. But they left me wondering how many other missing boys they and others had killed.

These unsolved crimes, like the abductions and murders for which Robert Black had been charged, had had a forceful impact on the psyche of the communities in which they had happened. The fact that there were unknown killers of children who were never discovered led the communities to believe that children were frequently being abducted and murdered. The reality is that these are still rare crimes.

But the fear of the crime outlives the reality of its rarity, and the unsolved killings throughout the 1980s prompted many people totally to change child-care arrangements and to restrict the movements of children. More important, they also led to thousands of other children being abused by seductive paedophiles simply because fear stereotyped abusers as 'stranger-monsters'.

The fractured nature of the multiple police enquiries into Robert Black was due in part to the absurd and apparently insurmountable parochialism within British policing – a loyalty among individual officers of all ranks to their own 'nick', then their own division and then to their own force. To some extent a product of the relentlessly macho culture that still riddles the ranks, this inability to offer automatic cooperation to officers from even neighbouring forces means that there has never been a truly successful national investigation into the activities of a serial offender. Put simply, many detectives are reluctant to share very much information with those whom they often view as 'rival' investigators. And so for all the genuine and impressive dedication of the detectives searching for the killer of Susan Maxwell, Caroline Hogg and Sarah Harper, there was never a chance of a single unified approach.

The emerging scale of Black's likely offending called for national response: but Black was not an isolated case. There are many paedophiles who abuse throughout the country rather than in one specific police district. The inability to coordinate investigations works in the favour of the sexual criminal. But if the forces were unable to put aside their distrust of each other in the Black investigation the prospects of a unified approach to the far more academic issue of profiling child killers and matching them to their victims were limited. The result was that the Child Murder Bureau covered areas also dealt with by Derbyshire's CATCHEM, which in turn overlapped some areas of 2AMIP's 'Operation Orchid'.

The Child Murder Bureau, none the less, was able to establish that by 31 July 1986 there were eighteen female child murders and abductions that remained undetected. The team in Bradford researched each case and drew up a map, three feet tall and two feet across on which each case was pinpointed. As the years went by some cases were cleared up: two men were convicted of three of the previously unsolved killings. So when, in the summer of 1990, Robert Black was arrested there remained fifteen unsolved abductions or murders of young girls to be considered, and at least two more abductions or attempted kidnappings had been added to the list.

Susan Maxwell, Caroline Hogg and Sarah Harper were three of the names on the map pinned to the wall in Bradford's central police station; Teresa Thornhill accounted for one of the attempted abductions. But the rest remained sad reminders of individual personal tragedies stretching back more than twenty years.

Most of the senior detectives involved in the joint enquiry harboured the suspicion that Robert Black might have committed several of the offences now staring back at them from the four-year-old map. At the head of the six-force investigation, Hector Clark was no less convinced – but proving Black's guilt was going to be no easy task.

> Black has not spoken to us about other matters, but it is inconceivable to think that he has not committed other offences. There are other children he's been involved with, and he is in my view a man of the most evil kind: he must be one of the most infamous murderers of all time.

And Clark's views were echoed in Leeds by John Stainthorpe.

> Robert Black is a very dangerous man, a very dangerous man indeed. I am sure there are other victims, other young girls he is responsible for abducting and killing.

Of the twelve names on Stainthorpe's grim list of unsolved cases, eight were marked as potentially the work of Robert Black.

The first, chronologically, was a young schoolgirl called April Fabb. A black-and-white photograph was tucked inside her file: it showed a girl with blond hair cut in a style that must have been in fashion almost a generation before. Stainthorpe checked the date on the case papers and understood.

Tuesday, 8 April 1969 was warm and sunny. The Easter Bank Holiday had been a glorious weekend, and the weather seemed set to continue for several days. April Fabb was on holiday from Cromer Secondary Modern School. She lived with her parents, Ernest and Olive, at 3 Council Houses in the tiny Norfolk hamlet of Metton. Just eighty people lived in the village, which was a little over three miles from the fading seaside resort of Cromer. Near by were larger villages – Roughton to the east and Sustead further west along the East Anglian coast.

Ernest Fabb was a builder's labourer. April was the younger of his two daughters. At almost fourteen, she was a quiet girl, shy and intelligent with a love of animals and an interest in stamp collecting and needlework. The house was happy: April Fabb was growing up much as any other youngster in the little hamlet.

At 2 o'clock that Tuesday afternoon she pushed her blue-and-white BSA cycle on to the lane that runs past 3 Council Houses. Her sister, now married, lived two miles away in Roughton. April had a belated birthday present to deliver to her brother-in-law – a packet of cigarettes, which she slipped into the saddle bag. She was wearing a green jumper and a wine-coloured woollen skirt, long white socks and a pair of wooden-soled sandals with red straps and brass buckles.

At 2.06 p.m. a tractor driver spotted her riding along the lane. A few minutes later she stopped at a farm on the Cromer road to talk to friends and play with their donkey. After ten minutes she set off again on her errand. At 3 p.m. her bicycle was seen lying on its side in a field beside the lane, half a mile from 3 Council Houses. The cigarettes were still in the saddle bag; there was no damage to the bike, no indication of a traffic accident, no sign of a struggle. And there was no sign of April.

Within an hour uniformed officers from Norfolk Constabulary had begun a careful search of the immediate area. But by dusk no new clues had emerged. At first light the next day the sweep widened to cover the fields, hedgerows, lanes and roads for two miles in every direction from where the cycle was found. A helicopter from the Air–Sea Rescue Unit at Coltishall, along the coast, quartered the ground from above.

In the meantime every inhabitant of the villages of Metton, Roughton and Sustead was located and interviewed. Gradually these house-to-house enquiries were extended to villages and hamlets further afield. Within a month more than 2,000 statements had been painstakingly handwritten and indexed at the central incident room.

Despite its intense efforts, Norfolk Constabulary never found April Fabb, either alive or dead. For twenty years her disappearance was to haunt the force – and the girl's parents. In a small house in Cromer a teenager's bedroom is kept remarkably tidy. On the counterpane of a single bed, propped against the padded headboard, a doll with wide and staring eyes sits next to a teddy bear wearing knitted overalls and a miniature bobble hat at a jaunty angle. Further down the bed a leather satchel is stuffed with school books at least a generation out of date.

For eighteen years Olive and Ernest Fabb preserved April's room just as it was on the day she disappeared. When they moved that year from Metton to Cromer the little shrine was simply transferred to a new location. Olive Fabb has never given up hope that her daughter might yet be alive. Now seventy-four years old, she is adamant that she won't concede that April is dead until her body is found or her killer convicted.

> I will never give up hope that April will be found one day. I still cling to the hope that she is alive and will one day come back. I think that somebody took her and is keeping her. She might be married now. I think all sorts of things sometimes – but I don't give up hope that she is alive.

Ernest Fabb, three years older than his wife, is more resigned to what he believes is obvious:

> It's a good thing that Olive does believe because it gives her hope. But I don't think April is alive. On the day, I thought she was abducted: after a time I realized that things were not very hopeful.

The death of a child is inescapably painful: glib and over-used phrases of sympathy can never articulate the depth of a parent's suffering. But when a child simply disappears, desperate and irrational hope adds an extra cruelty to the unhealing wound. April's mother says:

> Time heals a bit, but you don't forget – particularly at the time of her birthday and at Christmas. Her doll is still on the bed and her brush and comb are on her dressing table. I won't be turned from my view that April could still be alive.

Every twelve months during the twenty-one years between April Fabb's disappearance and Robert Black's arrest Norfolk Constabulary dusted off and re-examined the files. Each year, despite enquiries stretching across Britain and into Europe, the result was identical: no promising leads. Black's arrest changed all that. Although he had no driving licence in 1969 – and April had clearly been abducted in a vehicle of some sort – the *modus operandi* was remarkably close to his unique pattern of offending. And the fact that he managed to clock up a traffic-related conviction in 1972, two years before he obtained a licence, might make its absence in 1969 rather less significant. Stainthorpe marked the case down as a 'possible'.

He did the same with the next file he opened. Christine Deborah Markham was nine years old when she disappeared less than half a mile from her home in Scunthorpe on Monday, 21 May 1973. The Markham file was less revealing than April Fabb's, but there were enough similarities to forge a link between the two cases. Once again the attached photograph showed a girl with a short, almost elfin hairstyle: the child's eyes skewed sideways and were somehow all the more disturbing for being half-hidden from view.

Christine had vanished at 8.30 in the morning. She was on her way to the nearby Henderson Avenue School. The time of the disappearance was striking: between eight and nine o'clock is the busy morning rush hour in almost every town and city across Britain. With so much traffic and so many possible witnesses, the moment when she could have been abducted without attracting attention must have been brief indeed.

It was this element of opportunism, together with the now familiar lack of any evidence of a struggle, that pointed to Black's known pattern of abduction – a strong man grabbing a small child and hurling her into his van in a matter of seconds. Similarly the dead silence, the fact that no body had been found and the complete absence of any obvious lines of further enquiry all strengthened Stainthorpe's view that, at the very least, Christine Markham's disappearance needed to be put to Robert Black before too long.

The third case on West Yorkshire Police's map of unsolved cases was one that the joint enquiry into the Maxwell, Hogg and Harper murders had already, if briefly, considered. Like April Fabb and Christine Markham before her, Genette Tate was still recorded strictly as a missing child, though the detectives of Devon and Cornwall Police had long since given up any pretence of hoping to find the girl alive.

Genette disappeared in broad daylight between 3.27 and 3.32 on the afternoon of Saturday, 19 August 1978. Throughout the entire day only five minutes are unaccounted for: five minutes during which no one saw her except the man who abducted her.

Genette was thirteen years old but looked younger. Small and *gamine*, she had recently had her brown hair cut short. Photographs circulated after her disappearance conjure an image of a Mabel Lucie Attwell illustration for J.M. Barrie's *Peter Pan*. She lived with her father John, her step-mother and her older step-sister, Tania, in the village of Aylesbeare, a small, isolated and unglamorous modern working-class hamlet of 350 people. It has a pub at one end of the main street and a blue-and-white-painted village hall at the other. It is a close-knit community. Strangers tend to be noticed.

On that Saturday in August, a bright, warm and sunny afternoon, Genette was doing a friend's paper round on her new blue bike. The newspapers were loaded into a tartan pannier over the back wheel. Her step-mother, Violet, recalled: 'I had been working that day and I met John in Exeter. We saw Tania off at the bus station on a holiday. We did a bit of shopping and then drove home to the village.' At 3 p.m. Genette was riding along Within Lane, a quiet and narrow road lined with a handful of cottages and bungalows. She had posted papers through fourteen letterboxes when she reached the part of the lane where a gradient requires most riders to dismount and push their bikes up the hill. Two girlfriends joined her as she struggled up the incline, chatting as they went. Genette handed one a newspaper to give to her mother. When they reached the top of the hill, Genette climbed back on her bike and rode off towards her next delivery. It was 3.27 p.m.

Her friends were in no hurry. They dawdled and gossiped; they stopped and read the paper for a few minutes. By the time they rounded the next bend in the road it was 3.32 p.m. Facing them, lying in the middle of the tarmac, was Genette's bike, surrounded by scattered newspapers. Its back wheel was still spinning. That vision, captured later as a still photograph, has haunted Genette's family, the village of Aylesbeare and the rest of Britain. It is a peculiarly powerful image even fifteen years on: there is not a mark on the bicycle, not a sign that whoever abducted her had faced any struggle he could not overcome.

John Alderson was, in 1978, Chief Constable of Devon and Cornwall Police. A gentle man, but forceful in holding and expressing unusually liberal views for so senior an officer, he became personally involved in the hunt to find Genette, dead or alive.

> In the beginning, when we started our enquiries, we were confident that we could clear it up – that this was probably a local matter. We carried out routine door-to-door enquiries, we interviewed witnesses, particularly the two girls who had last seen her. We were looking for motor cars or anybody who had seen motor cars. Then we identified the vehicle, traced it and got as much information as we could. We also made enquiries with other police forces to see if there had been any similar crimes and checked to see if there was information we could exchange.

For months detectives could assume only that Genette had been abducted: they could not be certain the case was truly a murder hunt. But her body was never found despite exhaustive searches and the scene of her disappearance yielded no evidence.

Her family was questioned in microscopic detail. For a time her father, John, was chief suspect after confessing that he had sexually abused another nine-year-old girl from the area. But gradually the police came to the inescapable conclusion that

Genette Tate had been snatched – and, presumably, killed – during those five minutes in the mid-afternoon of Saturday, 19 April. If so, her abductor was highly skilled. Not only was there no trace of a fight, or any mark on the bicycle, but Genette's two friends never heard her scream. Whoever snatched Genette did so quickly and clinically – and Alderson was coming no closer to finding him.

> After a while we become nervous that we were on to a more difficult case than ever we had envisaged in the first place because our experience in rural areas is that you do clear up crimes; people are very observant in the countryside. We then really had to pull out all the stops. We had huge – massive – public support in search parties. They were called 'Genette's Army', a thousand people at least who turned out on weekends and during holiday times to search the moorland.
>
> We had mounted police; we had dogs; we had helicopters, frogmen, clairvoyants even. I can't imagine a murder that's had more attention than we gave to the searching. Because we were then after a body, if there was a body, and if we couldn't find a body, then had Genette been kidnapped and taken to distant venues – abroad even?
>
> But in spite of all our work we didn't have one clue. It's almost as if she disappeared into the sky: if you believed in that kind of thing, that's what you would think had happened.

For Genette's natural mother Sheila and the rest of her family, and particularly for Violet, the step-mother who had brought up the child for several years, the nightmare was unending.

> The first few days it was just one long succession of callers – police, press, the vicar, neighbours – all trying to help and being very kind. That's the thing that takes it out of you, not just the agony of waiting and not knowing what happened. At the end of some days it was exhausting.
>
> At night we went upstairs to try and sleep, but always kept waking up. It's a quiet village with not much traffic: if a car

stops or there's a bang in the middle of the night, we jump up in case it's Genette coming back.

For Sheila Tate, by then living in Bristol, the pain was magnified by a terrible sense of guilt.

She used to come to me for Christmas. I never decorated the tree until she arrived on Christmas Eve, when we would do it together.

The doctor has given me tranquillizers and sleeping pills. I haven't taken any of them. I'm keeping them by me just in case the news we all dread comes through.

If only I had kept her with me after my marriage broke up.

If only: the two most common words when a child is snatched from a family. Guilt mixes with recrimination, fuelling a self-destructive anger: bitterness between otherwise happy couples lies ahead. And yet, all the while, the true cause of the problem continues to live out his life.

As the days and nights dragged by with no sign of Genette, Sheila moved down to Aylesbeare to join the vigil in the home her daughter had made with John and Violet Tate. It was clearly an added strain, but the two women made an emotional joint plea: 'If anyone has got her, we beg them to let her go.'

For Devon and Cornwall Police the search now moved outside the geographical boundaries of its force's area and into the realms of intelligence files on known paedophiles. John Alderson was convinced Genette had been abducted – and, presumably, killed – by a sex offender.

I think what happened – putting all the possibilities together and ruling out whatever we were able to rule out – that a motor car was involved. Genette was enticed to speak to the driver who then dragged her in and drove away. At first I rather hoped that she had simply been kidnapped and that one day she would turn up, but as the days wore on, and the weeks and the years wore on, it seemed clear that she was probably the victim of a sexual attack and died a death no little girl should have to die.

Again, in the beginning we thought it was a local matter, and any paedophiles we had on our criminal records we would know. But naturally we then got in touch with other police forces, looking for information they had on paedophilic crime that might be helpful. There were one or two children of the same age who disappeared throughout this time, and we thought it might have been a series of murders. But we were never able to link them up.

We eliminated everyone on our list of suspects. We spent a lot of time doing that, and a few people couldn't easily be eliminated – they weren't able to provide alibis – so we kept them on the list. But gradually we began to believe that none of them was the person who had done it. And it's when you get to that stage, when you've done everything, that it hits you that maybe this is going to be a mystery that will only be cleared up when someone in prison for similar crimes decides to confess.

In Peterhead Prison Robert Black was setting out on the road that would lead to just such a confession. Not that it started that way, or that it was clear-cut beyond any doubt. But, inch by inch, he was leading me to believe that the man sitting across the scruffy prison table knew enough to solve the Genette Tate mystery. The process began with a topic of conversation that had become familiar to both of us: what was it that led Black to abduct some children and not others?

BLACK: How would you explain it that I've been in situations where I could have abducted and didn't?

RAY: I think that will be common. Nobody would abduct all the times they wanted to.

BLACK: I know there was once . . . I think it was on the beach in Bournemouth . . . there was a little girl who came up to me. She'd lost her mother. (*Pause*) I might quite easily have just walked away with her, like: she was very trusting. And I helped her find her mother.

This image of Black as the rescuer of a small child may seem, at first glance, unlikely. And he could, of course, have been lying about the incident. But I doubted it. Internal inhibitors operate in all of us, including Robert Black. At times he would have been in control; he would not abduct because he was scared of being caught. But he may also not have abducted because at that time, and for whatever reason, he did not want to. Interviewing sex offenders, I have often been struck by the way they control their desires, even when they are going through moods, emotional states or fractured relationships that might otherwise trigger off a bout of offending. Even the most violent man who has ever lived is violent for only a short time in relation to the rest of his life.

Another offender – another killer of children, a man who had raped and murdered – once reminded me that although he had progressed from exposing himself in public to killing, he still periodically exposed himself. It was the same with Black. I believed that his paedophilia, his confused and distorted 'love' for children, would still have been operating in between the abductions and killings. However, his contact with the little girl on the beach would have fed his fantasy life: the scenario of rescuing the girl would itself have become a fantasy.

This is a well-documented phenomenon and represents the complexity of paedophilic personality that the therapist, or the psychological profiler, needs to understand. In another case a man who snatched girls between Birmingham and Southampton told me how he fantasized about abducting children and forcing them into boats. In this fantasy he would then rescue the children from a paedophile who was sexually abusing them. But after he had rescued them, while he was cuddling them and comforting them, he would then strangle the girls and place them in the water. (This man, a former Category A prisoner, was released from prison a few years ago. I doubt if anyone knows where he is now.)

The process of enabling Black to be honest about his career as an abductor and abuser of children was a long one. It seemed to function best when I gradually persuaded Black to reconsider the date (after he arrived in London) on which he would admit to having first kidnapped a child. It had started, exactly as I had expected before our first meeting, with his claim that the Laura Turner abduction was an isolated occurrence. This had given way to an acceptance that the abductions had been going on for most of the 1980s. But with the trial for the Maxwell, Hogg, Harper and Thornhill cases approaching, I knew I had little time left in which to get closer to the truth about other abductions and murders. I let him know that I was aware of his game-playing. And I asked him again when he first had the idea of abduction. Suddenly he started talking about a paper girl, and I thought, 'What's this about?'

RAY: What was going on?

BLACK: I don't know. Maybe (*pause*) . . . there was that paper girl that went missing. I don't know where she was missing, like, but it was all over the papers.

RAY: Tate?

BLACK: Yeah. That was her name, yeah. She disappeared. She never turned up.

RAY: Yeah.

BLACK: I suppose they've started thinking, 'How did he do it?'

RAY: And how do you think he did it?

BLACK: Well, they found her bike, didn't they? He obviously persuaded her to get off her bike, or grabbed her off the bike, one of the two. Then got her into a vehicle and took her away.

RAY: Why do you believe that?

BLACK: It seemed obvious to me.

RAY: So you used to think a lot about that, did you?

BLACK: I probably did then.

RAY: So when you thought about that, when you thought about Tate, what feelings did it give you when you thought about you doing it?

BLACK: I think that was how I started off, like, with the [abduction] scenario. Like with paper girls, like, early morning. Going through, like, 'Is this an opportunity or is it not?'

RAY: And what would you do?

BLACK: If I seen a paper girl, like, I'd maybe watch for a while to see what sort of route.

RAY: And how many times would you watch or follow that route?

BLACK: Maybe just the once, or I might not be in that same place for months, and then not even at that time of day.

RAY: Right. So you have a fantasy, a general fantasy, about children, but the fantasy becomes centred on girls on bikes delivering papers. What were you saying to yourself at that time?

BLACK: Just working on (*long pause*) getting myself into a position where it might be possible to take somebody. The rare occasions when I did talk to girls in that situation, usually I asked directions or something like that.

RAY: Right. So you'd see a girl delivering papers, then what would you do?

BLACK: I'd park, watch where she was delivering. Or maybe, if there were side streets, I'd try anticipating, turn into a side street and park.

RAY: To wait for her?

BLACK: Yeah, to see if she came that way or something like that.

RAY: And when you turned into a side street and waited, what would you be looking for?

BLACK: To see if there was some place where there was no houses overlooking, or where I'd see either high hedges or walls where the people in the houses wouldn't be able to see out.

RAY: Then if the girl was riding or walking with the bike: which would you prefer?

BLACK: I suppose I'd prefer to catch her as she came out the gate, like maybe after delivering a paper or something. Before she got back on the bike.

There had to be a reason why Black should volunteer detailed observations about such a famous case, especially as it took his abductions back several more years. I immediately thought, 'Why has he told me this? First, it's put him back to 1978 and, secondly, he must know what I'm going to be thinking about his involvement in the case.' From the amount of information he gave me – particularly about targeting other girls on bikes delivering newspapers – I was certain he knew what I would believe. But he could simply have been trying to detain me at the interview a bit longer, to keep our relationship going by feeding me another titbit. That was the sort of game-playing I had to deal with all the time: he was sufficiently calculating to be extremely cautious about giving me morsels of information. So everything he did give me had to have reason, or at least emotion, behind it.

I thought back to the way he had told me about the abduction of the little girl from Greenock Park, the girl he took to the air-raid shelter, strangled and left for dead. He had slipped into his account the fact that he had led the girl past a policeman he knew. At first glance that might seem an anodyne, harmless detail, but what he was really saying was, 'Look how clever and bold I was in abducting this child under the eyes of the police.'

Black's statements about Genette Tate had, as on other occasions, made me wonder whether I was dealing with the type of psychopath who enjoys the 'game' of not being caught, who boasts of his exploits and the fact that at times he has the power to show mercy. Black had once described abducting two girls in Carlisle and then deciding to let them go. He seemed at times to emphasize his ability not to get caught. Was his introduction of the possibility that he had abducted and killed Genette Tate an example of this game-playing? So often the true meaning of what we say lies behind the actual words we speak – and Robert Black was no different to anyone else in this regard.

And so it could have been with what he said about Genette Tate. I wasn't about to accept this as a simple and unequivocal confession. The nature of what I do requires me to work in what we might call metaphor. It's a method that prompts me to consider all possible sides of a case. For example, just because a man is found pulling a knife out of a body doesn't necessarily mean that he put it in there. The fact that Robert Black was making me believe he had a hand in Genette Tate's abduction didn't automatically lead me to accuse him of kidnapping her.

But it did fit with the pattern of the man I had watched emerge during our sessions together. Black had clearly tried to distance himself from the pain and abuse he had endured as a child. Like many others, he had tried to store the memories in his unconscious mind. But for him the process had not worked. The pain did not stay in the unconscious, even if it ever got there: it motivated him; it leached through into reality and led him to seek to destroy the childhood he never had by destroying little children.

I was convinced that Robert Black hated himself and hated the young boy he had been. He hated not being wanted, he hated being betrayed and abandoned. He hated having a penis, he hated putting things into his rectum – but he felt he had no choice. He hated being unable to have a successful relationship, he hated being unable ever to have his own children. He hated having fantasies of pain, he hated the fantasy of the little girl unconscious in the cellar. He hated himself, his loneliness, his feelings and his powerlessness. But in abduction, in sexual abuse and in outwitting the police he became a different Robert Black. He became powerful; he became important.

He felt like no one else: he felt like God. God determines when life ends, and he, Robert Black, was doing likewise. We should not underestimate the power he must have felt: it replaced the emptiness of the abandoned small boy, the child who perceived himself to be perpetually unwanted. All this would have been feeding into Black's mind, conscious or unconscious, as he described the abduction of Genette Tate, as it fed into my mind listening to him. But I didn't simply think, 'Oh, thank God, I've got a confession.' That attitude would be very unhelpful in my work with men like Black. I just catalogued the information in my head, acknowledging that someone needed to explore it further.

Many months later John Alderson came to the same conclusion after reading transcripts of Black's discussion of the Genette Tate case:

> What struck me was that Black is a man with a preoccupation with crimes of this kind. What I know about him now would indicate that he should, in any case, be interviewed about Genette's disappearance. But without doubt what he said made it vital that this happens.

Although Alderson could not have known it – he retired almost a decade before Black was arrested in the Scottish Borders – by 1991 the joint police investigation into unsolved child abductions and murders had independently marked Black out as a prime suspect.

John Stainthorpe was particularly impressed by the similarities between the Maxwell, Hogg and Harper cases and the circumstances of the Genette Tate abduction.

> A girl is walking along a street pushing a cycle and suddenly she's snatched and the cycle left. Black was in the habit of snatching young girls off the street very quickly. I think it is likely – on a percentage basis around 60 per cent or even as high as 80 per cent – that Black was responsible for Genette Tate's abduction.

But it was not a simple case of abduction – or a simple case to prove at all. Although PDS's South Coast run took in Exeter, Plymouth and the villages near Genette's home in between, and although anecdotal evidence suggested that Black frequently drove that route in 1978, there were no surviving petrol or bonus-payment records that would have tied him to the area on the day she disappeared. Without them, a prosecution for kidnapping was unlikely, to say the least. But for a charge of murder – and John Alderson is convinced Genette was killed – the prospect of trial remains tantalizingly just out of reach.

> I would like to see the person responsible convicted. That would mean that Genette's death is vindicated, in so far as anything like that can ever be vindicated. I want to see criminal justice triumph over evil. But at this stage I still hope that someone confesses fully to having killed her.

Genette Tate's abduction marked the end of the 1970s list of unsolved cases. There would be more in the decade that followed, but there would also be a small, potentially crucial, difference.

The cases of April Fabb, Christine Markham and Genette Tate had one feature in common above all: their bodies were never found. In itself this is highly unusual: most murders, even the 6 per cent not committed by the victim's spouse, almost invariably lead to the discovery of a body. By 1987, a year after AMIPs, the specialist London murder squads, were formed, there had been only three successful prosecutions for murder when the corpse was still missing. But from 1980 onwards all the unsolved cases involved the discovery of the victim's body. I was now firmly convinced Robert Black was a serial child killer: the changing features of the unsolved cases led me to a disturbing conclusion.

I began to suspect that these old police files recorded an important shift in Black's pattern of behaviour. If, as we might assume, he abducted and killed April Fabb, Christine Markham and Genette Tate, he must have gone to some trouble to hide their bodies. But in the later cases – even the Maxwell, Hogg and Harper murders – the bodies were found very easily. It suggested to me that he had begun to need the extra kick of the discovery of his victims.

This in itself is not unusual: it is quite common, in profiling serial killers, to find that they have done their best to ensure that the bodies are discovered. The finding of the body, particularly when allied to an apparent inability on the part of the police to find the killer, gives men like Black added satisfaction. In its way it is a physical equivalent of the kick Black would have got from describing to me how he walked past the policeman to the air-raid shelter with his victim.

And if all that sounds bizarre and far-fetched, we should remember that the very act of abducting, sexually assaulting and killing a child is also truly bizarre. We, the general public, may think rationally, but these are not rational crimes. They follow their own twisted internal logic.

Hounslow Heath is an unlovely stretch of suburban scrubland at the south-west corner of the greater London sprawl. In the less urban eighteenth century it was notorious for highwaymen and footpads: those with even a modest sum of money to protect did well to avoid it after dark. By June 1980 the heath had acquired a new and inevitably grimy reputation. It was, local children and their parents knew, a magnet that attracted the disturbed and deviant: flashers were all too visible, rape far from unknown.

On Wednesday, 18 June 1980, Patsy Morris was found, face-down, in a small thicket on the square mile of scrubby park. She had been strangled.

Patsy Morris was fourteen years old. She was a lively girl and a keen swimmer who had won both bronze and silver medals in her sport. On the afternoon of Monday, 16 June, she had left Feltham School early, dodging a double history period (history was not a favourite subject) and headed towards her home across town in Cygnet Avenue.

In between lay Hounslow Heath. George and Marjorie Morris had consistently warned Patsy never to cross the park alone, and, so far as they knew, she had always obeyed them. For George, a former army chef, this simply added an extra layer of pain:

> I spent fourteen years bringing her up the right way, to be well behaved and polite and kind to other people, only to see her taken from our lives by a maniac. Please [whoever did this], please don't bring grief to another family. Please come out into the open and never do anything like that again. Please come forward and give yourself up to the police.

When she was found in the thicket Patsy had been missing for forty-eight hours. But whoever had killed her had made no real effort to conceal the body; there was no evidence of even a shallow grave. The body itself, though, offered a host of clues to the nature of Patsy's killer. Her clothing had been pushed upwards, revealing her thighs. Her tights, and the two pairs of knickers she was (for some unknown reason) wearing, had been pulled down to her ankles. A second pair of tights, one leg missing from the gusset downwards, was tied around Patsy's leg and wound upwards until it was knotted four times around her neck. An identical pair of one-legged tights was wrapped three times around both wrists in front of her body and then over her breasts. Although her knickers had been pulled down – strongly suggesting a sexual motive for the killing – there was no forensic evidence of rape. Whoever had murdered Patsy Morris found satisfaction without penetration. If not rare, this was certainly unusual: previous sexual assaults and murders on or around the heath had invariably involved the full rape of the victim.

The case bore some of the hallmarks of what John Stainthorpe had come to recognize as Robert Black's signature. That said, there were circumstances that, if they didn't rule him out, didn't quite fit the emerging pattern of his offences. There was, for example, no evidence that Patsy had been abducted in a vehicle or that her body had been transported any distance. None the less there was enough for Stainthorpe to mark the case down as a cautious 'possible'.

He did the same with the next file. Just after 9 a.m. on Saturday, 6 June 1981, Marion Crofts left her home in Basingbourne Close, Fleet, to attend a clarinet lesson at Wavell School in Farnborough. It was a relatively short and, normally, quite uneventful journey. As she left the house, Marion pulled on her light-fawn anorak over her jeans and white canvas tennis shoes. She slipped her clarinet, in its case, on to the carrier at the back of her blue racing bike and set off. She never arrived.

Marion Crofts was fourteen years old. The only photograph ever released, blurry and indistinct, shows her staring quizzically at the photographer. Her brown hair is cut in a slightly shaggy bob. She does not look her age.

The small towns of Fleet and Farnborough sit in a belt of military bases that straddles part of Hampshire. Marion's route that morning would have taken her along Reading Road South, then into Aldershot Road, Norris Hill and Laffans Road. To join Laffans Road, she would have crossed Eelmoor Bridge before cycling past the Royal Aircraft Establishment on one side and the Basingstoke Canal on the other. Between the road and the canal lie twenty-five yards of woodland. In these woods Marion's killer abandoned her body.

It is a surprisingly lonely stretch of countryside, little used by strangers to the area. At a little after 9 a.m. on a Saturday morning in June it was far from busy. None the less, a handful of witnesses did remember seeing at least two unknown men in the vicinity of Eelmore Bridge. The description of one in particular was familiar to police. Between 9 a.m. and 10 a.m. a man estimated to be between thirty and forty years old, 5 feet 8 inches tall, with dark hair and a full black beard, was seen just west of the bridge by the edge of the Royal Aircraft Establishment. It was not, of course, an exhaustive description: its bare bones would match any one of hundreds of thousands of men throughout Britain. But one of those men was Robert Black.

The forensic evidence gleaned from Marion's body fell into what was fast becoming a depressingly familiar pattern. Her jeans had been partially pulled off; her juvenile brassière had been pulled up over her emerging breasts. She had, a post-mortem revealed, been sexually assaulted. The manner of her death, though, was not immediately recognizable as Robert Black's handiwork. She had been battered around the face and head: the beating ultimately killed her. It was the one piece of evidence that contrasted with the other circumstances: all of these fitted Black's known *modus operandi.*

There was less doubt about the next case file. Colette Aram's body was found in a field near her home at Keyworth in Nottinghamshire on Monday, 31 October 1983. She had set out from her house twenty-four hours before at just after 10 a.m. on a bright autumn Sunday morning. Colette was sixteen and, in common with most other attracttive girls of her age, had a boyfriend. That Sunday she was walking, as agreed, to his house. The field in which she was found, naked save for her blouse and brassière, which were tied crudely around her left wrist, was not on the route. Her parents could think of no reason why she should have walked even close to that part of Keyworth.

Forensic evidence seemed to provide an answer to that

mystery at least. Tests showed that she had been taken to the field in a vehicle of some sort. They also showed that she had been severely sexually assaulted – possibly with an instrument of some kind – and strangled. Although Colette was sixteen, and therefore apparently outside Robert Black's known target age range, the use of an instrument to abuse her struck a particular chord in John Stainthorpe: precisely the same violent assault had been endured by Sarah Harper. This, coupled with strangulation as the cause of death and the fact that her body had been transported before being dumped, led the detective to consider Black a prime suspect. As telling was the location of Keyworth: the village was well inside the 'Midlands Triangle', the geographical area within which Robert Black had dumped Susan Maxwell, Caroline Hogg and Sarah Harper.

The last case on Stainthorpe's list of unsolved female child murders was dated December 1984. A photograph clipped to the file showed a pretty, smiling face, with an exaggerated kiss curl edging down towards one eye. The name on the folder was Lisa Jane Hession.

Saturday, 8 December 1984 was to be a special day for Lisa Hession. The fourteen-year-old devoted several hours in the afternoon to preparing for a party that evening. A group of school friends had organized an early Christmas celebration. The party was to be held at a house in Leigh Road, Leigh, a suburb of Greater Manchester. Lisa had been born in the area, attended the local Bedford High School and lived two miles across town in Bonnywell Road. She was a keen cross-country runner and had competed with the Leigh Harriers team.

A perennial and intractable dilemma is faced every Christmas by the parents of teenage children. Most will be invited to parties. Most will want to go – without their parents arriving to pick them up like the youngsters they no longer wish to be. Christine Hession was no less concerned than any other mother. She made Lisa promise to be home by 11 p.m.

Lisa was known at Bedford High School to be a fashionable dresser. That evening she wore a white, knee-length skirt above white, low-heeled ankle boots; her blue reefer jacket obscured a

T-shirt and a bright-red cardigan. To be on the safe side, she carried a light-blue collapsible umbrella: her hair had recently been streaked. At 5 feet 4 inches she was tall for her age. But she was, none the less, still a child – no match for a powerful adult man.

By all accounts Lisa enjoyed the party. She left the house in Leigh Road at 10.30 p.m. in plenty of time to walk home to the safety of Bonnywell Road.

When the 11 o'clock deadline passed, Christine Hession called the police. Within an hour Lisa's body had been found in an alley behind Rugby Road. She had been just 200 yards from her home when her attacker struck. Two local men found the body. Ron Parry and his son Ronald were out walking the family dog. The younger man ran to phone the police while his father tried in vain to give Lisa the kiss of life. 'The little girl was lying on her back. She was very cold. There was a thin black mark around her neck, and she appeared to have a black eye.'

A post-mortem showed the cause of death to have been asphyxia. But the marks on Lisa's body and the state of her party clothes gave Manchester Police a better picture of how she had died.

> Her clothes were in some disarray [Detective Superintendent Terry Millard told a subdued pre-Christmas press conference.] Her skirt was pulled up around her waist, and her panties were ripped. I believe it is likely that her attacker grabbed her from behind, closed a hand across her mouth and dragged her, struggling, into the alleyway.
>
> Her T-shirt was pulled tight around her throat. It is clear she put up a tremendous fight. She had scratches round her neck and throat, and these may have been caused as she tried to pull away the clothing. She also had bruising on her lips. This would indicate she had been roughly handled.

Terry Millard was sure of one thing: the motive for Lisa's attack had not been robbery – her purse, with money in it, was with the body when it was found. This, and the state of her clothing, suggested a sexual motive. But the pathologist made it clear that Lisa had not been raped. Whoever attacked her clearly achieved his sexual goals without putting his penis into his victims.

For Christine Hession, life would never be the same. Six weeks after Lisa's body was found, she pleaded with her daughter's killer to give himself up:

> I beg him to come forward so that no other mother has to go through what I have. If someone is sheltering him, like his own mother or father, I appeal to them to give him up. I ask them to have the strength to do that. I don't feel I can pick up the pieces of my own life until Lisa's murderer is caught.
>
> I went to look at her [in Leigh Infirmary] and she just seemed to be sleeping, except for the bruises on her lips where the man must have tried to stop her screaming. I wish I had reached to touch her. But I couldn't: I felt numb. Every man I see, I think, 'Did he do it?' I can't help it, and I won't be able to stop until he is found.

Finding Lisa's killer was, not unnaturally, uppermost in the mind of Detective Superintendent Terry Millard. He knew that the man who murdered Lisa was quite likely to attack other children.

> It bothers me a great deal that the person who did this terrible thing is still on the loose. That person must be caught – and soon. How could anyone kill a sweet schoolkid like Lisa? We are doing everything in our power to get him: we shall not rest until he is caught.

Greater Manchester Police backed Millard's words with action. Officers visited 1,300 homes, interviewed 6,000 people, took 1,800 phone calls from the public, fed 4,800 items of information into the murder-hunt computer, staged a reconstruction of Lisa's last walk home and sent 183 separate items of evidence for forensic testing. But all the effort – the late nights, the knocking on doors and the searching of records for known offenders – led nowhere. Six years after Lisa Hession was strangled in an alley in Leigh, Greater Manchester Police had no clue as to the identity of her murderer.

Detective Superintendent John Stainthorpe did. He closed the file and marked it carefully: the name of Lisa Jane Hession would be added to the list of the possible victims of Robert Black.

There were other files too. Some referred to sexual assaults after which the victims had simply been abandoned, others to abductions or attempted abductions across the length and breadth of Britain. And there were files from Interpol in France and the Military Police in Germany. Three French children had been murdered outside Paris in 1988, and a fourth was missing, presumed dead. Each of the three dead children had been strangled and sexually assaulted. For almost two years the French police had struggled in vain to produce a single profitable line of enquiry.

In Germany the British Army on the Rhine had monitored the efforts of local German police to find the killer of a ten-year-old girl who had been strangled and sexually assaulted in June 1985. Silke Garben's body was found in a stream close to the Army base. Her trousers had been pulled down, and there was evidence of violent sexual assault: the pathologist reported a 6-centimetre tear in the child's vagina. But what really drew Stainthorpe's attention was a brief explanation that, although she had been strangled, Silke Garben died of drowning: she had been alive when she was dumped in the water.

The Garben file and, with it, the French cases forwarded by Interpol, made uncomfortable reading. Stainthorpe knew that Black had travelled extensively – to Holland and Denmark in search of child pornography; to Germany and France, where the Raysons had a second home and Black himself kept a caravan, on holiday. He was forced to ask himself how many children had suffered at the hands of Robert Black. He had a terrible fear that when the Maxwell, Hogg, Harper and Thornhill trials were over, an investigation would be needed not just across Britain but throughout Europe as well. But of one thing he was absolutely sure: there must be an investigation. There could be no sweeping of Black's crimes under the convenient carpet of elapsed time and projected expense.

> Someone will have to speak to him about these murders. Someone will have to begin the job of trying to sort out which murders Black is responsible for. We must do this: we owe it to the parents of those children. It's important to those families – and it's the families we're concerned with now. We must put their minds at rest: if it's him, then we must get it sorted out.

In London Detective Superintendent Russ Allen, the senior murder-squad detective assigned to handle the Metropolitan Police's end of Robert Black's case, shared the same view. But he was far from sure that a full-scale investigation would be helpful:

> I looked at a number of unsolved murders and settled on one in my area as having the best chance of having been committed by Robert Black. In that case there was a particular piece of evidence which led me to believe that Black might have killed the girl.
>
> When she was abducted the girl was wearing a bracelet of a particular, if quite common, design. When we raided Black's flat we found, on the mantelshelf, an identical bracelet. It's not conclusive, but it is strong circumstantial evidence: my experience tells me that sex offenders frequently keep trophies of their crimes, and I suspect this is what the bracelet was.
>
> But, because there was stronger evidence in the Maxwell, Hogg, Harper and Thornhill cases, I took the view that the Metropolitan Police should wait until Black was convicted to take the case further. At that time I recommended that Black be interviewed. Were he possibly to admit the offence, then at that time the parents could be approached.
>
> The family needs to know why their child was killed, and by whom. They will feel tremendous guilt for the loss of their child – that they did something wrong. They don't always get through this. They have nervous breakdowns; they just try to survive. It's the not knowing, especially with an unsolved case: every time there's a knock at the door by police, it all comes flooding

back. They will relive the day of the murder time and time again.

So I think police must have a high degree of compassion before raising possibly false hopes, especially such a long time after the crime was committed. I take the view that one must really treat parents with kid gloves: they have to live with their grief.

In my mind Robert Black holds the key. But if he isn't prepared to admit it when the Metropolitan Police go to interview him, then I'm not sure I would support an investigation which would inevitably raise the hopes of those poor parents.

Both John Stainthorpe and Russ Allen have now retired from their respective forces. The process of bringing Robert Black to court has taken so long – more than four years – that few of the original case detectives remain. Some have died. Inevitably, that lessens the pressure for a new and costly full-scale investigation into Black's involvement in other murders, assaults or abductions. As he is serving life already, the as yet unspoken argument runs: why spend more time and money on trying to add more life sentences to his tally?

Just before the Maxwell, Hogg, Harper and Thornhill trial was due to begin, the man who headed the joint investigation also retired from office. But, before he left, Hector Clark was open and honest about the likely outcome of the battle between the parents' need to know who killed their children and the ferocious economics of public spending on long investigations:

Black hasn't spoken to us about other offences he may have committed. What exactly they are would depend on whether an investigation is conducted into all the outstanding child murders and abductions in the United Kingdom over the past twenty years.

Someone else will have to make that decision. But if you are asking me whether there would be any purpose served, my answer would be no, simply because Black is not prepared to admit his wrongdoings. Even if we were able to adduce some extra evidence to connect him with other murders, now that he is serving life I doubt very much whether, in the public interest, he would be taken before a court in the future.

The one reservation I have about that concerns the parents of these missing children. The parents of children who have been

> killed, or children who have been abducted, still have a right to know who was responsible for that death or that abduction. But it would be a very, very difficult task for anyone to undertake after the passage of such a long length of time.

It was the needs of the parents that I wanted to discuss with Robert Black as we sat down again together in the little interview cell at HMP Peterhead. Time was running short: any day now Black would be transferred from Scotland to Durham Prison in anticipation of the formal process of appearing before Newcastle Magistrates' Court to answer the charges against him. I knew that the English prison system was likely to be a good deal less accommodating: my visits would probably not take place when Black was in Durham. And even when, as was inevitable, he was transferred back to Peterhead to await his full trial for the Maxwell, Hogg, Harper and Thornhill cases, defence solicitors were likely, quite properly, to cut off my access.

We had been talking now for more than two years, session after session in which Black had steadily admitted to an ever-growing number of offences. It wasn't the numbers that bothered me: to some extent it didn't matter whether he had killed one child or a dozen, as I had come to believe. It was what drove him to kill that was vital to deal with.

In saying that, of course, I don't mean that the number of his crimes was irrelevant either to his victims or to their families. In a sense, it was for those families that I was working at that stage. The guilt and pain that would be tearing at them silently was something I knew Black had the power to ease. I wanted to make sure these parents – Liz and Fordyce Maxwell, Annette and John Hogg, Jacki Harper – understood that there was nothing more that they could have done to save their children's lives. And the most powerful way to get across that message was for Black to spell it out. I wanted them to hear it from his own lips. In the end I decided to put the issue directly to him.

RAY: Do you ever think about the parents? They all will feel that they have failed: they all will feel that in some way if they'd been different, their children wouldn't have been abducted. What can parents do to stop you?

BLACK: Never take their eyes off their kids, I suppose. That's about all.

RAY: Is that the only way they could have stopped it? By watching them? How realistic is that?

BLACK: It's not on, is it?

RAY: No. And imagine the guilt and the pain they feel – and you are the only person who can release them from all of that.

BLACK: I don't know. I offered to write to Laura's parents, and apologize, and tell them there wasn't anything they could have done.

RAY: They [the prison service] wouldn't let you do that, would they?

BLACK: No, they advised against it.

RAY: What about the others?

BLACK: I can't do nothing about the others. Not at this time anyway.

RAY: When?

BLACK: Maybe after the trials.

RAY: After all that? What can you do then?

BLACK: I don't know, really. I don't know that I can actually do anything. I can see a lot of point in it – like, you're sorry – but what good does that do? It can't . . .

RAY: It's about learning from you . . . to try and prevent it happening again: to stop other men doing what you did. And for you to own up to your responsibility. And it's about the parents. How could the parents have stopped you?

BLACK: To prevent something like that happening, you'd have to keep them tied to your apron strings.

RAY: That's because you're clever. Or do you think it's the easiest thing in the world to do what you did? Is it easy to do, once you put your mind to it?

BLACK: No.

RAY: What's difficult about it?

BLACK: The final step: the actual abduction.

RAY: Why is that the most difficult part of the process?

BLACK: I suppose because I know that the child is going to be terrified at that time.

RAY: Why do you think the parents couldn't have done anything?

BLACK: I don't know. Short of locking the kids up . . .

RAY: The only way of dealing with you was to catch you.

BLACK: I suppose that's one way of putting it.

RAY: Well, you weren't going to stop on your own, were you? What would you say to the parents whose children died – there were lots of them? What would you say to them as a person who has done this?

BLACK: The only thing I would say is, 'Don't blame yourself.' Because there was nothing that they could have done.

Later, as I listened at home to the tape of this interview, I realized that I had missed the significance of Black's words. Although I knew that a direct question about killing would produce a denial, I was amazed that he had accepted my questioning, questioning that implied his guilt. Robert Black might never confess directly and outright, but he was prepared to allow someone else to make the deductions his statements invited and not to challenge those deductions, once made.

8

The Politics of Paedophilia

Birmingham: Spring 1993

As I boarded the aircraft for Aberdeen for what was to prove the final time, I turned over all that Robert Black had said in the preceding two years. It had been a long journey for both of us, and I knew we were close to completing what we had set out to achieve. Black had gained some insight into the twisted darkness inside his own mind and had begun to face up to the horror of what he had done. I had learned much about a man whose personal story, and the story of the offences he had committed, was as harrowing as I had come across in twenty years.

But there was also a bigger picture that, through the gradual stripping bare of Robert Black, had come into sharp focus. Black's life and, with it, his career as a sex offender illustrated an almost complete failure by every part of the investigative and penal system in Britain. The failure in itself was not new: I had lived with it, railed at it, cursed it and ultimately devoted my life to educating those responsible for it. But most cases involved only one instance, perhaps two, of such signal failure. The unique lesson of Robert Black's three decades as a sex offender was that it mercilessly spotlighted the system's breakdown at each and every stage. Never before had I worked on a case that exemplified so clearly all that is wrong with the way we deal – or, more accurately, don't deal – with sex offenders. From the care system to the psychiatric profession; from the police service as a whole and individual experienced detectives in particular to the policies of the Home Office: in each case there had been a failure to understand the nature and behaviour of men who abuse children.

But this failure was neither especially blameworthy nor particularly surprising. It was simply a reflection of the wholesale public ignorance about this subject, an ignorance that is directly responsible for this nation's failure to protect its children. In saying this I'm not apportioning responsibility for Robert Black's crimes to any individual psychiatrist, police officer, prison officer, politician or bureaucrat. The blame for those offences lies squarely with the man who committed them.

But the Robert Blacks of this world are not going to stop abducting, abusing and killing children simply because we say they should. There will always be a responsibility laid on society to try to protect children from men like him and to catch them once they offend. And it is the wilful ignorance of the general public, stoked by irresponsible reporting and political bandstanding, that prevents effective prevention and detection. That is where we failed in this case: we, as a society, failed to protect our children from Robert Black in the only way that we could have done. We failed to prevent his offending – and then we failed to catch him.

In my hotel room in Peterhead, as I reviewed his notes and listened again to the recordings of my sessions with Robert Black, I could see that the failures began during Black's early childhood. A very real sense of rejection and loss surrounded his earliest years. Not only had his natural mother abandoned him but he was placed with adoptive parents whose own behaviour seems to have isolated the boy.

I couldn't be sure, but I was left with the nagging feeling that one or both parents had abused Robert Black – how else to explain Black's complete inability to remember a single thing about the man he grew up to call his father? This complete absence of memory was not natural, but it is a common symptom of some gross trauma to which the mind responds by simply blotting out all recollection. And, if that was so, then it happened before the age of five: that was when Jack Tulip died and Robert suffered loss once again.

Some people may think that if his adoptive father abused him, Black would have been glad to see the back of him. But the dynamics of sexual abuse are never that clear-cut: it is not uncommon for a victim to feel so bound to the perpetrator of abuse that guilt, and an overpowering sense of loss, accompanies the termination of the abuse.

Our training of foster parents has, over the years, improved, but we still need to help them deal with the sexual abuse of children under their care and offer them the support they need. We also need to be careful about how we select staff. We have a long way to travel, but, in the light of Black's story, it is interesting to note that the selection of foster parents is much more thorough than the recruiting and selection of residential care staff.

Of course, society as a whole can't be held to blame for the failings of individual families, adoptive or natural. Nor does abuse – if, indeed, it occurred – excuse Robert Black's subsequent career as a sex offender. But Black's case highlights a lack of sensitivity in abandoning him once again, as Margaret Tulip died when Black was just ten years old, to a children's home. Black told me that other families in Kinlochleven offered to foster him but that the social services refused because these families had several children of their own. This is impossible to verify. But I have to question the decision – even in the late 1950s, when we knew less about child psychology than we do now – to dump Robert Black in the contemporary equivalent of a juvenile workhouse.

The care system that so signally failed Robert Black has, in fairness, changed a good deal in the thirty years since he endured it. At the close of the twentieth century the emphasis throughout Britain has shifted from caring for children in medium- or large-scale children's homes to placing children (or groups of related children) with foster-parents. But care homes, particularly for the disturbed, disruptive or plain difficult, remain. And all too often life for the children in them is petty, punitive and unforgiving.

Sexual abuse of children, both by their peers and by adult care workers, is depressingly common. Paedophiles frequently seek out, and gain, jobs in child-care agencies. Once there, they typically continue to abuse, and their new victims don't speak out. The problem with children in care is that even if they do say they have been abused, they do not necessarily make good witnesses: the privileged legal hierachy views their frequently disturbed behaviour with suspicion rather than seeing it as evidence of an underlying problem.

And so it has become a sad fact that if abusers abuse criminal or disturbed children, it is highly likely there will be no criminal proceedings on the basis that a child who is anti-authority or delinquent cannot be believed if he or she says they have been abused. This can make care a dangerous place: children abused in care are often reluctant to report their ordeal. And small wonder: if it is difficult for well-adjusted youngsters, growing up in a normal family environment, to disclose abuse by an adult – and it is – how much more difficult to do so within a system which you perceive as impatient or hostile?

Despite repeated attempts by children's groups such as the National Association of Young People in Care or the Children's Legal Centre, there is still no effective or safe complaints system for young people in the care of the state. These children, frequently psychologically scarred by the very fact of their presence within the system, are some of the most vulnerable in our society. Yet we choose to deny them – unlike convicted adult prisoners in jails – a secure method of raising their voice when abuse occurs. In this way the scandals of 'pin-down' in Staffordshire or the monstrous regime of sexual cruelty headed by Frank Beck in Leicestershire were able to scar the lives of countless young people for many years.

I see many victims of our care system – and 'care' is often a sick joke, at best. As I looked over Black's experiences in care homes I recognized a familiar and depressing pattern. Why, for example, did the home at Redding simply expel him after his clumsy attempt at sexual interference with another child? Was this not simply a management decision taken with the cynical aim of causing as little administrative trouble as possible? Why was there no attempt to discover why this young boy was behaving in this way? Why was he sent to another care home without any check being made on the suitability of that home?

And why was the home chosen, the Red House, one with a reputation for punishment?

The answers seem to highlight the problem that exists today: that the actual needs of children in care, whatever the reason they are placed there, come second to the convenience of the adults who manage the homes or run the care system. Yet we still have the temerity to be surprised when children emerge from care unprepared, unsupported, angry and, quite frequently, destructive. This must not remain an academic debate. For a child who is sexually abused, and then placed into care, and then abused again, the effect is devastating and all but certain to blight his or her future.

Robert Black left care, by his own account, a sexually dangerous adolescent. Not only had his own sexual problems been ignored but they had been compounded by the abuse he suffered at the hands of an adult staff member. Worse, he had been, under this man's twisted tutelage, required to lure, groom and present for abuse his successor.

I was hardly surprised by the almost immediate sexual assault of a young girl that ensued. Indeed, given what I now knew about the man, some formative incident must have taken place at some stage in Black's life. The incident in the air-raid shelter during which he strangled the girl, masturbated and left her for dead became his main fantasy during subsequent masturbation.

I had the feeling, during our interviews, that this was in some ways the blueprint for his later offending. He was telling me about something that had happened twenty-seven years before, yet the fact that I could feel it, experience it, showed how real and fresh it was for him. If it had been only a distant memory that he was grasping for, he would not have been able to get in touch with his feelings so clearly and so memorably.

What did surprise me, however, was the sentence that Black received for abducting, abusing and strangling this seven-year-old girl. My overriding reaction when I heard about this from him was anger. And the twin targets of my anger were what he had done and the system that dealt with him. We have to ask how, when a fifteen-year-old boy takes a little girl to an air-raid shelter, abuses her and nearly kills her, the judicial system can do nothing more than admonish him after deferring sentence for a year.

I found the answer in the psychiatric report that described the incident as 'isolated' – which is exactly what Black, like all sexual offenders, wanted the system to believe. At the same hearing a probation report gave an opposing and, as it would turn out, much more accurate picture of Robert Black. But, as is so often the case, the judge listened not to the probation officer but to the psychiatrist.

Judges have posed a major problem in child-abuse cases for more than twenty years. Before the 1970s, even in that liberal decade, the 1960s, when Robert Black made his first court appearances, the issue was one of those subjects their lordships generally viewed as better left unaired. They presided over a series of crucial procedural obstacles to the pursuit of successful criminal cases, particularly when the victims were pre-pubescent children. The loose canon of legally unenforceable guidelines that determined the presentation of evidence in court – the so-called 'Judges' Rules' – simply forbade children under the age of six to appear as witnesses. They were considered too young to be able to tell the truth, even about the abuse they had endured at the hands of adults.

These guidelines were abolished in 1988, but many courts remain obdurately closed to young witnesses. Even when cases involving older children came to court, the child victims were required to give evidence against their abuser under his watchful (and generally intimidating) stare. Worst of all, many judges, all white, middle- or upper-class men in those days, clung to a belief in the 'predatory Lolita' – the sexually active child who lures otherwise innocent adult men into her clutches.

Put so bluntly, it seems an untenable position, yet many judges presiding over sex-abuse trials have expressed precisely such distorted views of the sexual exploitation of children. One, Judge Brian Gibbens, summed up thus in the case of a man who had had sex with his friend's seven-year-old daughter: 'It strikes me, without belittling the offence, as one of the kinds of accident which happen in life to almost anyone, although of a wholly different kind.' Judge Gibbens's comment was no mere isolated idiocy. It was the product of the British judicial system. The judge made his remark not in the dark ages before the 1970s, when the issue of child abuse was seen as too unpleasant to be aired, but in the early 1980s. A full decade had passed since the rest of the country had come to accept the disturbing reality of child abuse. Yet judges like Gibbens remained ignorant of this change of view.

Throughout Britain judges have traditionally been deemed to be above the need for special training. Until the 1980s they were assumed to have gained all the knowledge they would need on the bench during their careers as barristers. Yet many of the judges trying criminal cases have worked predominantly at the commercial bar, presenting cases in which money, not the value of life, is at stake. Even today, after countless official enquiries into the prevalence and handling of child-abuse cases, their lordships are required to undergo no more than one week's compulsory training every five years.

The result is, simply and depressingly, that some of the men and women responsible for sentencing sex offenders may be as ignorant as the judge who gave Robert Black a deferred sentence for abducting, abusing and leaving a seven-year-old girl for dead in the air-raid shelter at Greenock Park. We have, apparently, learned nothing. And I have a terrible sense that the system will continue to let this happen because it does not understand sexual offenders – and makes no effort to understand them.

Robert Black's life story reinforces the point about all such men: by ignoring the reality of their sexual offences, hoping senselessly that it will quietly go away, the criminal justice system allows their desires free rein. The failure of the courts to recognize that first prosecuted offence for what it so clearly was – attempted murder with a sexual motive – ensured that Black continued to abduct and abuse for another twenty-seven years.

Even during the year of his deferred sentence, he admitted to me that he sexually abused girls on his visits to blocks of flats either as a butcher's delivery boy or in one of his periods of unemployment. We simply have no idea of how many children suffered at his hands as a result, but by his own suggestion it could be as many as thirty or forty. And when Black was next arrested, for his sexual assault on the six-year-old girl in Kinlochleven, the system once again broke down. When Black was sent to Borstal for twelve months nothing was done to attack the roots of his offending. He was given no treatment at all and, immediately after his release, teamed up with another former inmate to commit joint rapes.

Of course, I wouldn't have expected him to be given treatment at that time – the concept of working with men like him had not yet emerged. But today, twenty-seven years on, almost nothing has changed. We still ignore the vital need to treat, not simply punish, the Robert Blacks of this world. Even when it became clear that treatment could break the cycle of offending, nothing was done about providing it. In prison it still remains a luxury offered to only a minority of sex offenders. People are blind to the fact that if we don't do this work, we will have more abused children, society will become even more unsafe and men like Black will develop into offenders.

The crass stupidity of our nation's wilful blindness has haunted me throughout my career. It is ultimately a political issue. Working with men like Black is not seen as vote-winning: how much easier to pander to some base popular reaction and call for the castration of all sex offenders, as if that would actually solve the problem. I was once talking to a politician who told me: 'Ray, there are no votes in working with sex offenders.' I said that I'd make the issue a vote-loser if he didn't support change.

We simply cannot continue doing what we have done for years – what we did, albeit briefly, with Robert Black. Locking a man up for a little while, doing nothing with him and then letting him out again is quite stupid. And it's no use suggesting that we execute offenders. Offer that as a possibility, and we will see a dramatic increase in the number of children killed by their abusers. After all, why be hanged on the evidence of your victim if you can dispose of that victim with no extra penalty?

Nor, in any event, do I believe the victims' families would necessarily support such a move. The parents of at least two of Robert Black's victims, Fordyce and Liz Maxwell and Jacki Harper, say they do not support the death penalty for the man who killed their daughters. The years since Sarah's abduction and murder have given Jacki time enough to reach a conclusion that is considered and, to my mind, rational.

> Something has to be done with people of the same ilk as Robert Black. They usually start off with minor offences and get worse and worse and worse until ultimately they do kill children. If they were caught earlier, and given the correct treatment, maybe it would be stopped and children wouldn't be being abused and children wouldn't be dying.

It took until 1991 for the Home Office finally to recognize the wisdom of what Jacki Harper saw as simple common sense. It established pilot programmes to treat sex offenders in sixteen prisons throughout England and Wales. Within a year the department's junior minister, Peter Lloyd, was able to boast about his government's commitment to the programmes:

> The prison service has a duty to help prisoners towards leading law-abiding and useful lives after release . . . It is important that all prisoners have the opportunity to make the best of their sentence so that their time in prison is not spent in a negative way waiting for release. Sex-offender treatment programmes are already running at fourteen centres, plus Grendon and Wormwood Scrubs, and they can treat over 400 prisoners a year.

But, however welcome the initiative, such figures represent only a small proportion of the population of child abusers in prison at any given time. In the spring of 1994 the Home Office admitted that less than 10 per cent of convicted child sex offenders were in the (voluntary) treatment programmes running at its sixteen trial prisons. It also announced that there were 2,200 such offenders in cells in England and Wales.

Peter Lloyd may be right to say that the units *can* treat 400 men a year. But they don't. This isn't all the Home Office's fault. Prison is a very difficult place in which to conduct sex-offender work because, to produce change, the therapist needs to discover vulnerability in the offender. This is unlikely to be forthcoming from most offenders because they have to survive in a system that, whether we like it or not, they interpret as abusive. How can a man in prison, often angry with the conditions in which he is held and fearful of the other inmates, allow himself to be vulnerable enough to change? It can be very difficult to overcome the dilemma of requiring vulnerability in a man who is trying to survive in a system that runs on daily brutality.

In addition to this in-built problem the Home Office has built its own barrier. Quite simply, most sex offenders in prison will never be eligible for places on treatment programmes. Most sex offenders receive sentences of less than four years, yet the Home Office enforces a rule that requires a longer sentence if the offender is to qualify for a place. It makes no sense. I can only assume there is a hidden economic or political agenda at play.

That agenda, increasingly overt rather than hidden, was expressed by the Prime Minister himself in the spring of 1993. In a lengthy interview and briefing session with the right-wing *Mail on Sunday* newspaper John Major announced a new direction for his government's policy. Henceforth there was to be 'a little less understanding and a little more condemnation'. That seemed to be crazy, to be quite the most stupid remark, even for a band-standing politician. To use an analogy, we were all supposed to be very busy jumping into a river to rescue drowning children, yet no one was to do anything about the man just around the bend up-river who was pushing them in.

When are we going to face this issue and address the problems in a sophisticated and concerted way? I know why we don't: ultimately no one wants to be seen to be 'soft' on sex offenders, and everybody is terrified of being held accountable for men who re-offend. But the tragedy is that unless we work with these men, they *will* re-offend. That's what the Robert Black case should be teaching us: had someone worked with him early on, many children might still be alive. But they didn't – and we, as a society, still fail to demand this most basic of policy changes. Instead we appear to believe that it is much better to lock them up, do nothing with them and then release them at the end of their sentences. At least that way, when they do re-offend no one can be held accountable.

The frustration I have long felt with the apparent lack of effort made to combat offenders' distorted sexual beliefs in prison was mirrored in every aspect of Black's career as an abuser and abductor. His case is an object lesson in how to permit the development of a serial child abuser and killer. For more than a decade he was allowed to amass a collection of 110 child-pornography magazines and fifty-eight films or videos. During the first three years of his collecting habit there was no specific law that made child pornography illegal. Instead it was covered by the catch-all clauses of the Obscene Publications Act, which outlawed material that tended to 'deprave or corrupt'.

But in 1978 the Protection of Children Act specifically outlawed the taking, showing or distribution of indecent photographs of children. Although simple possession of child-pornography magazines, films or videos was not illegal (an Act closing that loophole would not be passed until 1987), the means of acquiring them was banned. The Act, which started life not as a government measure but as a Private Member's Bill, was not immediately popular. Fuelled largely by ignorance of the true nature of child pornography – that to produce it requires the sexual abuse of a child – and backed by references to the apparently successful experiment by the Danish Government in 'liberalizing' its pornography laws, the decade had seen a gradually increasing belief that perhaps this material was not as bad as all that.

This view reached its apogee in the 1979 report of the government-appointed Home Office Committee on Obscenity and Film Censorship, more usually known as the Williams Committee after its chairman Professor Bernard Williams.

Between 1977 and 1979 the committee visited the main production and distribution centres for all pornography in Europe – Holland and Denmark. There is a certain irony in the fact that as its members conducted their lofty academic analysis of *Lollitots*, *Teenage Sex* and *Lolita*, Robert Black was routinely travelling to the same locations to purchase the ideal titles for a rather less intellectual study.

The Williams Committee also took evidence from a number of experts on the issues of pornography and sexual behaviour. One, Professor Trevor Gibbens, Emeritus Professor of Forensic Psychiatry at London University, summed up the mood of the decade. His evidence was quoted in the committee's final report:

> Professor Trevor Gibbens told us that he thought young girls often had the ability to exploit what they saw as a 'good racket' and were quite capable of still growing up into well-adjusted women. This did not mean that Professor Gibbens was arguing that the use of children in pornography was anything but undesirable, but that he was suggesting that long-term damage to those involved was more doubtful than is widely assumed.

Such naïve ramblings would, perhaps, have mattered less had not the latter part of the 1970s seen a simultaneous convergence of three vital accelerating factors in the growth in child-pornography consumption.

The first was the great Danish experiment – the legal freeing of companies like Rodox/Color Climax to exploit children sexually and to make money by selling the resulting celluloid. The second was the greatest single technological advance in the distribution of obscene material: the advent of the cheap video camera. And the third was the corruption of the one police squad that could have, should have, laboured to prevent child pornography coming into Britain.

The Obscene Publications Branch of the Metropolitan Police is now known within the Force as SO14 (Special Operations Unit Number 14). It is based in an L-shaped office on the seventh floor of New Scotland Yard, with adjoining offices for civilian staff and a tiny cubby-hole where seized material can be viewed. It is a dedicated unit in every sense of the word. New recruits to the Met may snigger about the opportunity for SO14 officers to view 'dirty' videos, But this nudge-nudge attitude dissolves during the first few frames of the first viewing of the first child-pornography cassette. It suddenly ceases to be such a great joke. For the men – there are rarely many women officers on the team – of SO14 this material is quite frequently stomach-churning in its gynaecological detail. But it is the images of childhood destroyed – pictures of children's faces – that have the longest-lasting effect.

In 1976 SO14, however, had yet to be born, at least in its present form. The squad that did its work was known as the 'Dirty Squad', both because it covered the squalid Soho-based sex industry and because it was financially corrupt, accepting substantial bribes from those it should have been investigating. The result was the free flow of obscene material into Britain. And with the hard-core adult films and magazines came child pornography.

Both the Post Office and HM Customs and Excise testified before the Williams Committee that they rarely managed to intercept any child pornography bound for British paedophiles. Customs was, in any event, rather more interested in expending its intelligence and operational efforts on stemming the flow of clearly illegal drugs than attempting problematic prosecutions under the less precise Obscene Publications Act. As for the Post Office, it had all but abandoned any attempt to prevent the importation of child pornography. According to the Williams Report:

> The Post Office Act . . . empowers the Post Office to detain and dispose of any prohibited articles in postal transmission.
>
> Representatives of the Post Office made it plain to us that this prohibition was not enforced to any significant extent because it was not possible to do so.
>
> A sealed postal packet rarely announces itself as containing prohibited material, and although the 1953 Act gives the power

to open and dispose of any postal packet posted in contravention of the prohibition, this power does not extend in the Post Office's view to the opening of packets on suspicion . . .

Cases which do come to light, numbering no more than fifty a year, are usually those where a package bursts open in the post or has to be opened because it is not capable of being delivered . . .

However, the Post Office told us they had misgivings about removing items from the post in this way on the basis of their own judgement – which they did not feel competent to make – rather than the judgement of a court . . .

Accordingly, since the law gave them a power rather than imposed an obligation, the Post Office determined (after 1978) that they would no longer, on the strength of the Post Office Acts, dispose of indecent or obscene material coming into this country from overseas.

Behind its leaden prose Williams was reporting a crucial, and previously unannounced, policy change. From 1978 onwards the Post Office simply abandoned its responsibilities to prevent the importation of child pornography. Since the mail is the chief method by which paedophiles obtain the magazines, films and videos they need to sustain their distorted sexuality, this amounted to an open invitation for trade in all obscene material. It was one that Robert Black accepted and vigorously exploited, and it was to take another eight years – eight years of unfettered importation of the grossest photographic records showing sexual assaults on very young children – before there would be any attempt to halt the tide.

Iain Donaldson was known affectionately to his friends and colleagues as the 'Moose' a nickname earned by his loping 6 feet 5 inch frame and booming Scottish voice. In 1985, as the new head of a reconstituted Obscene Publications Branch, Donaldson began to redirect its efforts away from adult pornography and towards cutting off paedophiles from their 'oxygen supply' of child pornography. He inherited a branch that had just two officers investigating child pornography and at least five times that number policing the tawdry adult market. Within four years he had reversed the position.

> We adapted our resources to target child pornography as a number-one priority. Eighty per cent of the squad's efforts went into tackling it, and in the years since 1985 it has expanded its expertise, its intelligence, and its prosecutions have been quite notable.

Notable sometimes, however, for the wrong reasons. In 1988 Donaldson's team prosecuted Professor Oliver Brooke, a leading London paediatrician, for purchasing, commissioning and trading in child pornography. It was to prove a salutary reminder of how far Britain's judges lagged behind the growing understanding of child pornography. Brooke received an initial twelve-month sentence but appealed against it. His case came up before the most senior criminal judge in the country, the then Lord Chief Justice, Lord Lane. He reduced the paediatrician's sentence by half with this ringing exposition on the nature of the (grossly explicit) material:

> It is not inappropriate, perhaps, in view of the puerility of this kind of behaviour, to compare it rather to a schoolboy collecting cigarette cards in olden times . . .

Reverses like that became simply part of the territory for Donaldson and the Obscene Publications Branch: every time they took a step forward, there seemed to be a wilful ignorance pushing them back again.

> The effort and the dedication required of the team was – is – tremendous. They've all got their own children, so, psychologically, it's important for them to feel extremely committed to combating this abhorrent crime. You have to remember how terrible the visions they have to see every day can be.

Gradually SO14 gained recognition as the leading edge of law-enforcement effort against child pornography and paedophilia. It built up an impressive card index of almost 5,000 known offenders, had a team of twelve officers working full time to penetrate the secretive circles of paedophiles who traded in child pornography and built up a case load of potential investigations that would take a minimum of twenty years to clear.

But there were frustrating restrictions. They were, and still are, prevented from tackling cases of child sexual abuse unless child pornography has been generated. They have no power of arrest (although plans have been laid before Parliament to change this). Most frustrating of all, they were forbidden to take on cases outside the Metropolitan Police area. Although this rule is occasionally bent, SO14 is paid by the Met and seen as a resource for the residents of the Greater London metropolis. If it receives intelligence about paedophiles and child pornographers outside its boundaries, it passes that on to the relevant police force.

But no other police force in Britain has a dedicated child-pornography squad. Cases – and they are rare beyond comprehension – are handled, almost as an afterthought, by generic vice squads more used to arresting pimps and prostitutes on street corners than to conducting long-term investigations into secretive paedophiles.

> And yet [Donaldson admits, with a weary shake of his head] child pornography is certainly a problem outside London. In fact, it's an immense problem. Yet the people [in other force areas] who decide on resources have got all sorts of pressures on them, and people with other problems are lobbying Chief Constables to devote resources to other things.

Yet ask Iain Donaldson – ask anyone who has seen child pornography and knows both how it was made and the probable results of its widespread availability – if there could be any higher priority than protecting children from it, and the answer is a slow, insistent shake of the head.

SO14 continues to function. Room 717, New Scotland Yard, remains a dedicated child-pornography unit. But quietly, insidiously, change is coming. Officers there report a new lack of support from their commanders: its staff are no longer permitted to publicize their work. That work has never formally been recognized as a force priority: some of SO14's most experienced officers fear that by the end of the decade Britain's sole concerted effort to tackle child pornography will be a mere ghost of its current self.

And in the summer of 1994 the Commissioner of the Metropolitan Police made it known that he wanted the Obscene Publications Branch disbanded and its work parcelled out to a variety of different squads. Those squads are already overworked. They are also inexperienced in the detailed task of investigating child pornography.

There is no good reason to abolish SO14. Just as there is no good reason for all other British police forces to opt out of child-pornography policing, even if it didn't take the abuse of a child to produce it (and it does) and even if didn't take up valuable police resources (and it does). Despite all that, we have to recognize two vital truths.

First, that child pornography is one of the factors that make men more, rather than less, likely to abuse children. And, secondly, that in a crime the detection of which relies currently too much on the victim's complaints, child pornography represents evidence. Most paedophiles collect it: many actually make their own, videoing or photographing themselves abusing children.

One of the best ways to protect children is to investigate and find child pornography. Yet we simply don't do this. If the Metropolitan Police had had an effective and uncorrupted child-pornography unit in the 1970s, the flood of explicit films and magazines, from *Lollitots* to *Lolita*, that Robert Black sought out would have been very much riskier to obtain. Had the isolated efforts of the Obscene Publications Branch been matched by commitment and adequate resources in the Home Office, it is possible – even likely – that Black's child-pornography orders would have been intercepted and his name once again noted as a danger to children. And if each and every police force outside London matched even the Metropolitan Police's limited efforts, the number of men like him – men who abuse in the relative security of public ignorance and official inertia – would first be recognized and later, perhaps, reduced. There can be no good reason for failing to resource this properly. After all, what it amounts to is child protection: very simply the best way of making our children as safe as we can.

That it doesn't happen is a reflection both of the political process that affects the treatment of paedophiles in prison – a shameful disregard for the priority I am certain should be attached to this need – and of a wider lack of understanding. Our society simply does not understand paedophilia because it deliberately shuts its eyes and ears to the problem. But if you don't understand something, how can you combat it? The widespread failure to understand the nature of child-sex offenders is thrown into sharpest relief by the failure to catch Robert Black during the eight years he was hunted for the abductions and murders of Susan Maxwell, Caroline Hogg and Sarah Harper.

As our prison sessions were drawing to a close, Hector Clark was preparing for Black's trial. Part of the process inevitably involved a series of briefings and background interviews with the press. These were covered by a necessary caveat: they were to be published – under British court rules they could only be published – after the conclusion of the trial. By this stage Clark would have retired.

Most journalists who were granted an audience in the Deputy Chief Constable's spacious and comfortable offices overlooking the playing fields of Edinburgh's prestigious Fettes College asked a variant on one vital question: how could Black have been missed in such an exhaustive investigation? It was a question that Clark must have expected, for the answer was remarkably similar on each occasion: the words formed almost a mantra that might, if repeated often enough, obscure the failings the question sought to explain.

> If Black had come within the remit [of our investigation], it would have been because of a number of reasons: someone told us – and they didn't; he had a conviction that made him

significant – and he didn't; he lived within an area that we were looking at – and he didn't.

There are so many people throughout the United Kingdom. If someone doesn't tell us what they suspect, how are we to find out? We just ask questions. We listen to what we're told. We gather evidence. No one ever told us about him. No one drew him to our notice. He had convictions that, whilst they were sexually related, were not serious enough to warrant bringing him into our enquiry.

This version of Black's life and convictions, and its function as an excuse for the investigation's failure, drew a sharp response from John Stainthorpe.

That's nonsense. Once a child molester, always a child molester. Speaking as a practical policeman, they never stop, they never change. They develop, and the offences become more and more serious. Black should have been arrested years ago, with his history and convictions. Why he wasn't brought to our attention much earlier I shall never know.

Just who failed to bring the name of Robert Black to the attention of Hector Clark and the joint investigation into the Maxwell, Hogg and Harper murders is a subject none of the affected forces chooses to discuss.

Certainly, Strathclyde Police would have held, on their Local Intelligence files, Black's earliest record for sexual offending against children. And while the first conviction for lewd and libidinous behaviour might have led to some confusion, the 1967 charges of indecent assault against the six-year-old girl in Kinlochleven should at least have made him a suspect. West Yorkshire Police had, after all, asked all forces to comb their files for just such records. But Black accumulated convictions in other parts of the country as well. Most were for motoring offences – and in the archaic tradition of British policing, traffic violations are not recorded in the same files as a criminal's more serious records.

None the less, given the urgency with which an itinerant

known paedophile was being sought, it is hard to explain how Local Intelligence Officers in any one of half a dozen police forces failed to identify Black as a potential suspect. The Metropolitan Police had even carefully noted on his 1979 assault conviction that he was a van driver travelling the country. Ultimately what stands out is not that Robert Black, paedophile and itinerant, was unknown to the police but rather that despite his convictions, the regional intelligence systems were unable to recognize him in their own files.

It generally comes as a shock to new officers in the Metropolitan Police Obscene Publications Branch to learn, first, that there has never been a national database of even convicted – much less suspected – child-sex offenders and, second that national and regional intelligence or records systems are accessible only by the name of an individual. To access, for example, the vast database of the National Identification Bureau, which stores every criminal record in its secure computer files, an enquiring detective must have the name of a suspect, which works well when the investigator has a suspect and wants to match his known record with a new offence or string of offences. But to detectives investigating a case of serial child abductions or murders, NIB's gigabytes of computer records are simply useless: the very thing they seek – a suspect's name – is the only useful key to the system.

There are, it is true, more refined profiling computer tools: CATCHEM in Derbyshire can pinpoint the statistical likelihood of a suspect's being the perpetrator of a new murder, and Crime Pattern Analysis, controlled by the Home Office, frequently proffers suspects' names to senior detectives investigating a series of linked offences. But none has the necessary systems to allow an officer to punch in the details of the case and ask the computer to search all the records of known similar, or even potential, offenders.

Instead officers like Russ Allen, formerly a detective superintendent with 4AMIP, one of the Metropolitan Police's eight specialist murder squads, have been forced to undertake laborious and time-consuming leg-work:

Every divisional police station throughout the country, and there must be several thousand such stations, has a Local Intelligence Office. So if someone's stopped in the street and relevant information is gleaned, it is fed into the LIO.

I always took the view that if I wanted information from a Local Intelligence Office, I would send my staff personally to the divisions. To start with, my officers would know exactly what they were looking for. But, more important, this doesn't put additional workload on the LIO.

If I simply ring these people up, listing the information I require, I'm a voice at the end of a phone to officers who've already got a full day ahead of them and who would find it increasingly difficult if I gave them a long bit of searching to conduct on my behalf. Quite simply, it could lead to gaps if I was to rely on someone else doing this work. And I know that if my staff have gone down and done it, then the work's been completed – and completed to my satisfaction.

There are more than 100 LIOs within the Metropolitan Police Force area, enough to pose a daunting problem for anyone with the urge to search their files individually. But multiply the capital's complement of Local Intelligence Offices by a factor of ten to cover the whole country, and the obstacle becomes frankly insurmountable. To visit and flick through the files of every LIO in Britain would strain even a major investigation to breaking point. Most such nationwide enquiries rely on telephone or written requests. And, inevitably, such requests either fall on deaf ears because of inter-force rivalry or are pushed to the bottom of an ever-growing pile of paperwork. Yet the regionalized LIOs are the eyes and ears of the British national intelligence system. As Allen knows only too well, even a system as genuinely sophisticated as Crime Pattern Analysis relies on LIOs sending their intelligence up a convoluted chain of communication.

CPA's information comes from the Local Intelligence Officers evaluating the intelligence that they have and then feeding it up. They have certain criteria for the intelligence to meet before it warrants going into the CPA database, but once those are met it is vital for the LIOs to be religious in sending data through. Because an investigating officer like me could lose a case should that not have been done.

Allen is a cautious man, a career detective who moved from 4AMIP into the rather less dynamic world of financial security for London Transport before emigrating to Botswana. He does not, with ease or enthusiasm, expose the gaping holes in a system that he served for most of his adult life, but even he is forced to admit that, at a generous estimate, at least a quarter of Britain's LIOs at some stage fail to send through crucial intelligence. In West Yorkshire Allen's opposite number, John Stainthorpe is rather more blunt.

It was crime intelligence that let us down in this case. While computers like HOLMES are invaluable tools in an investigation, without an effective computerized crime-intelligence system to back it up you're fighting with one hand tied behind your back. Without a computerized intelligence system which can be updated on a daily basis you've got to rely on people trawling through the files manually and being alert enough – and, indeed, interested enough – to pull out the relevant document. The whole thing's a joke.

Remember, it wasn't police efficiency that caught Robert Black – it was the quick thinking of a member of the public [in the Scottish Borders village]. Without him, Black might still have been at large today. And yet had Black been on a computerized criminal intelligence system, his name would have popped up like a cork out of a bottle.

By a remarkable coincidence, the first breach in the previously impenetrable wall of Home Office complacency over this problem occurred within days of Robert Black's arrest for the Laura Turner abduction.

In August 1990 the Association of Chief Police Officers delivered a report to the Home Secretary calling for a new national and computerized crime-intelligence network. In itself this was far from new – the police service as a whole had called for organized national intelligence gathering for at least fifteen years. But in the summer of 1990 the Home Office listened. Within three months the Home Secretary announced that a new criminal-intelligence unit, fully computerized, with a national remit and funding from both central government and regional police authorities, would be swiftly created.

On 1 April 1992 the resulting organization opened its doors for business. The National Criminal Intelligence Service (NCIS for short) is based in an anonymous office block just off the Albert Embankment in London. Five regional offices – in Bristol, Birmingham, Manchester, Wakefield and London (a second unit) – divide the country geographically.

NCIS's statement of purpose announces that it exists to 'provide a quality service in gathering, collation, evaluation analysis and development of relevant information and intelligence about serious crime (excluding terrorism) and major criminals of regional, national and international interest,' and 'by the dissemination of that information and intelligence to the appropriate law-enforcement agencies, to facilitate the bringing to justice of offenders.'

Under the NCIS umbrella 400 dedicated police and civilian staff were divided into eight major areas of crime-intelligence gathering: drugs, counterfeit currency, public-sector corruption, football hooliganism, stolen cars, international criminal intelligence, the British branch office of Interpol and the National Paedophile Unit. The new service was given its own section of the Metropolitan Police Intelligence Computer, known as INFOS – a vast and almost unimaginably powerful mainframe originally based at Putney. According to NCIS's promotional brochure:

> INFOS is a free text system based on a well-tried and flexible data-retrieval software package. It is employed in many other intelligence and information-handling applications and has been modified over the years to suit the particular need of each user.

The same brochure set out the antecedents and aims of the National Paedophile Unit.

> The Unit has its origins in the Obscene Publications Branch of the Metropolitan Police.
>
> It was set up to research and develop intelligence on paedophiles and others involved in the making, importation or distribution of pornography.
>
> Up until 1992 the details were held on a card index system, but these are now being weeded, updated and superseded by incorporation into the INFOS computer system.

Like many of her colleagues in the open-plan NCIS offices, Louise Ellis moved across from a civilian job at New Scotland Yard to join the nascent service. A young and friendly woman in her late twenties, Ellis heads the National Paedophile Unit and is happy to demonstrate how quickly a computerized request for information can be satisfied.

> First, I'm going to input a name into the system. And it tells me now that this person is known to us for activities involving abuse on children and has also come to notice for the receipt of child pornography.
>
> It's giving me a description of this man, any marks or special features that would identify him, and all of his history as far as where and when he has been arrested in the past.
>
> I can now make that information available to the police officer who made the enquiry and he will be able to use that as he feels appropriate, whether that is as a reference point or to add more to the story they've already got on this man.

The entire process takes only a matter of seconds. Better still, Ellis is able to start a search by punching in 'key words' – salient details of an offence, such as the known use of a Transit van – and emerge with a list of paedophiles known to use such a method. It is precisely the system that was so badly needed on the Maxwell, Hogg and Harper cases:

> Paedophiles are very much a national problem, and they don't stay in one area for any length of time. So it was felt that a

national unit needed to be set up to look at this problem and to try to keep tabs on the location of these people so that we're aware of their activities and where they were going on at any particular time.

Ellis has done her homework: she has studied the nature of paedophilia and the difficulties associated with policing the desires of a large number of otherwise anonymous men:

The first thing is that, in my experience, most paedophiles do continually abuse. Their methods stay much the same, although they do progress in [the seriousness of] their offending the longer they get away with it.

It's very important to look back over someone's history of offending because there could be gaps – for example, long periods of time spent in prison – which could break up the offending pattern that you may at first see. It doesn't mean they have necessarily stopped offending. You shouldn't rule someone out simply because they haven't come to notice recently. Currently on our database we are holding approximately 5,000 names of people who, we know, are involved in paedophile crime. I believe there are more than 5,000 such people: these are just the ones we are aware of and are currently looking at. I think it's impossible to put a final figure on how big our database should be, on how many names we should be holding, because we are still very much in our early stages. But I would say that there should be roughly double that 5,000 figure on the database eventually.

To former officers like Russ Allen, NCIS's National Paedophile Unit is the answer to the criminal-intelligence problem faced by detectives dealing with serial offenders.

Any senior investigating officer from any force can access that information base and, from there, draw out intelligence information to assist their investigation, which might help tie in offenders with offences from all over the country. I could go to NCIS and the Paedophile Unit and find details of known offenders I was looking for. Most certainly I could.

If only that were true.

The theory and practice of the National Paedophile Unit are depressingly far apart. First, and most fundamentally, it is not a national unit at all: neither Scotland nor Northern Ireland has elected to join the NCIS intelligence network. Inevitably that means that, apart from some *ad hoc* telephone contacts, the vast swathes of intelligence gathered by police in those countries are denied to officers like Louise Ellis. Worse, the system is not compatible with any other police computerized enquiry or intelligence system. Ask Louise Ellis about the technical compatibility of her database with these systems, and her response is almost farcical.

> The NCIS computer system is not compatible with any of the other currently existing databases. It is not compatible with HOLMES; it is not compatible with NIB either.
>
> There doesn't appear to be a reason why it's not compatible. It's just that it was the system that was available and would perform the functions that NCIS wanted it to perform at the time.

Without computer compatibility, all data transfer has to be handled manually. In essence this requires officers to cling to the very traditions that so fatally flawed the Maxwell, Harper and Hogg cases. In particular it ensures that NCIS cannot, in any direct way, access the wealth of criminal records held by the National Identification Bureau. Instead Louise Ellis has to rely on LIOs volunteering the names and histories of sex offenders – details that she then has to record manually on the NCIS database. Since part of the reason for the Unit's existence was to bypass this need, it seems perverse that the old system is still operating two years on.

Perhaps even this hurdle might be surmountable with enough staff. But the National Paedophile Unit is grossly under-resourced. For much of its first two years Ellis battled on either alone or with one assistant. In late 1993 she was granted an additional (untrained) staff member. She does not expect her team to grow beyond three. Just how low the Paedophile Unit ranks in the scale of Home Office funding priorities can be seen by comparison with the Football Unit in an adjoining office. According to the NCIS brochure, 'The Football Unit provides a central point for collecting and analysing intelligence about persistent football hooligans and gangs, especially those who travel throughout the UK and abroad.'

According to Louise Ellis the Football Unit runs on a regular staff of between eleven and twelve officers. Yet the Home Office's own figures reveal that football hooligans count for but a tiny fraction of the total number of known paedophiles in Britain today. In the 1992/93 season there were 4,588 arrests in or around football grounds across the country. Fewer than 200 of these were for potentially serious offences; the vast majority were for drunkenness (1,522), disorderly behaviour (820), threatening behaviour (635), breach of the peace (354) or running on to the pitch (286).

Despite the common view that great gangs of armed tribal thugs roam the country on Saturday afternoons, throughout the entire 1992/93 football season just thirty-two people were arrested for possession of an offensive weapon – a figure that retreats into triviality when compared with assaults during an average month of Saturday nights in any one of Britain's major city centres. The reason why football hooliganism has been accorded such high priority, and has been awarded such generous funding that it can afford eleven or twelve intelligence officers at NCIS, is simply that its eradication has become a political imperative. Politicians perceive there are votes in the issue. Children, abused or otherwise, are completely unenfranchised. The contrast is stark.

We need an appropriate national paedophile response, and we aren't getting it. We need to change what we're doing. The resources committed to drugs and their users swamp what we do for children. Don't we have any sense of what the abuse of children creates? What do people expect the end result to be? The outcome of this careless deficiency of policy and practice can, paradoxically, be detected by its absence at the National Paedophile Unit in NCIS's London headquarters.

In December 1993 Louise Ellis sat at her dark-brown

terminal and, punching in a password, accessed the Unit's section on the INFOS database. She was looking, by request, for information on one Robert Black, van driver, of 7 West Bank, Stamford Hill, London, and lately to be found c/o HMP Peterhead. It was not a successful search: 'Robert Black is not recorded on the NCIS database at this time. He has never come to our notice and the information that is available on him has never been submitted to our office.'

The fact that the subject of the longest computerized manhunt in British criminal history (an enquiry sabotaged by the lack of a computer sufficiently well programmed with data to pick up Black's previous convictions), a man presently serving a life sentence for a near-fatal sexual assault on a six-year-old, a man charged with three murders and four abductions, a man with whom a succession of police forces across Britain and Europe would like to discuss unsolved crimes against children, was not on the National Paedophile Unit's computer nearly three and a half years after his now infamous arrest, speaks volumes about the efficiency and resourcing of the Unit.

Dark comes swiftly to the north-eastern coast of Scotland. In the little cell that had served as safe ground for our sessions together, Robert Black and I were close to the end. Once his trial started, I would be prevented from seeing him again.

He had never confessed, in so many words, to any murder. Yet he knew that I was convinced he had killed many children, including Susan Maxwell, Caroline Hogg and Sarah Harper. I had promised Black, from the outset, that I would keep no secrets and tell no lies. I knew now that I had to spell out my beliefs one last time, both for Black's sake and in the faint hope that even now the man might make some halting confession to the families of the murdered children. It was to be a lengthy conversation but one not tinged with anger: I felt sorrow, pain, even privilege because I had come close to the man and had begun the process of helping him face the desires that drove him.

RAY: At least I've got the truth about you.

BLACK: Mmm? You want to share it with me?

RAY: Because I know the real Robert Black.

BLACK: You want to tell me about him?

RAY: Yeah. Yeah. You just tell me when I get it wrong, OK? Robert was a lonely boy, an abused boy. A boy who was obsessed with sexual behaviour and behaviour that he didn't understand. A boy who didn't know what it was like to be really loved or cared for. A boy who didn't receive much affection in care. A boy who had a lot of loss and bereavement in his life. A boy who was removed into care. A boy who was abused in care. A boy who carried on his obsession with girls and with abusing girls and with abusing himself. He was trying to make sense of his fantasy life, his sexual life, his ordinary life. It was all mixed up.

He did something when very young that he found very hard to deal with: he didn't know what he'd done. He thought he'd killed a little girl. He became obsessed with the fantasies of that. He couldn't get it out of his head; they kept coming into his head at various times, and he abused lots of other girls. He abused a girl from a family he knew and went to Borstal.

I don't know what sort of time you had in Borstal but it couldn't have been nice for you. You couldn't have liked the loss of your liberty and you couldn't have liked to be locked away. You came out. You were frightened.

BLACK: Mmm. I was glad to be out.

RAY: You left and you went to London. You'd been abusing in different ways – watching, touching, pornography. You got obsessed with it. You started following and abducting girls, wondering about girls, talking to girls, wanting the circumstances to be right.

You've had an obsession with orifices. You've given yourself probably quite a lot of pain, maybe even to the extent that you've bled because of what you've been doing to yourself.

I think you picked up a girl. That girl died. I think you got frightened; I think you got control again, did other things, but I think the same thing happened again. And the same thing happened again. And the same thing happened again.

The same thing happened again and you got caught. And

you don't like yourself. You don't like what you do. You don't want to face what you do.

That's what I believe. And I don't think you can deny what I'm saying.

BLACK: I don't think I ever thought of myself as lonely at the time, like. Looking back, yes. But at the time, no.

RAY: I'm right, aren't I?

BLACK: Some of the time . . . some of the time.

RAY: Most of the time. Why can't you tell me?

BLACK: What do you want me to tell you?

RAY: Well, out of all the things I gave you in that story that you could have disagreed with, the one you picked on was loneliness.

BLACK: I thought you were going to say something else then.

RAY: Did you? Well, I didn't.

BLACK: I didn't deny it because I can't deny it.

EPILOGUE

Newcastle Crown Court, Thursday, 19 May 1994

> Robert Black . . . You are an extremely dangerous man. You are already detained for life in Scotland. I sentence you on each of these ten counts to life imprisonment. I expect that you will be detained for the whole of your life, but . . . I propose to make a public recommendation that the minimum term you are detained is thirty-five years.
>
> *Mr Justice Macpherson of Cluny, trial judge*

Robert Black's trial lasted five full weeks. He was moved, under strict security, from Peterhead to Durham Prison on Sunday, 10 April. The hearing began four days later.

He faced a total of ten charges: three each for Susan Maxwell, Caroline Hogg and Sarah Harper – their abduction, murder and the prevention of a lawful burial – and one for the attempted abduction of Teresa Thornhill.

Throughout the trial Black spoke only twice. On the first day he confirmed his name and current address and entered a plea of not guilty. Thirty-six days later he reacted to the jury's unanimous guilty verdict by staring at the assembled police and murmuring, 'Well done, boys.' In between he had not uttered a word. He had, as was his right, chosen not to give evidence on his own behalf. While the prosecution introduced a parade of witnesses to support its case, Black's defence had called only a handful.

The case against Black was based on two carefully dovetailed planks. The first was the circumstantial evidence – witness sightings, PDS records and petrol receipts – that placed him at or near the place where each child was abducted within a significant timescale. Added to this, the same sets of records placed him close to where their bodies had been discovered. On its own this evidence might or might not have been sufficient. But the prosecution sought, and was granted, leave to introduce the evidence of Black's abduction of Laura Turner. This was highly unusual. In most trials the court is at pains to ensure that the jury is not told of the defendant's previous record. Only when a verdict has been brought in does the judge tell them what, if any, crimes the man in the dock has on his record. But English jurisprudence allows previous convictions to be introduced when the trial judge is satisfied that they amount to evidence of system – a pattern of offending so unusual that it amounts to a trade mark. It is a tactic most frequently seen in fraud trials where financial criminals use a definable system to cheat their victims. Its use in such a high-profile serial-murder case was bound to cause dissent.

Black's lawyers attempted at a series of pre-trial hearings to resist the prosecution's request for evidence of system to be allowed. The defence employed both English and Scottish lawyers and had already sought, without success, to have Black tried in Scotland. They argued that since two of the cases with which he had been charged, Susan Maxwell and Caroline Hogg, began either in Scotland or on the border with England, its courts should take precedence. (Whether by coincidence or not, Scottish law does not allow the introduction of evidence of system.) When the defence bid failed, the lawyers served notice privately on Mr Justice Macpherson that if Black were convicted, an immediate appeal would be launched, citing the evidence of system as grounds for an unfair trial.

For the families of Black's victims, the trial was an ordeal to be undergone with ever-increasing trauma. Liz and Fordyce Maxwell had originally planned to be abroad on holiday when the case began. But a much delayed start, and the sheer length of the hearing, meant they were back at home when the Crown led its first witness. By the end of the trial, the Maxwells were together in court with Annette Hogg and Jacki Harper. They sat stiffly in the public gallery as the jury of six men and six women were sent out to consider their verdict.

The jury took three long days to deliver its conclusion. At a little before lunchtime on Thursday, 20 May, the foreman stood up to read the verdicts. One woman jury member wept freely. Liz Maxwell gasped as the first 'Guilty' was firmly delivered: Fordyce broke down in tears. A friend grasped Annette Hogg's arm: she whispered, 'I'm fine,' as Caroline's verdicts followed. When the charges relating to Sarah Harper produced the same result, Jacki cried uncontrollably. Later she and Liz gave separate interviews to the phalanx of more than 100 journalists and cameramen, each expressing their delight at the result. 'Every parent,' Liz Maxwell said in a quiet and dignified voice, 'can rest more easily knowing that Robert Black is in jail for the rest of his life.'

But how easily can – should – parents rest? Robert Black may, assuming he does not win his appeal or escape, stay in prison for the rest of his life. But what of the other Robert Blacks, nascent or fully developed? How safe are children from them?

On Wednesday, 29 December 1993, I locked the heavy green door of 25–33 Park Road, Moseley, for the last time. I turned and strode briskly past the bored prostitutes patrolling their street-corner beat: I was walking away from the major part of my life. Officially, at least, the Gracewell Institute would live on until the end of the year: the formal date of its demise would be listed as 31 December. But for me there was no point in lingering: the offices were silent, the staff dispersed.

The men, offenders all, who had been their clients were scattered to the winds. Some of them had been returned to the communities they came from or into other types of hostel accommodation. Many of the staff were made redundant. Gracewell had been an attempt to protect children by working with men who were determined to abuse them. And now it was over.

Gracewell was a dual-site operation, a hostel and a day clinic. In May 1991 we had sought, and been granted, registration by the regional health authority as a nursing home. We wanted the registration to give our work some official monitoring and oversight. We were accountable to the authority for all aspects of the service we offered. Strictly, we were not a nursing home – at least as far as that phrase is normally defined – but the authority wanted to be flexible and, with the blessing of Whitehall, was prepared to register us.

But if this group of professionals were happy to accept us, the local community around us was not. Although, to our knowledge, no offences had been commited by any of the men while they were with us, our growing public profile had begun to foment a degree of controversy among people who believed that treating sex offenders is always and inevitably wrong.

Gracewell had earned only plaudits from police, probation officers, social services departments and the courts. Even the Home Office had made favourable noises and had begun an assessment of its techniques. The Sex Offender Evaluation Programme that evaluated our work was to show clearly both the importance of Gracewell and its effectiveness. Yet among the multi-ethnic Moseley community – a community that crosses most social, racial and financial boundaries to yield a rich cross-section of the British public – a handful of residents began a campaign to force the clinic away from their streets.

Much of the protest was peaceful – if ill-informed and resting on blind prejudice. Some was not. Just after we closed our doors one evening in 1992 I heard the sound of an explosion in the porch. There were two of us left in the clinic: the offenders had not been in the building that afternoon, as it was Friday, and the second half of the day was devoted to working with abused children and their mothers. The last had left less than an hour earlier. We ran back downstairs. In the porch we were greeted by a wall of flames 9 feet high. We managed, eventually, to extinguish the fire and walked through the charred woodwork to look outside.

A man was standing watching us. I walked over to him and asked if he had seen what had happened. Quite calmly, he said he had laid the fire and pointed to an empty petrol can lying in the bushes near by. I was stunned and asked him why he had done this, and he said simply, 'There were perverts in there.' I explained we had only mothers and children that afternoon and suggested that, as he had tried to burn us down, he should come and look around inside. It was the first time he had ever been in the building, the first time he gained any insight into our work. When he had seen round the clinic I gave him a cup of coffee and called the police. He and I sat together in reception as we waited for the officers to come and arrest him. It seemed farcical. Not for the first time, I wondered why I did this job.

Not all the protests were so extreme. But the campaign to close Gracewell, based on the danger presumed to be posed by the men, heightened. Local councillors were lobbied. Soon a planning loophole emerged. By December 1993 Birmingham City Council had sent us a letter formally giving notice of a decision it had reached. The letter said our planning consent was unsuitable and that the clinic would have to close.

There was a certain irony in the decision. It appeared that Gracewell was offering our clients too much care. Our treatment programme and our twenty-four-hour supervision meant, in the planners' eyes, that we no longer qualified as a hostel, were therefore in breach of our planning consent and would have to close.

It was depressing. We had existed without a problem until the campaign began. Now we were to be closed on a technicality. The decision-making process inside Birmingham City Council became a simple response to the residents' wish that Gracewell should go 'somewhere else'. And yet where were we to go? This was the classic argument – 'Not in my backyard'. There is no such thing as 'somewhere else': there is only another community across town, or across the country, to which the debate would be transferred.

What is most absurd in the debate is the notion that there is somehow a location that is 'suitable'. In the terms of the protesters, there can be no such place because there is no specific planning-permission category of sex-offender hostel and because the only suitable place for a community treatment centre is in the community – somebody *else*'s community.

The council decided that our work should be done in hospitals; the residents announced that it should be done in prison. The result was a joint determination to close us down. Yet when Gracewell closed neither of those options was a possibility. None of the residents in the clinic could be sent to prison – they had either already served their sentences or never been given a term of imprisonment. And no hospital would accept them on the very reasonable grounds that none showed any evidence of definable illness, physical or psychiatric.

The closing of Gracewell, the only residential centre working with paedophiles outside prison walls, was caused not by any flaw or mistake in its operation but rather by irrational and implacable opposition to its very existence. The outcome was predictable. I stood and watched as the men whom the staff and I had laboured to control were simply returned to where they came from or the referring agency. It appeared that Birmingham City Council and the residents it represented preferred to have offenders living anonymously in the community, unsupervised and untreated. They had no means of knowing where these men would go: for all they knew, or apparently cared, some of the offenders could have slipped into bedsit accommodation in Birmingham itself. How safe would that have made the community?

It was, quite simply, madness. Every day other sex offenders (not the men resident at Gracewell) go into social services properties for meetings with council staff. Sometimes the police are called in to supervise these meetings. And yet at the end of them the same men will walk out alone and return to the community with little or no supervision. Sex offenders live in hostels all over Britain. Sex offenders leave prison and move into bedsits across the country almost every day of the year. There is virtually no attempt to monitor or supervise their subsequent movements and activities.

I sought to offer something that made the community around Gracewell safer by taking the men inside a clinic that did supervise them and, above all, worked to break their cycle of offending. By closing Gracewell the council and the residents did not protect one more child. In fact, the reverse is true: they put children at risk.

If the men who were at Gracewell were intending to abuse after 29 December 1993, they have all been in a position to do so more easily. The referring agencies who sent the men knew that they could offer only a fraction of the control and treatment that we were able to offer. And other men who would have come to Gracewell cannot now do so: if they were a risk inside a supervised clinic, they are a much greater risk untreated, unmonitored and at loose in the community.

The decision to close the clinic was, in its widest sense, political: it was engendered by a lust for votes. Once politicians abrogate their wider responsibilities in pursuit of easy electoral advantage, then care in the community – for the disabled, the mentally ill or sex offenders – stands no chance of success. Care facilities face the constant risk of closure and resettlement. And, in the case of sex offenders, planners are championing the wrong cause. Sex offenders need secrecy; they need a lower level of supervision: Birmingham's actions ensured they got it. The paedophile community had long sought to have Gracewell closed down by both legal and illegal means. It's a sad encapsulation of the wilful British ignorance about sex offenders that in closing Gracewell the city council did paedophilia's work for it.

And the more I looked at the closure and its repercussions, the more I saw this picture of society's closed mind in microcosm. It seemed not to matter that Gracewell had existed to protect children, nor that it had lived up to this aim. In the muddy battleground of public opinion truth was fiction and fiction truth.

The campaigners had used as a justification for their noisy crusade a claim that Gracewell's methods were ultimately unsuccessful and that men leaving the clinic stepped across its threshold to abuse again. In support of this (quite false) allegation they cited the case of a man called David P., who had recently been convicted on two separate counts of rape. Joyously, the campaigners, with a journalist and TV access programme in tow, reported that this man had been at Gracewell and had left and raped two women. Therefore Gracewell must be a risk.

In fact, David's case demonstrated the precise opposite: he had, certainly, been to Gracewell – but only for assessment. An admitted abuser of his step-children, he was seeking access visits to them and, quite properly, his local social services department was seeking a report on the threat he posed. David was a violent, abusive and dangerous man. In the course of his assessment he boasted that he had arranged for a social worker's car to be blown up, for the windows of the social services building to be smashed and for the department's phones to be cut. Nor was this mere bluster: all the incidents had taken place.

When David threatened Gracewell staff with similar treatment I promptly terminated his stay and contacted the social services department, asking for their client to be removed. David had been with us ten days. He had undergone no therapy, and his assessment report made dismal and depressing reading. A high risk – but, of course, a man who, when we threw him out, was a free man, out in the community. Fully nine months later he raped an elderly woman and a young woman in her twenties. He was arrested and is now serving life. Neither he nor his victims, his family or social workers have ever alleged that Gracewell somehow failed to correct his behaviour. Yet this was the foundation of the argument that Moseley community could never be safe with Gracewell operating in Park Road. It seemed almost perverse – not just that David's experience was distorted and twisted (that much goes with the territory and we could have expected it) but that there could be such wilful ignorance in the community and in the council chamber.

We need to be clear about this issue. Our society does not kill paedophiles or lock them up for ever and a day. These men are left in our communities, dangerous and in need of intensive treatment to reduce the likelihood of their offending. Most sex offenders will never be convicted, yet the social services need appropriate risk assessment. Without this, they have little alternative but to move children into care. Despite this, no community is prepared to allow clinics to operate: we tried to move Gracewell to a large mansion in another county, well away from schools and children's playgrounds. That community's response was – quite literally – to set fire to our buildings, which prevented the project from going ahead.

The reaction to Robert Black's conviction was depressingly predictable. Newspapers talked of a 'sex monster' and a 'beast', as if the calling of names could somehow either explain him or protect children in the future. But there are two images that remain with all of us who have been involved in the investigation into Robert Black's life and crimes.

The first is Sarah Harper's white-marble gravestone in Bruntcliffe cemetery, above Morley – not for the message carved on it, 'Asleep in the arms of Jesus', but for its place between two other stones. To the left lies 'Leah Johnson – mother': an old stone for a woman who lived a long life. On Sarah's right is the headstone for 'Joan Jeffers – 60 years'. The two seem to sum up the tragedy of a life cut short, a life that ended before Sarah had the chance to grow into womanhood or to have children.

The second image is a flickering and much shown piece of television archive video-tape. It shows the Maxwell family on the day of Susan's funeral. Countless cameras covered the event in dazzling sunshine at the tiny church at Coldstream. Fordyce remembers almost nothing of the jostling and pushing as journalists and photographers vied for position. Liz can recall every moment but is sure, beyond doubt, that the family was right to hold a public funeral: 'I suppose if we had said that we wanted no publicity, then that could have been arranged. But in a way we wanted to tell people: "This is what it comes to. This is following a coffin. This is burying your child."'

The strength and courage of Liz and Fordyce Maxwell, the gritty determination of Jacki Harper, should be a lesson to all of those who are willing to indulge a selfish desire for vicarious retribution and let it override the practical need to work with men who abduct, abuse and kill children. Robert Black may be in prison, but men like him are all around us. How can our society not see this? It's almost as if, by blindly clinging to their ignorance, people believe they are safe, but instead they are increasing the risk to themselves, their children and families across the length and breadth of the country.

The lesson needs to be learned, and maybe Robert Black's story is a way of starting the process: in telling it I certainly hope the public will begin to listen and understand.

If we can't protect our children twenty-four hours of every day, and we can't, we must work with offenders to reduce the risk that they will abduct, abuse or kill. There are thousands of men in Britain, at large and unnoticed, who are on the same path as Robert Black. Some are at the start of the journey, some close to the terrible, dark place he inhabited. A few will already be child killers like him. Unless we intervene in their lives, these men will become what he became. And other parents will, like Liz and Fordyce Maxwell, like Annette and John Hogg, like Jacki Harper – like all those affected by Robert Black's crimes – have to make the slow and bitter journey to their children's graves.